Tales From A Mad Man's Wife

A Memoir

D1545965

Marilyn Miller Skylar

First published by Dog Ear Publishing
4010 W. 86th Street, Ste H
Indianapolis, IN 46268
www.dogearpublishing.net

ISBN: 978-1-4575-2419-6

This book is printed on acid-free paper.

Printed in the United States of America

For David
To help him remember

Acknowledgements

*S*ince most everything I have written came from the depths of my memory as well as the clippings and scrapbooks found in long sealed boxes, I needed some verification from friends to be accurate. It took some research, but thanks to my computer I found the following willing souls to approach.

Many thanks to Joe Sallay, Bob Chism, Jerry Grilly, Leonard Cohan, Ernie Perlmuter, Byron Krantz, Bob Miller, Ed Spizel, Larry Enfield, Bill Metcalf, Lee Pitt, Bill Levy and Dick Wingerson. Sadly,some very dear friends who helped me recall incidents like Ed Eigner,Steve Lebby, and Paul Goldner have since passed away.

I also want to thank my children, Claudia, Dean, and Stephanie, the latter having formatted my manuscript and coordinated the photos in order for the publisher to work on it. Steph, you are an angel to take this on despite your busy corporate schedule. Claudia and Dean ...you both are cyber geniuses. I couldn't have managed without your help.

I told David's story as I saw it. Please enjoy the book.

Intro

I realize there are people who never watch television in any shape or form. However, a large amount of individuals do watch TV, especially shows that seem more hip or cool, or whatever the adjective is of the moment to describe a show with sexy overtones like "*MadMen*."

I am writing this memoir to describe what it was really like for "mad men" in the 50s and 60s, and later. My subject is one close to my heart. His name is David Skylar, and he was a really good advertising executive. This book is not only a labor of love; it also took a heck of a lot of labor. You see, I was not able to get any feedback from this wonderful man, who happens to be my husband, because a stroke in 2004 wiped away memories of his past life.

Fortunately, I have a good memory. I also have scrapbooks filled with newspaper clippings that his secretaries throughout the years meticulously kept. Some events could not be verified. There is hardly anyone left to do the verifying. I did find a few hearty souls like Joe Sallay, Bill Levy, Ed Spizel, Jack Byrne and Ernie Perlmuter, who checked out some puzzling facts.

Advertising is a tough field. The business has taken its toll on a lot of good people. Basically, I was on my own to write David's story. But you know what? I was mostly in the story too, so I guess it was no trick to remember.

When David's roommate Bernie introduced us in college, he told me, "This guy is better for you than Ben," who I was dating at the time. I used to sit around between classes with Bernie and he was my good buddy. I had no idea who his roommates were or where he lived.

He knew all of us quite well. I was skeptical, but an arrangement was made to go out with Bernie and his date the following weekend. We met at a graduate house where his girlfriend lived. While the other couple needed privacy, David and I awkwardly waited in an adjacent room where people were dancing to Chinese music. We attempted to dance as well. It was a very unusual way to start a friendship. Eventually, we all went out to the local bus station where the guys had prepaid dinner tickets. I felt terrible to learn I had used some of my date's precious rations. That was the beginning, and except for five months while he finished school and I went home to find a job, we have been together ever since. I am telling you all this because David literally had no possessions except for khaki pants, shirts, and his army trench coat. He worked hard and achieved his goals, not so much for acquisitive reasons, but for the challenge he enjoyed in reaching them.

I may quote some of his "bon mots" from time to time in these tales, but right now I have found a postscript he wrote after an exceptionally great story he had written for the town radio station, as well as the *Columbia Missourian* daily newspaper. He was called at 3:00 a.m. to cover the story of two escaped convicts, and that is quite an unusual call for a journalism student. He joined the highway patrol in the search and brought back a great front-page story. All the other reporters looked up to him as being hot, and the faculty went all out for him in every respect. That night, without having any sleep, he wrote me the whole story and the subsequent praise he received.

Here was his postscript: "My head is still not too big for my hat, but it sure feels good to know that you're top man in the school."

David seemed to be top man from then on, except for a few instances. See what you think.

When I met David he was teaching tennis at Stephens College.
Surely a creative way to supplement his GI allowance and meet girls!

David's Beginnings
(Notes found that he prepared in the 1950's)

I've used the line: "I was born in New York and raised in the Air Force." That's almost true. I took advantage of the "R.A." program New York public schools offered before World War II. "R.A." means rapid advancement; you can go as fast as you are capable. I graduated from Stuyvesant H.S. when I was 15 and a half years old, and immediately enrolled at City College of New York (CCNY). I had two years of engineering studies before I joined the Air Force when I was 17 years old.

I flew B-17s before I started shaving regularly. I had a fifty mission crush in my hat, a few ribbons on my chest, and was cocky as hell. I also learned how to drink, gamble, chase women and shave. I survived World War II, but almost didn't survive being discharged. I remember that I shook in 1946 when I took off my fancy officer's uniform and became just another 21-year-old in New York City without an education, without a job, and with a lot of hype and expectations. I didn't know what I wanted to do, but I knew I didn't want to be an engineer anymore. Twenty-two months of army technical schools to become a pilot bombardier and radar technician took that career drive away. Army aptitude tests pointed me in the direction of "working with people," whatever the hell that means.

I went back to CCNY for one semester and decided that New York City was not for me anymore. I'd seen a good part of the country and the world, and NYC was too much of everything I didn't want. Luckily, I had friends who were in Columbia, Missouri at the University of Missouri...

David enlists in the Air Force.

First officer's uniform.

Chapter 1

*T*he day I was introduced to David Skylar, I knew he was
going to be a person of interest to me. He was lean and
tough, and very hungry in every aspect of the word. He was
very different from the guys I knew in Shaker Heights, Ohio. He
was a New York kid who enlisted in the Army Air Corps at 17,
after having attended college for a year and a half. It must have
been the right move, because he grew five and a half inches during his three-year tour of duty. He went in a scrawny boy and
came out a six-foot hunk. That's what I saw when I first laid
eyes on him. He was a power to be reckoned with, especially
with those nicer-than-Sinatra blue eyes and long blond lashes.
But he was still skinny and without the money to buy a decent
meal.

I'll skip lightly over that meeting at the University of Missouri. We dated for two semesters and then I graduated and
went back to Ohio. He still had summer school and another
semester to go, since he wanted his BA as well as his BJ degree.
He was able to accomplish this with his pre-war credits from
CCNY.

We each wrote daily letters, but it was a very lonely time
for me. David was thriving in his new-found success as a star
reporter for the *Columbia Missourian*, a student-run newspaper.
Every news assignment that he received turned out to be a front-
page story. He was the first student reporter to travel the state

chasing bad guys, as well as rejected Russian war brides. It boggled my mind that he even got the first expense account given to a student writer. He got huge headlines and bylines. I was so jealous. After all, I had already graduated and had a lowly job as a copy boy for the *Cleveland Press*. It would become obvious later that David was meant for an exciting career. There would be no filling paste pots for him. Eventually, he graduated and headed to Cleveland, my hometown.

Chapter 2

*H*e traveled with his two best friends whom he knew as a child in the Bronx. There was Chester Feldman, who had been stationed at Missouri in the V12 program of the Navy during the war. He liked the school so much that he returned as a civilian. When David found out he was given a chance to play basketball there, he contacted Chester to find a place to live. He ended up in a rooming house with Chet and four other veterans. Once he was settled, he arranged for another friend, Lee Pitt, to join the crowded space. The three New Yorkers managed to graduate at the same time.

After graduation the friends started driving home via Cleveland. Although they had planned to stop for a day or two, it didn't work out that way. It seems that they had a minor accident on the way and the car needed body work badly. When they limped into town I was upset, but my brother suggested they bring the car into the repair shop at my family's bottling plant. It took a few days, but the repairs were made gratis. I guess I forgot to mention that the car belonged to me—I had loaned it to David for strategic reasons. We had decided to marry in March, and I wanted to expedite his leaving Missouri as soon as possible. He was to take it to New York, get his act together, and bring his mother back for the wedding. I was probably a jerk for giving up my transportation to work, but that is what love was all about in the ancient days of the late 1940s.

When we married as planned in the spring of 1949 we moved in with my widowed mother, who was not well and needed constant care. While I continued with copy boy chores, David looked for a job—sort of. He was pampered and fed by my mother and her housekeeper. He also played a lot of golf with some clubs he bought while in the Air Corps. A job he had been told would open up at the *Cleveland News* never materialized. No other jobs in print journalism or public relations turned up for five months.

With Lee at a new job on the Guam newspaper and Chester starting out with TV producers Goodson and Todman, David was getting a bit edgy. We had already applied and were accepted to Columbia University for our master's degrees when the big break occurred.

The biggest ad agency between Chicago and New York gave him a chance to freelance articles for their industrial clients. These articles were really technical and beyond the scope of David's knowledge. By researching the subjects and making them understandable, they were well accepted by the trade journals, popular news magazines and periodicals. He received $50 an article, which was big money in those days. Since he wrote so well and knowledgeably, the agency decided to offer him a full-time job. He became the assistant to the public relations director. The job paid $60 a week. It was a comedown financially, but a giant step in the right direction. He became a "mad man" as ad men have come to be known at the present time.

The legend began. I basked in all his glorious feats, but there are so many stories that I'd better get on with it!

David's roommates in college. Jim Shea, Lee Pitt, Bernie Rubin.
Absent is Chester Feldman.

David's stag night.

5

Recycled wedding picture.

David with first boss Ed Powers.

First year of marriage.

Chapter 3

*I*n one of the earliest moments of his career, our hero had to consume a lot of alcohol. He was given several accounts where his clients got drinks named after them for obvious reasons.

One lunch with a man named Glenn Martin from a company called BF Goodrich lasted over three hours. Young David, who thought he knew everything about handling clients, had to match drink after drink with this man to prove he was made of the right stuff. After all, he had to get his presentation across, so he drank one Martin Martini after another until he thought he would burst. He did make it though, and if I'm not mistaken the slogan "Smileage" was conceived either above or under the table. There is still a tiepin with the name engraved on it somewhere in David's drawer.

That experience trained him for a really big, first negotiation. As the representative from the ad agency for Society for Savings Bank in Cleveland (the forerunner of Key Bank), he sat in on the negotiations of the sale of the Terminal Tower and Hotel Cleveland to the Sonnabend family of Boston. Just as he was getting his bearings in the biggest agency between Chicago and New York, he was given the job of observing Cleveland's first major real estate turnover in modern times.

It was rumored that A.M. Sonnabend, a millionaire realtor, was in competition with Hilton and Sheraton to see who could add the most hotels to their chains. After Conrad Hilton bought the Waldorf Astoria in New York, A.M., or Sonny as he was called, bought the Van Sweringen properties, which included the Terminal Tower, three office buildings, and the 1,000-room Hotel Cleveland. The negotiations for the sale were long and bar-happy, and David became the golden boy of the "main man," Mervin B. France, head of Society for Savings. David drank next to Mr. France hour after hour until the deal was made. He somehow managed to arrive home in the middle of the night before he tossed it all! That was the first and last time I ever saw him sick from drinking.

Chapter 4

O nce Mr. France got a hold of our boy, he never let go. He used him as a sounding board, and when the old Society for Savings filed to become a national bank, David made excessive trips to Columbus on the bank's behalf.

Mr. France also steered many of his clients to David for advertising and PR. At the time you would have thought this young man was the only one at the agency. He performed so well that he became a vice president when he was only 33 years old. But I'm getting ahead of myself. So much happened prior to that promotion.

The aforementioned "Sonny" Sonnabend took over the Cleveland Properties for only eight million dollars. He changed the name of his company to Hotel Corporation of America. It became a client of Griswold-Eshleman, vis a vis David Skylar, and became one of the country's leading, upscale hotel chains. The hotels had Charterhouse Restaurants in which mouthwatering prime rib of beef was served. A brilliant creative guy, Jack Gilbert, was called in to work with David on a menu for the restaurant. They gave a name to all the choices on the menu, and by the time they got to the baked potato they were giddy with laughter. They came up with naming the potato after the owner and his wife—thus the name "Baked Potato Sonesta" was created after Sonny and Esther. Later the hotel chain changed to the Sonesta Hotels. Who would have thought?

About that time David and Jack met some wealthy relative of the Sonnabends, who was probably an investor. He was quite blustery, yet gullible, and the two guys took the opportunity to tease him in any way possible. One morning at breakfast during a brainstorming discussion about commodity futures, David looked at Jack and then said, "I believe the coming market is in caraway seeds." The man got up suddenly and went to the nearest phone to call his brother. The next thing they knew, he had "cornered the market on caraway seeds."

Chapter 5

$\mathcal{T}$he Hotel Corp (HCA) turned out to be David's most enjoyable client in those early days of his career. During the fifties his own family was growing, as well as the company's hotel expansion. Each venue that HCA purchased was visited by David and his family. Most of them were upscale properties and well-suited for vacations. In 1956, the Edgewater Beach Hotel in Chicago was packed with candidates of the Democratic Conference held that summer when the Skylar family arrived for its second visit. Our son Dean was three, and our daughter Claudia was four and a half. Despite the fully booked vacation, we were shown a beautiful corner suite that was saved for hotel dignitaries or consultants and special friends. Our daughter ran into the second bedroom and wailed, "Our own TV isn't in here like last time!" We explained that it was needed for the future president—she wasn't too happy to give it up.

Two years later, Sonnabend also purchased the Whitehall in Palm Beach. Again we all flew down. In that era it seemed that old world wealth had not given away completely to the "nouveau riche," and our stay was quite staid and old fashioned. There was an evening of talent by residents during our visit. People got up and sang, recited, whatever they wanted to do, and then our seven-year-old got up and said she wanted to play the piano. We were startled when she sedately went to the piano in the large banquet hall and played the piece she had just learned the week before at her first piano lesson! The next day it was noted in the *Palm Beach Post* society column.

It was a different world then, and the "mad men" of the day conformed to it. It would be hard to find a successful man of 33 today with two young children, a "homemaker wife," and a house in the burbs. The television sitcom showing early ad men is not exactly accurate. Most of the agency's personnel were married. The married young account executives all seemed to socialize together. They also included representatives of *Time, Life, Sports Illustrated,* and a bundle of industrial magazines. Most had young families and were not about to run around to bars with their wives. However, they did a lot of entertaining at home. A weekend party was always the big excitement of the week. Sometimes babysitters were not available. It was not uncommon to see three or four babies laid down to sleep on a king-size bed. Mothers and fathers took turns checking on the offspring.

At one point the friendly associates formed a bowling group, since the sport was in its heyday in the 1950s. The wives really looked forward to the competition. There were eight couples, and four of the women were named Marilyn. It was very confusing until they all started using other nicknames, like Marlie, Mar MJ and Lyn. No ad man was as dissatisfied as the present-day TV portrays them!

Chapter 6

One day in the early months of David's career, a young man came to the reception desk and asked to see someone about starting a public relations campaign for his company. The receptionist didn't often have walk-ins (it seemed so gauche), and she asked him to wait a moment while she consulted her notes to see who was in the office. It so happened that young David was coming out of his small office behind her and she called out to him. She whispered to him when he came to her that someone was in the waiting room, and told him he was the logical person to meet the man. He went back to his desk and a lean, dapper, Italian-suited guy walked in and extended his hand. "I'm Sam and I need a PR program for my company." That was the start of a brief friendship and a briefer business relationship.

Nobody remembers what kind of company he had, but they do remember his car. I, especially, was impressed when he invited us out to dinner and picked us up in his chartreuse Cadillac convertible. Then he asked us what we'd like to eat, and when we told him steak would be fine, he pulled up a contraption that was some kind of early car phone and called our favorite restaurant. Even unimpressionable David rolled his eyes.

To make a long story short, a great campaign was created for him, many meetings took place, and many invoices were sent. Then he disappeared with all the ideas, no bills paid, and no more client. That was a good lesson for a young man in the advertising field: Know with whom you are dealing before you open the flood gates of information.

Chapter 7

One of David's most endearing early jobs was setting up meetings for his PR clients. In the mid-1950s, his clients were almost strictly of industrial leaning. Many were simply associations of companies rarely known in the business world, but whose products were essential to American industry. For example, there was the National Clay Pipe Institute, the National Welded Steel Institute, the National Electrical Manufacturers Institute, all inclined to find the most exclusive golf and tennis venues for their annual meetings. Many of the members were small-town folks who really lived it up when they got together at places like Pebble Beach, the Wigwam in Litchfield Park, Arizona, the Broadmoor in Colorado, and, of course, The Greenbrier.

David would set up the agendas, the speakers (he was always one of them!), any tournaments, prizes and promotions. Of course the secret of his success was to keep every item in the program brief so the men could have lunch and get to the first tee quickly. Those were the days when trips of such nature were charged off on one's taxes, or in David's case, charged to his expense account. Then, of course, came the wives. It was hard to believe that someone from an obscure town in Indiana could have such magnificent gowns and jewelry. I guess owning the biggest company in town allowed the women to "do it up regal." Since I tagged along with David to help entertain the ladies and promote the great brilliance of the ad agency, I had to look good, too. During that period of time I had the most expensive wardrobe of my life. And David, too, wore different tux shirts every night. The ladies especially liked his ruffled, royal blue shirt. It matched his eyes.

All this sort of B.S. was a sign of the times. Everyone seemed to prosper. Companies were beginning to listen to the PR and advertising groups who showed them how to make their businesses thrive.

Chapter 8

Several months after joining Griswold-Eshleman Ad Agency, David suddenly looked around and saw that his coworkers and those on the board of directors were all WASPs. I said suddenly, because he was too engrossed in whatever he was doing to think about religion, race or ethnicity of any kind. He was born Jewish, but never received any formal instruction in the religion.

Then something occurred that made him realize he was "different." The owner of a printing company that did most of the agency's work took him aside. He said, "David, did you know you are the first Jew to be hired by Griswold?"

"I just suspected that recently," David said.

"The anti-defamation league has tried for years to get people in the establishment agencies with no luck," the owner said.

"Well, are you telling me I broke the barrier?"

"You definitely have opened up an industry for people of our faith! Up to now we have started small agencies of our own, and of course *we* don't *discriminate*," the owner pointed out.

Shortly after this interchange, people applied for jobs that had been warned off before, and some of them were hired by Skylar. They were not Christian. One was a creative artist genius by the name of Dave London. Another was a young man named Steve Lebby, who probably was the super salesman of the sixties.

There were one or two others, but definitely Griswold was still a bastion of Christianity. You will understand later why I brought up this issue.

To resume the early ad-ventures, I will have to go back to when Mr. France (the bank president) introduced David to the Stouffer Brothers. They, too, embraced Skylar's talents, not only for commercial use, but for their charitable endeavors. Vernon Stouffer was an active board member of the Cleveland Zoo. He decided to take some prominent people with him on a safari to Africa to bring back animals for the zoo. It became a big deal when he came back with his assortment of wild animals. I remember a picture of him in his safari clothes—a very pompous little man, but very generous as it were. One of David's duties was to promote the whole safari and later the attendance to the zoo. He came up with a musical ditty that was played constantly on the radio: "It's the zoological thing to do! Visit the Cleveland Zoo." Another good client for Griswold stuck fast for years.

Chapter 9

*I*n any office complex there are going to be a few people who are a little strange or slightly different from the norm. At Griswold-Eshleman there were two such account executives that fit the category. I will give them different names to "protect the innocent."

There was "John" to begin with, who was a large and jolly kind of guy. He was known for his sense of humor and his capacity for liquor. He was a true family man with a stay-at-home, but very bright, wife, and five little boys about a year apart. I don't know much about his advertising talents, but he was certainly the life of every social event he attended. One evening he had a group of his agency pals over with their wives, and he served drinks like there was no tomorrow. He kept telling his wife not to serve dinner yet, and soon it got to be after 10:30 with guests feeling no pain.

Suddenly, John got up, excused himself, and went upstairs. His wife started getting food out on the buffet. Ten minutes later, John came downstairs again. He was in some scruffy flannel pajamas. His wife was horrified when he decided to "moon" everybody. "Please don't go," she begged. "He's just having fun." Everyone looked at everyone else. In a few minutes some couples started leaving. Soon all the guests had departed. No one knows what went on in that house later.

Another time John bumped into David in the elevator after work. The early offices were located in the terminal tower, which was connected to the then-Hotel Cleveland. There was a small bar at one end of the dining floor. It was sort of a "patio" bar. John convinced David to join him for a drink. After a while they both got a bit silly and decided to invent a new drink. They told the bartender to add a pinch of this and a dash of that, and after several experimental drinks they decided they'd found "the one." Now they had to come up with a name. John looked over and saw David's *Time Magazine* cover. It showed the Freedom Fighters of Bosnia, John said, "That's it! We'll call it the 'Freedom Fighter Martini," and anyone who drinks it can go home and slap his wife." Nice man.

A few weeks later when David was in Columbus, a bartender told him of a new drink called the Freedom Fighter and David broke up laughing. Such things travel fast in the agency business.

The final, sad part of the story is that this macho guy, this family man, turned out to be gay. His wife divorced him. Later we heard from another city that he had taken his own life. The whole episode was beyond belief. I spent forty years looking for "Jane"—his wife. I finally found her with the help of the Internet. I located one of her sons, who explained that she had remarried, lost her husband, and was now in a retirement home.

Chapter 10

The other young man who seemed very out of place at Griswold-Eshleman was from some place in New York State. He had a very devious agenda. He planned on taking over any of his colleagues' accounts as soon as he was able. As I recall, he had financial problems and often borrowed money from fellow workers. Apparently he was quite talented, but for some reason he misdirected his talents.

Although not too friendly with his male associates, he didn't seem to have trouble with the secretaries. After a while he started seeing one of the girls quite regularly, and it became obvious that he was serious. One evening David had just called to say he would be coming home in an hour when the troubled employee came into his office and asked him for an unusual favor. It seemed he had made an afternoon appointment with a local judge to marry him and the young secretary, but he needed a witness or best man to go with them to the judge's chambers. At first David looked at his watch and said he couldn't make it, but after seeing the disappointment in the man's face he agreed. I received another phone call telling me to postpone the final roasting minutes for his favorite prime rib and explaining the unusual request. Nothing really surprised me anymore.

When it got to be 7:00 p.m. I had to feed the children. The beef was not done, so they got hamburgers. At eight I decided to resume cooking the roast. At nine o'clock David came through the garage entrance and headed to the front of the house, at the same time calling out, "We have company." He went to the front door and opened it to the newlyweds, who were flying high! They had insisted that David celebrate with them after the ceremony. I was livid!

At one point, after listening to the ridiculous conversation, I looked at the young woman and saw that her wig was crooked. I told her so! She shot back and said, "So is yours!" I had just had my real hair done that afternoon. When the couple finally departed, David and I ate dried-up roast beef with no conversation.

Chapter 11

*L*ooking back on the 1950s, I realize that those years were the most significant part of David's development as an advertising executive. The post-war excitement of new products taken from wartime inventions and their marketing was in every commercial endeavor. Competition was fierce and everyone wanted to prove his cleverness in bringing products to the market.

In the case of the Cleveland bank Society National, the goal was to get the most depositors in the shortest amount of time, since it had only recently reverted from a savings institution. In March 1954, David and D. James Pritchard, vice president of the bank, found themselves in St. Louis listening to an obscure piano player whose syrupy smiles and fluttery crescendos were wowing little old ladies wherever he appeared.

David had heard about him and convinced Jim Pritchard to go along with him to Missouri to check out this entertainer. What they saw overwhelmed them: A pudgy faced young man with glossy, black wavy hair who played semi-classical and popular melodies with a dramatic flourish of hands and body as he led the audience into his charms. Though the two advertising types were not exactly carried away, they saw the possibility of using this man's talent for the bank.

After sitting through two performances they were able to contact the pianist's brother, who acted as his manager. They told him they had an idea that would make him more known nationally, and made him a proposal to come to Cleveland and do a live television broadcast, which the bank would sponsor. The idea clicked with the entertainer, and now David and Jim had to get past Mervin B. France, the president of the bank. Although Mr. France usually went along with David's advice, this was a trickier deal than usual. Bear in mind that he was a very macho conservative gentleman who usually slept through the opera openings that he'd attend with his wife every year in a very prominent box. Films were gathered to show him, and each time he viewed them the remarks and slurs that came out of his mouth were not to be believed. Finally, he capitulated and an arrangement was made with Channel 5 in Cleveland to televise a national network presentation of an evening with this celebrity. It was the first time Liberace did a live show on TV.

Needless to say, the studio audience went wild, as did the national audience. Those invited to the show were Society friends and neighbors. A huge party was held for a more select group after the screening. All of a sudden, Mr. France and all of his high-level and social friends became believers. Every person at the party wanted to be photographed with "Lee," as he eventually became known, and Mr. France of the former slurs did a real turnaround. When "Lee" said to him after the party how much he admired his fancy watch, Mr. France took it off and handed it to him, saying, "Please take it; it's my pleasure." David and Jim just stood there gaping.

The offshoot of this big event, of course, was Liberace's jumpstart to great fame. For the bank there was also something special. David conceived the idea to have Lee cut a special 33rpm record with "Liebestraum" on one side and "Roll out the Barrel" on the flip side. That record was given out free to any new depositors of $50 to the bank. Society National gained several million dollars from this one promotion.

David and Marilyn with Kathryn Pritchard and Liberace.

David with Jim Pritchard, Liberace, his brother George & wife, and Lee's manager.

Chapter 12

$\mathcal{F}$rom the very beginning of David's advertising career, interesting clients appeared. It must have been the post-war "let's catch up" feeling that prevailed at the time. Companies both big and small were clamoring to move their products out to the world. Of course the new invention of television had already fueled the trend. Being the new fair-haired boy at the agency helped David get the cream of the new clients. One morning a call to Charles Farran, Griswold's president, from a Detroit drugstore owner caused a big stir at the agency.

The man was negotiating to buy a huge drugstore chain in Ohio that had been in business for half a century. Farran called David into his elegant corner office and told him about the man's desire to use Griswold's expertise to guide him through the transition of ownership. "What do you think, David?" asked Farran. "Can this guy be for real?"

"Well, who knows? You say he only has two stores—discount ones at that. Maybe he inherited the money. It's going to cost big bucks to buy Standard Drug. I'd better take a look," mused David.

"Okay, that's what I needed you to say. He wants to give a tour of his methods at the stores to anybody who gets up to see him. And he wants to do it right away," said Farran.

"I'm on my way. What's his name and phone number? I'll call him back now," said David. After setting up an evening meeting with the druggist, he decided he would drive the 150 miles to Detroit so he wouldn't have to worry about airport delays or other problems. It took about three and a half hours to make the trip.

When he arrived at the man's office, he was greeted by a nice-looking, slim, no-nonsense girl in her early thirties. "Hello," she smiled. "You are nice to come see us so promptly. Bernie will be back any minute." David thought it was interesting that she referred to her boss by his first name. Later, he found out she had just been made a vice president of the company. When Bernie Shulman made his appearance it was not as a striking, dominating entrepreneur. He was of average height with partially balding, dark hair. He had average facial features and talked very softly. An unusual characteristic was a shortened arm, which obviously was a birth defect.

Almost immediately he started to talk about his discount strategies. He asked his visitor to tell him how much he paid for various products, and after he was told he bragged about how much lower prices were in his stores. The first store they traveled to really boggled David's mind. He had never seen such low prices before. Most drugstores did not have discounts in those days. Since he was always a bit skeptical about new business practices, David requested that they visit the second store thinking that maybe they hadn't had time to copy the markdowns. However, when they got there it was all the same. Good prices, great promotions, and definitely a money making proposition. Now it was easy to see that Shulman must have made his money by being one heck of a businessman. He also had a partner named Sid Dworkin. After having dinner and discussing plans, it was too late to drive home. David called me and said there was a man with incredible plans who was heading for big-time success. He was right.

Shulman bought the Standard Drug Company and changed the name to Revco, which was the name of the Detroit stores. Revco expanded to other venues, topping 2,500 before it went bankrupt decades later. However, in the first five years of expansion into Ohio, David handled all the advertising, PR and crisis management. He oversaw the sale of all Standard equipment and furnishings in Cleveland. We ended up with one of the original roll-top desks that the store owned, and an antique clock that had "Coca-Cola" written on the face. I had the inscription erased, because my family distributed beverages from another manufacturer. Little did I know then that the value of the clock had been considerably diminished.

The takeover of Standard Drug went smoothly, and David maintained a good relationship with Shulman and the company for several years. For reasons unknown to David and me, Bernie Shulman took his own life sometime in the mid-sixties. His original partner, Sid Dworkin, took over the helm of Revco until it ran into difficulties through financial problems with one of its subsidiaries. Sid Dworkin became an even better friend and client for David. At one point he wrote a brilliant speech for Sid on the safety and purity of generic medicines, which he presented to the AMA national meeting. It was just one of the many jobs he did for Sid during his tenure at Revco. This friendship continued until Sid also passed away.

Chapter 13

*T*oward the end of the 50s, business was booming and David was called upon more than ever to solve problems for major clients. Also about this time we saw Griswold-Eshleman beginning to expand their facilities both locally and nationally. They moved out of the Terminal Tower building into the new Illuminating Co. modern quarters at 55 Public Square. The company was growing so fast that it soon took over another floor. It was definitely the hottest agency outside of New York.

For David each day brought more exciting challenges. He became an expert in any kind of business he was called upon to promote. He believed that an intelligent businessman could head up any kind of company. After all, such a businessman would know how to surround himself with the right people. As an account executive, he researched his clients' products carefully and could create interesting ads. Sometimes it was difficult to come up with copy for ball bearings or extruded aluminum, but somehow the words began to flow. He believed that if he could edit *The Dairy Goat Journal*, which was his first job while in school, he could write anything.

As the agency grew, more and more consumer accounts were serviced. Companies like the Hoover Co. and Kitchen Aid became well publicized. There were many ad agencies in Cleveland, but only a few were New York branches and could get the prestigious accounts that Griswold claimed. At this point in his life, David wanted to give back some of the good fortune he was achieving. He taught classes several times a week at the Cleveland Advertising Club, and he joined groups that promoted the welfare of the sick and elderly. He was called upon by political groups, as well as politicians, to solve their problems. He was apolitical; it didn't matter if the democrats or the republicans asked for his help. It was all the same to him; a problem to be solved.

Some of us saw him as the brain behind the brains of many Cleveland dignitaries. To this day people do not know who wrote the speeches for the president of May Company or the chairmen of Society National Bank, among others. At a huge Growth Board banquet the aforementioned retail president stepped down from the podium and walked through the ballroom toward his seat amidst thunderous applause. When he reached David's table, he leaned over and said, "Thanks man, I couldn't have done it without you." That was the first I knew of such activities. He never told anyone. So many prominent men trusted him to keep their reputations intact. Soon he was a confidant of many mayors, senators, judges, and governors. One mayor, Carl Stokes, the first black head of a major city, enjoyed his company a lot. They often had quiet lunches when Stokes would have his limousine arrive at a prearranged corner to pick David up and whisk him off to a down-home eating spot where they would be given an out-of-the-way table for serious conversation. Carl had problems with some of the establishment, and David acted as a conduit to them. On the lighter side, they seemed to share the same taste in clothes. One day he got into the limo and saw dapper Carl in the exact same tan, western-style suit he himself had just purchased. They laughed about it and said it was a good thing David was not wearing his that day!

George Voinovich, a former United States senator, also benefited from David's expertise when he was campaigning for governor and later. When President Eisenhower came to Cleveland for a major re-election fundraiser, David was called upon to handle the whole affair. This included setting up the invitation list, the security, and the major publicity that was needed. To my dismay the whole affair occurred on a day we were to introduce some old friends to the joys of the Greenbrier resort. As it turned out, I drove with the couple to W. Virginia, and the next day I met the train from Washington from which David had to transfer. He was still in his tux with his shirt unbuttoned and a loose tie. He hadn't slept at all since leaving the very successful event. He didn't even have a bag, as I had brought all his clothes and golf clubs in the car. It was a great beginning for a much needed mini-vacation.

Most of the Skylar vacations included some degree of business participation. That suited us fine, because there was more pleasure than business. Vacations such as these were really considered some kind of perk, since salaries in the advertising business were relatively low in the Midwest.

Be that as it may, friends who worked in other fields did not seem to have the same advantages as we had. David worked long hours, and for some reason he never thought too much about his remuneration. Often I would ask him if he remembered to pick up his paycheck when we were just starting our family, and he promised sheepishly to get it the next day. Even so, we never lacked any creature comfort. We lived in a wonderful suburb and were happy with our situation. Then an interesting thing occurred.

David with Senator George Voinovich at the time he was Governor of Ohio.

President Eisenhower thanks David for a tremendous fundraiser which he organized.

James Hagarty thank you photo.

David chats with Leonard Berstein at opening of Severance Center mall.

David with former Cleveland Mayor Ralph Perk.

David with Senators Howard Metzenbaum and George McGovern.

Chapter 14

One evening when David returned from work at a reasonable hour, he seemed particularly edgy. I wasn't sure what he had on his mind. After dinner he finally explained that Charlie Farran had invited us over to his home the following Friday evening. "Hey, that's great! "I said. "So, what's the problem?" I could see by his hesitation that something didn't sit right with him.

He looked me in the eye and said, "I have a feeling that he wants me to move out of the Cleveland office." I saw that he had mixed emotions about such a move and told him that I felt the same way.

"Look, David, let's just wait and see what he really wants when we get there," I cautioned.

The big evening arrived and I dressed in what at the time was considered "elegant casual," a simple tweed suit with a short-sleeved cashmere sweater underneath, a single strand of pearls, and my wedding ring. I was emulating the boss's wife, who was always immaculately dressed for any occasion. We were greeted warmly and were surprised to see that only one other couple was in attendance, and it was Farran's stepson and his wife. After a half hour of small talk we sat down to dinner at a beautifully appointed table where the hostess herself did the serving. After the main course I stood to help clear, but was refused. Then the fun began.

The boss sat back and said, "You know we just bought an agency in Chicago?" David shook his head yes. "We need someone to run it, and I feel you would be the right person," Farran said.

David looked at me as if to say, "I told you so," and responded in a surprised tone. "Hey Charlie, this is quite a surprise and I am not sure what to say."

"Just say you'll do it," Farran laughed.

"I need some time to think this over, Charlie, okay?"

"Okay, but give me an answer by Monday, if possible," Charlie said.

The rest of the evening passed quickly with no more discussion of the issue. When we arrived home we talked through the pros and cons, and decided that moving at that time was not feasible for our little family. We had often heard that if one turns down a so-called promotion it might never be offered again. We also knew that a wrong move in any career was often regretted. The whole weekend was fraught with worry over the reaction to our decision.

On Monday morning David walked into Charlie's office and proposed his own idea about Chicago. He told Charlie he would spend three days a week there until the office was reorganized in the Griswold style and a local manager could be hired. After much discussion Charlie agreed, and so began David's commuter life.

Every Sunday evening he would take the Rapid Transit to the far west side airport and board the flight for Chicago. On Wednesday evening he would board the flight for Cleveland. Sometimes he would leave on Tuesday and board the plane for Cleveland on Friday. Sometimes the planes were lined up for takeoff by the dozens, and he arrived home at midnight or later, exhausted. He never complained about his job, and in fact thrived on the challenges. It wouldn't be long until he traveled east instead of west.

In between flights the home office required the rest of his time. There was always some kind of crises going on that only he could handle. Even in these early years he became an expert in crisis management, which he defined as the handling of a situation in which the government or the media interferes in one's business. One such event was at the May Co. under Frank Coy's leadership. Apparently it was a minority group that organized a "dirty tricks" program against the store. Restrooms were vandalized and trash was strewn about when no one was looking. The papers printed stories of unrest at the store.

David had a simple solution. He arranged for one or two minority sales persons to be hired for main floor departments that were clearly visible from the front entrance. Soon the vandalism stopped and order was restored. From then on there was no more discrimination in hiring employees—a solution that should have been found years before, and a solution that changed the practices of business in the city.

It was soon apparent that this unrest spread to the banking industry. Jim Pritchard, who was vice-president of Society National at the time, called on David one day to discuss the low percentage of minority depositors. This seemed a strange development. The bank had always been a total community presence since its school savings program began a half century before. David told Pritchard he would start investigating the problem immediately.

He began to meet with minority leaders who had worked with him before. One after another took him to the same restaurant in midtown that these men felt they could trust to secrecy for their meetings. David got his fill of spare ribs at the time. What came out of the talks was "the black face in the window" proposal. I cannot say for sure that it was David's idea, but it sounds like his usual to-the-point pronouncement. And so Society National Bank also began hiring African-American tellers. Soon the percentages changed.

Chapter 15

*A*short time after he made a deal with his superior to commute to Chicago, David received a phone call in the office that was completely unexpected. It was from the president of a major ad agency at the time known as BBD and O. If my memory is correct, it stood for Batten, Barton, Durstine, and Osbourne. The CEO asked if David would be interested in working for him in New York. After some discussion it was decided that David should fly in to see him and check out the lay of the land, so to speak, and it should be done as soon as possible.

On the way home that night he thought about what it would mean to go back to his hometown as a big-time advertising man. He could feel the blood flowing in his veins with just the thought of such a lofty job. Dinner was over quickly that night, as he went to the phone to make a reservation for the next day. He always had his secretary take care of such matters, but this had to be done from home for obvious reasons. He never had to report his whereabouts to anyone, but he did want to let Blanche Young, his secretary, know that he had personal business out of town. If anyone wanted him, she would let him know. She would never give anyone information about him. She treated her young employer as the son she never had. She made things easy for him.

That was a sleepless night for both of us. I realized the exciting possibilities for my husband. I also thought about the new home we had just remodeled and the perfect suburb in which we lived, and that the house was just across the street from his mentor, Mervin France, the new chairman of Society National Bank. Mr. France had been delighted when he heard we wanted to buy a house near him. I remember when he said, "It's location, location, location when you are looking for a house." It was the first time I'd heard that expression, and it was followed by a generous bank loan on his part.

When David awoke the next day he had already set up his guidelines for a move while he was attempting to sleep. Now he put his thoughts down on paper before he took off for the airport. The little-over-an-hour flight was smooth, and he caught up on his lost sleep. When he arrived at the hotel that was arranged for him, he had a message waiting for him that asked him to be at the agency's office by 12:30 p.m. He freshened up and caught a cab. He didn't expect such immediacy.

When David was ushered into the large, opulent, corner office of his interviewer, he was almost ready to accept any terms just to get into the agency. He was even more sure that he wanted to move when he was offered twenty-five thousand dollars a year salary. That was a ten-thousand dollar raise! In the late 50s that was considered a substantial amount of money. He still had to check out some other issues that he so carefully had itemized, and he told the CEO he would let him know in two days.

When he got back to the hotel he started to make calls. He learned from friends that the best places to raise a family were in the New York suburbs, like Westchester County or the Connecticut area. Another possibility was northern New Jersey. This meant a commute of at least an hour on a train. There was no way he would drive those distances every day. Besides which, the real estate was twice as expensive as the area around Cleveland. The new house in Shaker Heights was only one-half block from the Rapid Transit stop where he could hop on a rapid car and be in his office in 25 minutes. Another issue he checked out was the price of domestic help in the New York area. This also proved to be twice as much as he was now paying. Live-in help at that point in time was $43 a week in our new home, which even after extensive remodeling only cost $54,000. He crossed off item after item.

The day passed quickly after making so many calls, so he decided to have dinner with an old schoolmate and fly home the next day. The friend didn't help his decision-making at all. He kept talking about how hard it was to live comfortably on his income! By the time David got home the next day, he had already made his decision. After hearing all the pros and cons of the offer, I agreed with him wholeheartedly. With two primary school children and a baby on the way, I was not about to give up my so-called creature comforts. Two days later he called that magnificent ad agency with his regrets. As it turned out, he ended up working in New York soon after. That's another whole story.

Chapter 16

Afew weeks before the short trip to New York, I forgot to mention our first cruise vacation. David always came up with interesting ideas, and who was I to debate any of them. No one I knew at the time had been on a cruise, and it all seemed so movie magical to me. We hired a nurse for fifty dollars a day and we set off for New York to embark on the SS Brazil, which was one of two ships owned by a small shipping line. We were getting away from it all.

What a short-lived thought that was. We got to our stateroom, left our suitcases unpacked, and went out to explore the promenade deck. Sitting on a deckchair all bundled up in a blanket with a drink in his hand, was our insurance agent! He also lived one block away from us back home. His wife was not with him. Even though he was much older than us we knew him well, since his youngest son was the age of our son, Dean. We also knew him to be a heavy drinker. When he told us that his wife had a broken leg and couldn't take the trip, we both mentally rolled our eyes in disbelief. How could a man just leave his wife in such distress!? It was too bad, as he latched onto us wherever we docked and we couldn't shake him. We managed to meet some nice young couples though, and thoroughly enjoyed the ports of call. In those days the ships only held about four hundred passengers or less, and got into interesting Caribbean ports. It was also at one of these ports that an official came on the ship with messages. I'm not sure how the system worked in those days, but people were not contacted except when they reached a port. David received the surprise of his young life.

The telegram handed to him read, "Congratulations! Stop. The Board has just elected you a vice-president. Stop. A celebration is in order on your return. Stop. Signed Charles Farran." We will always remember Trinidad for that message. David had just turned 33. He was the youngest VP the staid old agency ever had. We didn't wait to celebrate!

In those days the shopping was fun and different for us. The island stores didn't become tee shirt havens until many years later. Then, unlike now, David enjoyed shopping. He bought watches and native shirts, and English tweeds. I bought embroidered tablecloths and dresses with matching hats, and cashmere sweaters, and little watches with different colored bands for every day of the week. You would have thought that the promotion brought great wealth. It didn't, of course. Everything was so cheap in the islands then. Shopping was the thing to do! One of our new acquaintances, who had cruised before, warned us about duty charges and gave us her instructions about debarking when we got to the States. I can only tell you that even in the cold weather I was overheated wearing four cashmere sweaters and a blazer, plus my beaver coat. David also looked much heavier than he was. As I look back, we were still rather naïve.

We have been on many cruises since, and never shopped like we did then. In fact, in later years we never even got off the ship in the Caribbean. We did in Europe, of course, but that was new to us. We got home and distributed all the gifts, and David got down to business again. He felt rested and certainly more confident with his new position.

Chapter 17

One of the employees that David especially liked was a big, jovial, unusual looking young man named Joseph Madigan. He was trained by David, more or less, in the rudiments of public relations, but he had a built-in ability to charm his way into getting anything from his sources. He was a Notre Dame graduate married to a St. Mary's graduate, the daughter of a well-known Cleveland attorney. Joe seemed to know everyone in town. It was a surprise, however, that he decided to promote his boss in the media even more than was needed. One after another blurbs appeared about David in gossip columns of the local newspapers.

Actually, the items began even before Joe's efforts. Milt Widder was the columnist for the *Cleveland Press*. In 1954, under the headline of Literati, he wrote: "Adman Dave Skylar wrote the piece 'We Didn't Touch the Outside,' a feature in current *American Home*. It's about his and his wife's (Marilyn) remodeling of the interior of a Shaker home." This was not exactly earthshaking news, but lots of people read it.

Another notice by Sidney Andorn, a columnist for the then viable newspaper the *Cleveland News,* called attention to me, but it was slightly inaccurate. It read: "Talking of gestures, a nice one was tendered this week by Liberace, no less, to Marilyn Skylar, wife of Dave the ad-man who had charge of Liberace's tour when he was lately in Cleveland. Mrs. Skylar had admired a pair of cufflinks the entertainer was wearing. So in the mails this week came the cufflinks made into earring for Mrs. Skylar."

It sounded so special, but Lee had dozens of these cufflinks and earrings made up for people with whom he did business. Unfortunately, I didn't treasure them enough and the gold print of the man at his piano has mostly worn away. I can only find one of David's cufflinks that were sent at the same time. The small insertions in gossip columns continued, but got more interesting when Joe took over the task.

A typical non-story tidbit occurred one day: "At the VIP-studded Health Council Welfare Federation luncheon at Hotel Carter yesterday, ad exec Dave Skylar admitted he was helping push the latest fashion for men—the wide lapel, double-breasted suit of yesteryear. However, Dave's isn't fresh from Carnaby Street—he got it out of the mothballs at his house."

The big flurry of articles came when he first became a vice president. In 1958, it seems as if every publication in the field, as well as the local media, wrote glowing stories about his promotion. As we look back we realized that the agency founded in 1912 never had a 33-year-old vice president before. The stories all included his membership in the Public Relations Society of America, Sigma Delta Chi (a national professional journalism society), and the Cleveland Advertising Club. They went on to say that he was chief instructor during the Ad Club's 1956 and 1957 sessions of the advertising school, and was continuing on as faculty advisor for the coming years. His service on many health and welfare boards was noted. This was just the beginning of his local notoriety.

Probably the nicest account appeared in the *Griswold House Organ* (WGOH). It was written in the form of a letter to the three ladies who acted as his secretaries: "Open Letter to Blanche Young, Cynthia Moore and Coleen Reardon. Dear Ladies, Please don't say anything about this 'til Monday afternoon—you wouldn't spoil a WGOH exclusive scoop—but we wanted you to be among the first to know that your boss is now a Griswold-Eshleman Vice President. That's right! Today, Dave Skylar becomes a vice president at 33, the agency's youngest. Blanche, you remember when Dave joined the company in 1949 as an assistant in our public relations department; and during the past nine years you have no doubt observed his general travel plans: fast and up. Dave worked on every PR account in the shop over a period of years; then, because he's a curious, eager-to-learn type of guy, he got into advertising and eventually became Mr. Farran's assistant on the B.F. Goodrich account. Other accounts he has served include National Clay Pipe, Nema, Society for Savings, American Vitrified, Osborne, Denison, and many more." The writer went on to name all the memberships in organizations, his previous work as a reporter and editor of a farm magazine, and the fact that he flew in heavy bombers over Europe as a bombardier-navigator and general morale builder.(I wonder where they got that from!) The rest of the letter remarked about his family and the big, black, moyen poodle, Suzette, who flunked obedience school. The letter closed with: "Anyway girls, just wanted to let you know right away. I know you join us all in wishing Dave sincere congratulations and good luck."

Joe didn't have anything to do with that piece, but there was a lot more he did drum up. Sometimes when I asked David about an item he would say, "I have no idea." In later years there were a few items that were embarrassing. There was an insert in one of the columns with a sketch of David on the side. It read: "Greater Cleveland has been known as a vibrant advertising and printing center for many years. Its fame will spread as far as London when David Skylar, Vice President of Griswold-Eshleman, speaks before the London Economic Institute (that's the ad club of the English capital) next Friday. This HALO OF THE WEEK to Skylar, who is one of the young men in the advertising business who has helped Cleveland's reputation. He is the author of a number of books, was partially responsible for the Cleveland Orchestra brochure that spread our fame behind the Iron Curtain two years ago, and his advertising genius has helped a number of civic drives, including the United Appeal of '66."

Most of the above was true except for writing the many books. I am not sure where that information came from. He has written dozens of articles and given an untold number of speeches, but he never had time to write even one book. When asked by friends and co-workers why that was, he merely answered that he preferred to communicate his ideas while they were fresh in his mind. And communicate he did. Every organization in town sought his help. He thrived on his successes. It took a lot of effort to perform these extracurricular activities while commuting to Chicago and New York. It was certainly ego building, but not necessarily lucrative. However, there were always perks—lots and lots of perks came with the job!

David with Joe Madigan and MJ Klyn, his associate.

Chapter 18

Vice President Skylar was given even more responsibilities at the agency, and he was also given more perks. One of the most enjoyable was the privilege of attending the annual convention of the AAAAs (American Association of Advertising Agencies). In mid-century it was held at the elegant Greenbrier resort in White Sulphur Springs, West Virginia. Only the top agencies in the country had memberships. Usually the major executives or owners of each company attended the event, so it was quite a coup for Charlie Farran to ask David to join him and his wife. Of course, I was included in the invitation! It probably was more exciting for the wives than the execs themselves. The women had to plan their wardrobes, after all. Since this was a first-time adventure for me, I went all out to show what a successful man's wife should wear. Of course, Irma Farran had to look the most regal of our team. She was the boss's wife! I simply followed suit in whatever she suggested. It was a great learning process.

Since the men didn't like trains, and the airlines did not have direct access, we drove down from Ohio. The first time we drove the Farrans down in our Ford Country Squire station wagon. It was a tedious drive, but the end game was worth it. This first time, I believe, I was in awe of all the big names I met, who up until now were only names in our big cocktail table book called "The Art of Advertising." I don't think David had the same feelings of excitement that I had. He felt he was one of the big boys now.

After the usual registration procedure in the lobby, we were accompanied by an old-time bellhop that showed us to our room. It was a beautiful corner room recently redone by Carleton Varney, a high-end interior designer at the time. The style was very British country and extremely colorful. The bellhop started to unpack for us, but we declined this service. He looked a little miffed, but he got a very large tip anyway. We checked our clothes after he left to see if anything needed pressing, and then settled down to rest and read the program of events issued to us when we arrived. That evening was more or less business casual, because people arrived at all hours from across the states and it wasn't always easy to get dressed up after a long trip. But from then on each day became more formal. All of the women involved, most of them wives, had to make immediate appointments at the beauty salon! There were scattered women advertising executives, but in those days it wasn't the norm.

At dinner the first night we sat at a table away from the other attendees. It was not a mingling night. Charlie Farran pointed out some of the illustrious names to us and we just took it all in. The guys wanted to pack it in early. Work began at the crack of dawn and included attending seminars, having lunch, and getting their foursomes together for the various tournaments. It was tough. All seminar leaders were urged to get everything on the agenda done efficiently so the golf and tennis could get going. David saw it was just like all the institute conventions he'd attended, only on a grander scale. It was going to be a blast.

The next day dawned clear and a bit chilly. A perfect day for golf! Unfortunately, it was perfect for the men only. If the ladies wanted to play they had to tee off almost in the dark, when it was colder and quite misty. Tennis was an option in the morning, but I still hadn't met anyone with whom to share a court. Sleep was my first choice at that point, and then reading the new books I had brought with me. Personally, I didn't care for ladies lunches or craft lectures and the like. Evenings were bound to be more fun. I looked forward to them.

The second evening passed rather quickly. A prominent politico made his rather boring speech after dessert that almost put us to sleep. By then David and Charlie had arranged to sit with other couples, and our new friends suggested we have a nightcap together. They also had been at this function in prior years, and told us an interesting tidbit about W. Virginia gambling. They suggested that the next evening we should go to the local casino. You have to understand that gambling was illegal in West Virginia at the time. I was all for the secrecy involved. Things were looking up.

The next night we found a big black limousine waiting for us after dinner. I found out later that it was a shuttle limo that made several trips a night from the resort to this place. It was just a place, to be sure; a charming, white clapboard, single story house that was well landscaped with tall trees and beautiful foliage. We weren't certain what to expect until we walked in the front door and saw a mini Las Vegas setup in the over-sized living room. The croupiers were LV styled also, but a bit stern looking. We saw dozens of people from the meeting, and it occurred to us that it was a private deal for the Greenbrier and no townies were admitted. We quickly got into the swing of things; David went to the craps table and I headed for my favorite roulette. As I was reaching over the people closer to the board to put my chips down, I felt someone looking down my dress. He made some remark and I ignored him. Later I found out it was a well-known agency man from New York City.

As we gambled with the custom-made chips we noticed a disturbance at the front blackjack table. A man was lying on the floor not moving. Everything stopped. As the manager was trying to revive the victim, in marched four state troopers with a gurney and hustled the poor man out of the room. The gambling went on as if nothing had happened. We later learned the man had a heart attack, but we never found out if he had died. We quit at that point and hustled into the limo. A couple of years later we learned that the little operation was out of business. The law caught up with it because it sent some of its chips through the US mail, and that was a no-no. We had brought our two chips back with us thinking we could use them again. The staid old Greenbrier lost a great attraction.

The final night of the meeting was ball gowns and black tie. The jewels on some of the more mature agency wives were magnificent, if not a little gaudy. It was obvious that postwar advertising was indeed quite successful in some areas. We actually danced away the night and David, who is not the storybook romantic, acted like he enjoyed this whole finale. In subsequent years we became the blasé middle-aged folks who brought along a younger couple. One time I tried to do a makeover for a lovely young wife who dressed like a frumpy old lady. I didn't have much luck. It was sad to find out that her husband left her behind as he moved up the ladder.

There is one funny story about the Greenbrier that I will never forget. David's agency had just bought a small agency in New York. The two principals and their wives came to the meeting where we met them for the first time. When we came down to breakfast I noticed one of the wives was wearing riding clothes. I was wearing a skirt and sweater. I chatted with her and asked if she enjoyed the trails that I'd heard were beautiful. I said I would like to ride with her the next time she went. She sort of looked over at her husband, who laughed heartily, and said in his New York accent, "Are you kidding? She has never been on a horse in her life. She just heard that riding pants were the only pants allowed in the Greenbrier dining room in the morning, so she bought two pair. A new classy agency wife! The following week David had to start his eastern commute to get the new Griswold-Eshleman branch in shape.

Greenbrier dinner with Griswold-Eshleman members only with AAAA.

Chapter 19

*L*ooking back on the sixties, it seemed as if David was always going or coming from some place. It got even more apparent when Griswold-Eshleman bought or merged with a New York agency called Mogul, Baker, Byrne, and Weiss. It certainly was not one of the big, well-known shops, but it had a creative presence in the big city and a couple of interesting clients. It was 1968.

Charlie wanted David to go to New York to take over the office, but he felt he could do the job just as well in three days a week. So began the eastern commute. Flying out of Cleveland early Monday morning, spending the next three days in New York, and back home again late Wednesday night or early Thursday morning. Naturally he went directly to the office, so it wasn't for another 12 hours or so that his family saw him. The main reason for his monitoring of the new agency was to get it synchronized with the methods of Griswold's home office. There was also the name change and client recognition of the new owners. Since David was by now executive VP and still Director of Client Services, as he had been for years, it was up to him to bring the new addition up to speed.

One of the interesting clients was a men's clothing store called Barney's. It was named after Barney Pressman, who was probably the PT Barnum of the men's clothing industry. He had been a client of the New York office and listened to the ideas that Jack Byrne tossed around, and consequently became quite successful. His son Fred joined him in the business. On one of his first trips, David met the Pressmans. He got along fine with them, and it was obvious that they would remain with GE as long as Byrne was on the account. David visited the Pressmans every chance he got. He also bought lots of suits! One of the first stories David told was of the way Barney would stand behind David as he looked in the mirror, grasping the voluminous folds of the pants in his fist and telling him how perfect the suit was for him. David was a 44 jacket and 36 pants at the time, and needed considerable alterations. I believe the very first suit he bought was a double-breasted Pierre Cardin with a very fitted jacket and side vents. Somehow Barney Pressman brought to mind the joke of the old salesman that yelled, "Turn on the blue light, Sam! The man wants a blue suit."

One of the other clients that David befriended was Ed Carey, the head of Carey Limousines. He and David hit it off so well that before long Skylar was added to the Carey Board of Directors. It is essential to have such a perk in New York, and we both took advantage of that. When I joined my husband in the Big Apple, I liked to go down to the garment district where I had a lot of contacts with the designers' workrooms. I remember bringing a friend from home with me, and hopping in and out of a car while the chauffeur had to circle and maneuver in the crowded streets while we tried on clothes. When I was not visiting, David would spend many after-work hours with Ed in Irish pubs playing darts. Boys will be boys. But the funniest story was in Boston when David got a Carey car to drive him out to see our daughter Claudia when she was a freshman at Wellesley. He found her dorm, but she was not home from class yet, a young girl told him. He waited about ten minutes and then saw his oldest child sauntering toward the dorm building. He got out of the limo to greet her. When she saw him, she shook her head in disbelief. He went to hug her and she said, "Daddy, what are you doing in that limo? It's so embarrassing!" He wanted to take her out to lunch, but she was ashamed to be seen getting in that vehicle. He knew he had raised her to have good values, but not that good. It took a lot of convincing to get her to join him for lunch! From then on he requested a simple Buick sedan for his transportation.

One other Carey story should be told. One time in New York, David asked the driver to go to the Bronx. He had the idea to see if his old birthplace was still there. As they came closer to the area the driver was getting more and more stressed, and he finally said to David, "I'm sorry, sir, I cannot take the chance of driving into that neighborhood. It is too dangerous." As David noticed the bombed-out look of the streets around him he heartily agreed, and they turned right around and headed for Manhattan. And this was in a normal unostentatious car. Forget nostalgia.

Other New York stories go farther back, at least to 1963. That was a very good year.

David joins his elders on the Board of Griswold-Eshleman.

Chapter 20

$\mathcal{E}$ ven before the New York agency was acquired, David made frequent trips to the big city for other clients that had branch offices there. That was also the heyday of the Plaza Hotel, one of the major hotels of the Hotel Corporation of America. The manager of the Plaza, Neal Lang, was a legend in the field. His sophistication and savvy innovations made the Plaza known throughout the world. In 1963, the place was booming, and Skylar had a great time consulting with his debonair client.

It seemed that one trip was to coincide with David having to meet his daughter's train from summer camp in Maine. After gathering all the bags, he whisked her off to the Plaza where he was going to meet with Neal before flying out to Buffalo, where he was to join me and our other two children for a brief weekend of work and play. The evening before they left, David took Claudia out for dinner and decided that they should get to sleep by ten, as they had an early flight to Buffalo. Claudia fell asleep quickly, but David had some work to do before he could call it a day. Around midnight, just as he was nodding off, someone knocked on the door. David hastily threw on his suit pants and opened the door to a fierce-looking man with a bulge under his suit jacket indicating a gun holster. "What's up?" David asked.

"I understand you have a young lady in your room, sir, and we don't condone that behavior in this hotel," said the man.

"What are you talking about? I have my daugh..." and he started to laugh. "Okay, I get it. What does Mr. Lang want?" he said.

"He wants you to come down to meet Leo Le Fleur, who has been entertaining in the Edwardian Room. Mr. Lang is having a party for him," the security guard said.

David said he would be down shortly and dashed off a quick note to Claudia, telling her how to reach him if she woke up. The party was going strong when he joined the group and before he realized it, the sun was about to rise. He hastily excused himself, hoping to grab at least an hour of sleep. When he got back to his room, his child was still apparently asleep.

A few hours later, father and daughter were leaving the hotel when the desk clerk handed David a large envelope. He stuffed it into his briefcase assuming it was some information he had wanted from Neal. Not a word was said about the night before as they rode out to La Guardia for the short flight. David did catch a few winks, as was his usual airplane habit.

When they arrived in Buffalo we were waiting to greet them along with the Madigans, who had driven us there. Joe was working on the Charterhouse account with David. The manager, Albert Elevic, was another old timer in the hotel business who befriended David and Joe, and comped them all the way. We'll get to that later.

That morning, however, Claudia ran down the steps of the plane breathlessly exclaiming, "Mommy, Mommy, Daddy got up after I went to sleep, and he went out and didn't come back till almost morning." I asked her to slow down and tell me again what she had said. I remember looking at David with great animosity and wonderment. My first reaction was anger that he had left his child in a hotel room alone, and then I started thinking of what he could be doing in the middle of the night. I didn't speak to him on the way to our quarters.

When we got there he seemed to remember something. He opened his briefcase and pulled out the envelope he was given at the Plaza. "See," he laughed, "now you know who I was with last night." He handed me a photo of him and Neal Lang pretending to vacuum the lobby. They were acting up for the photographer after an evening of partying. Neal Lang was a very funny guy. David always told that story and joked about his little girl with the big mouth that almost got him in trouble with his wife!

The rest of our weekend was fun. The children swam and watched TV while the adults sat around and just relaxed. There was one mystery I haven't solved to this day. In the picture David is wearing a short-sleeved shirt. How did he have one? When did he buy it? He hates short-sleeved dress shirts. That is just one small puzzle I cannot solve. I can't ask him, since his past memory is gone due to a stroke.

Neal Lang was a good client for David. He was also a good friend. He made David's days away from home very pleasant. He also needed companionship when his English wife, Suevie, took his son home to England from time to time. Eventually there was no more wife. His little boy, who was called Nello, was the prototype for Eloise at the Plaza. He was a real little character. I'm not sure if his mother had custody or not. The few times that I saw the boy, he was full of life. He used to wear nightshirts remade from Neal's shirts with Neal's monogram on them. To this day David has all his shirts done in the same monogram, which are two initials in the center of a circle of French knots. Neal was his stylish mentor. My next tale about New York also concerns Mr. Lang.

David with Neal Lang, manager of the Plaza Hotel, in a noctural vacuuming of the lobby.

David with Albert Elevic, Charterhouse Motel manager and Jayne Mansfield who promoted openings back then.

Chapter 21

The Hotel Corporation of America was constantly growing in its early years. New ideas for dining and entertainment rooms were always on the corporate agenda. One of the most elaborate dining schemes was first used, I believe, at the Edgewater Beach Hotel in Chicago in the 50s. Palm trees, exotic plantings, and Polynesian-type food attracted diners who sought a different venue for their celebrations. When one left the lobby of the hotel and walked into the Kon Tiki world it was a magical transformation. It was almost fun doing ads for the restaurant.

One of the ads that David created even won a national award. It was on billboards as well as newspapers, and caused a sensation in the advertising world. It showed a baby bottle with an olive in it and the headline was simply: "Take your baby to the Kon Tiki." The ad first ran in Cleveland when Kon Tiki opened in the Hotel Cleveland. It was later used in other locations. Years later we saw various bars and restaurants copy the idea in one form or another. David also worked with Jack Gilbert on exotic menus for the room. Too bad no one thought to record their hilarity as they made up unusual names for the food offerings. I can only tell you 50 years later that they enjoyed their work tremendously!

One day Neal Lang called David and asked him when he was going to be in New York again. David answered, "I'll be there whenever you need me."

"I need you now. We just booked Eartha Kitt into the Persian Room, and I convinced the Sonnabends that she is a great draw for the hotel. I need you to come up with a great ad to back me up."

"Hey, that's easy. I'll get on it right away. Give me a couple of days to set up and I'll get back to you on my arrival time," he said.

Since the Plaza was then the most elegant of HCA properties, it was almost a privilege to work for it. There was talk at the time that Neal was at odds with the owners about which groups and conventions should be booked at the exclusive hotel. Neal was turning down business that he deemed unacceptable for his hotel. He also felt that bringing in celebrities as guests, as well as entertainers, would restore the original prestige of the hotel.

David got right to work on the assignment. He researched all he could about the entertainer. He then realized that most people had heard of her and there didn't seem to be a need for describing her background or her talent. *I'll keep it simple*, he thought, and an idea popped up that convinced him he had really done it this time. He sketched out what he wanted and took it to the art department for finishing. He called Neal and told him he would be on the early plane the next day.

In the morning, on the way into town from La Guardia, he wondered briefly if the tone of the ad would be approved. But knowing Neal as well as he did, he felt confident that he would get it. David passed through the lobby nodding to some of the staff that he knew, and took the elevator up to Lang's suite. It was a spectacular suite that had been negotiated when he contracted to become general manager. David rang the doorbell and Neal answered the door in an elegant smoking jacket and slacks, obviously not yet dressed for work. He greeted his ad man and friend with a hearty handshake.

"Have you had breakfast yet? They will be bringing up some shortly. Anyway, how about a Bloody Mary beforehand? Then we will get to work. I ordered some eggs benedict and plenty of toast—enough for everybody," he quipped. David wondered who "everybody" was. Did the owners decide to attend the ad meeting? Did Neal's wife come in from England? He wondered about all this silently. It wasn't the time to ask questions.

David removed the ad copy from his briefcase as Neal put the drinks on the table. He stopped short as he glanced at the presentation.

He whistled and said, "What have we got here!? That's fantastic. I love it!" Then he read the full newspaper page layout. At the bottom of the page which had a shadowy seductive photo of the singer it read: "Have Eartha Kitt for dinner tonight...in the Persian Room at the Plaza Hotel." David beamed with pleasure as his simple idea was accepted."

"I'm glad you like it," David said. "What do you think Eartha Kitt will say about it?" he asked.

"Why don't we just ask her?" he said with a twinkle in his eye, and called out loudly, "Eartha, come here a minute. I want to show you something."

In about 20 seconds the bedroom door opened and out comes the chanteuse herself dressed in a nightgown and extremely feminine negligee. She was a petite woman, but her charms were very evident. Neal introduced her to David and showed her the ad. Her great big eyes got even bigger, and she laughed girlishly.

"Sonny, you got my number. I love what you have done," she purred. And with that she leaned over and grabbed the Bloody Mary that David had not touched.

"You have your answer, Dave," Neal remarked, and just then there was a knock on the door. Two waiters brought in the sumptuous late breakfast. David ate enough for three people himself, but then again, he always had a hearty appetite when things went well.

The ad took a full page in the *Times,* and Eartha had a very successful run at the Plaza. Just recently I learned from some old-time hotel man (they are few and far between) that our dear friend Neal Lang left HCA in a mutually agreeable way. He was even given a going-away party. Paul Sonnabend took over until a new manager was hired. We lost track of Neal after that. David lost a good friend.

David with Hotel Sheraton Cleveland manager, Allen Lowe, receive the grand prize advertising award for Kon-Tiki campaign in 1961.

Chapter 22

*A*lthough David did not belong to a club in his early working career, he played an awful lot of golf for business. He was very lucky that Charlie Farran, his boss, arranged for him to use the facilities of Canterbury Golf Club whenever he entertained clients. Usually that's a no-no unless the member is in the foursome, but in this case it was undisputed. Charlie was president of the club. No questions asked. David was well known by the starter and the caddies, as well as the grill room servers. Years later when I played in ladies district tournaments, I would be approached by the Canterbury starter to find out how my husband was doing.

It was natural then for him to wish Cleveland could have a professional golf tournament of its own, so when he heard about an inquiry being made by some acquaintances, he checked into its authenticity. It turned out that one of his long-time friends was at the same club as the group making the inquiry. These members of Beechmont Country Club went to Michigan for three days to talk to PGA officials about the rudiments of golf tournament startups. When they returned to Cleveland they got the board to okay the tournament, and a contract was signed with the member that bought the so-called deal for several years of events. Immediately the committee was formed and David became the public relations and advertising director of the project. His good friend, Dick Perlmuter, and his family's company did all the printing thanks to David. The first Cleveland Open was touted as the first $110,000 golf tournament. It was the hottest sport event to hit the city in a long time.

David was able to get top sponsors, and not surprisingly they were mostly his clients. One of the main ones was Society National Bank. He also obtained the sponsorship of Coca-Cola, The May Co., and D.O. Summers, a dry cleaning chain. It wasn't a hard sell; everyone wanted to get into the act. David had a lot of details to work out. He had to plan schedules for interviews of the golfers, as well as their individual transportation and locker room needs. He actually set up a table in the locker room to answer questions or offer assistance to any of the participants.

Questions like "where is the best barbershop" or "where is the best place for a steak dinner" were answered promptly. The guys really appreciated the extra attention. Our son Dean became a gofer, and at the end of the tournament he was rewarded a white hardhat that was signed by every major player of the day. He also became the proud owner of all of the scorecards. He still hasn't parted with them.

The night before the pro-am, David had an open house at our house. He invited all the golfers and sponsors for a stag party. I had left town that morning to take our daughter to camp and missed the whole thing. To this day I can't imagine how David managed the party as well as taking care of three-year-old Stephanie and 10-year-old Dean. I guess it is good that I will never know!

As part of the organizing team, David did not have to pay for his round for the pro-am which was expensive. He drew as a partner Tommy Bolt, who was known as a hot-headed golfer. The other amateur was Vince Marotta, who was later known as Mr. Coffee after his great discovery. I have not found out who his pro partner was. As the first groups of committee members went off you could see the nervous looks on their faces. The fans were lined up on both sides of the tee, and they had never had an audience before. Some did well, but others did not. David, who was a decent enough golfer, walked up to the tee with a terrific swagger and hit a ground ball that hardly went past the crowd line. Although embarrassed at first, he laughed it off and had a magnificent second shot. From then on he played a very nice game. Somewhere about halfway through the game, the terrible tempered Tommy broke one of his clubs on a tree and it was downhill from then on.

The tournament was a great success. The fans were delighted to see their new idol at the time, Arnold Palmer, win. I've been told that David and Coca Cola convinced CBS to wire up the whole golf course for the very first televised tournament that was the forerunner of all our present golf viewing to this day. It was also interesting to find out that there had been a skirmish between Lee Trevino and some drunk at the club, and a problem with NAACP about a locker room attendant.

I also learned that the host club made $50,000 on the deal. The printers made money on the program and other printed materials. The promoter, of course, had to make his share. David Skylar? Nada. But he always worked for the challenge, and he felt that he done a good job. The original club didn't step forward the next year. The members had thought the pros would be friendlier to them, and they were disappointed enough to vote against hosting the second year. It was not till 1971 that they tried again. In 1964 and 1965 the tournament was played at a municipal golf course, then a country club on the other side of town for two years. After a few more starts at semi-private courses it came back to Beechmont Country Club. Unfortunately, Paul Warren, the original franchise owner, passed away and his wife sold off the package.

David and golfer Tommy Bolt at first Cleveland Open.

Senator Metzenbaum and David with pros at the Cleveland Open.

David with Vincent Marotta (Mr. Coffee) and their pro-am partners.

Chapter 23

Throughout the sixties David managed to continue his charitable work despite all the agency responsibilities. I wondered how he could maintain his health as well as his equilibrium. The city leaders, many of whom seemed to be Griswold clients, called upon him constantly to serve on the non-profit organization boards that proliferated in Cleveland at the time. There is no doubt that he believed in helping these groups in any way he could. It was amazing that the community leaders listened to what he told them. His efforts on behalf of his company's clients in both business and civic matters were intimate and vastly complex. While most advertising and public relations men have specific spheres of operation, David seemed to be everywhere and did everything—always in the background. He had a reputation for almost shocking candor; honesty was basic to his relationship with his clients as well as his friends. In a profession known for soft answers, he had this gift of blunt straightforward speech.

In 1965, David began to make speeches about citizens becoming more active in their communities. One of his early efforts he titled: "Arise Ye Women of the World." To better explore his thoughts at the time, I would like to quote some of his passages in a speech to one women's group.

"It seems to me that every season is open season on women, but more so today. The cry of distress is sounded every time you turn around. The so-called experts tell you that our culture is engulfed in grief because American women have declined to grow up; have refused to seek their own identity and have failed to pursue a career outside the home. I think this is nonsense. Not only is this off base as a theory, but it distorts the facts. It's true that US women in the 50s and 60s have taken a temporary breather in their pursuit of freer, fuller lives as career girls, but it's false to claim that a whole generation of brain-washed child brides has been forced into a housewife trap as confining as a concentration camp.

"Further, the experts say your only salvation lies in a full-time profession or a high-level creative job. Since most women don't have the talent or education for this kind of job, the gloomy message is unavoidable. There is no escape.

"But when we look at the facts and sweep all the gloomy generalizations aside, the clear and uncontradictable truth about women in America today is there is no one kind of woman and no single pattern of living."

He goes on to say that women who were weary of baby talk, but were unable to break out into the working world, found that their moment came when their youngest child entered first grade. He noted that almost half the mothers of school-age children were out of the house by then and on a job. He said that was an unprecedented and unmatched event in wartime. He felt this statistic disproved the notion that most women are condemned to a domestic life.

The choices for women's participation in business and the community were many, and continue through their later years. Many women, he said, were working their children, or even their grandchildren, through college. Others are involved in community projects: city-wide art shows, recordings for the blind neighborhood, improvement groups, and the like. David even quoted Mary Beard, who said in her book *Women as a Force in History*: "The dogma of woman's historical subjection to man must be read as one of the most fantastic myths ever created by the human mind."

When David made the statement that tests were done to show that women were as intelligent as men, and slightly more so, the women in the audience applauded wildly. When the ladies went home to report the speech, their husbands were not so approving. It was not a myth that many men of the day still hired women for the most part as office workers and very few got executive positions.

So you see, David Skylar was quite different from most of his fellow workers. He was able to convey his progressive thoughts to most of his clients. Gradually, old-fashioned advertising became lighter and less technical, and more profitable. Two years later another speech was a big hit with the ladies. This one he titled: "Have an Affair with Cleveland." He expanded on the idea that women feel they are unfulfilled in their home or in a lower-echelon job in the business world, and suggested they have an "affair" with their city. He specified that it didn't matter if you belonged to the Alka Seltzer or Pepsi Generation, you had to get involved and participate in something worthwhile. So guess what?" All this positive thinking was for real. I ended up as the "better half" of two charitable fundraising groups.

First came the Heart Fund. I don't know how it came about, or who suggested it, but somehow Mr. and Mrs. David Skylar were the first husband and wife team to share the chairmanship. I have a feeling my husband suggested it. I guess I might have suspected that at the time, but good little wife that I was, I never argued out of it or complained. Actually, he really needed my help. With all his other activities it was a wonder he did as much as he did. He made all the decisions and got the corporation guys involved, and I had to attend meetings and meetings, and more meetings, since over 37,000 volunteers had to be inspired, as well as organized, to do neighborhood canvassing on Heart Sunday. The goal was $888,000, a sum that was to finance all the heart programs for the coming year. It doesn't seem like enough money, but in those days it was considered a huge amount, at least 39% more than the year before. Cleveland in those days always came through with charitable giving, so the goal was reached and then some.

I should tell you right now that I was perfectly happy being a bum, taking care of my home and family, and doing occasional stints as a substitute reporter. I also became a stringer for my old work place the *Cleveland Press*, and later the *Cleveland Plain Dealer*. I loved to play tennis and golf, but I hated luncheons and meetings. Committees met and nothing ever seemed to get done. Now you know that my husband got me into my community activities. When he told the various women's groups to get involved in the community he wasn't kidding. I was the guinea pig. Eventually I did enjoy doing certain projects. The women's City Club had me write a big show for them, but it got canceled when the president had a heart attack. However, working with the big projects came sooner than I thought. We became the co-chairmen of the Cleveland United Appeal Metropolitan Division. That's the division where all the population is called upon to give their time and money. The "little guys," I called us. No big corporate pledges, just small contributions to add to the fund. That was a job to end all jobs. Literally. After that campaign I didn't do too much community service. David, however, continued helping out wherever he could.

Getting back to the United Appeal campaign, I must tell you that no campaign before or after had the pizzazz that enveloped that one in 1969. It was all because David used every one of his public relation tactics to inspire the thousands of volunteers. He helped me write my speeches, as well as his, and sent me on daily trips to outlying sections of the city. The job isn't only during the campaign; it starts four months before the actual door-to-door canvassing. We had to meet the section managers and their captains, and so on down the line. I had to blend in with the neighborhoods that I visited. It's a bit simpler for the men. They just wear the same suits wherever they go. Women have to tone down or up, depending on the group. I kept track of any problems, but it was not so difficult if the captains were doing their part.

Most of my speeches were gatherings in someone's home. My pep talks seemed to be received enthusiastically, but there was one home in my own neighborhood where I was upstaged by a coffee pot. The captain/hostess was Ann Marotta. When it came time for refreshments she was busy showing all the ladies the new invention that was going on the market soon by her husband's new company. It was to be called Mr. Coffee. It was hard to continue UA details when the volunteers were so excited about the invention.

David, who was executive vice president and still director of client services at Griswold-Eshleman, by then had a private goal in mind. He had served as PR director of the campaign since 1966, when it hadn't made its goal and he was determined to do all he could with his metropolitan division to change the trend. In a *Plain Dealer* article, the general manager of the Community Chest that puts out the United Appeal said that there was too much divisiveness in the community. He was referring to the article that said that there were conflicts between the rich and poor, between ministers and their congregations, between blacks and whites, and between central city dwellers and suburbanites. The newspaper went on to say that the conflicts were deeper than those aforementioned. It believed people were leery of duplicating their private gifts with the government subsidies. The closing dinner was where the results were to be announced. When the Metropolitan Division was called to announce its total donations, David and I didn't just stand up and report. We marched in with a loud musical presentation of the Amazing Mets, with our whole group of volunteers led by David in an authentic Mets baseball uniform and me in a Oscar De La Renta dress. Nobody thought to give me a Mets uniform also.

(Thanks dear.) Anyway, we went over the top in the gifts, and I believe a lot of that so-called divisiveness ended.

David was soon to embark on a different phase of his career. But once an ad man, always an adman, no matter what you end up doing.

Heading the march of the "Amazing Mets" United Appeal campaign.

We got the final goal announcement off to a booming start.

Chapter 24

In the summer of 1965, the Skylar family went on an extended tour of the United States. It was probably the first and last time we were all together. Here's how it all began. Claudia, age14, came home from school one day and announced she no longer wanted to go to camp. "Camp is boring and I want to go someplace different. All the kids I know do exciting things in the summer, so why can't I? Lizzy is going to Las Vegas to see her grandparents. That sounds neat."

"Yeah," said Dean, "camp is dumb. I want to go to Disneyland. Mark is going as soon as school is over."

"Me too! Me too!" called out little five-year-old Stephanie. "I want to get a Mickey Mouse hat and go on the wheel thing that goes around and around."

"Okay kids," I said, "we'll have a family meeting after dinner. We'll see what your daddy thinks, but I want you to know that I don't want to take a trip just because others are doing it. We must do something that we really want to do for our own sakes."

That evening Big Daddy was greeted at the corner when he got off the rapid transit. Claudia on her bike, Steph on her mini two-wheeler, and Dean on his precious skateboard. It was quite a sight to see, and David asked them how come they all came to greet him. "We just want to tell you that you have to convince Mom to go on a trip this summer."

"That shouldn't be too difficult," said David.

When they got to the door I was waiting, and received my quick hello kiss from the weary worker, who then asked, "What's up with the kids?"

"Oh, they are hoping to get out of camp this summer. They want to go places," I said laughingly.

"So what's the big deal? As a matter of fact, I was going to talk to you about taking some time off myself to travel," David said. "Let's eat and I'll tell you what I was thinking about later."

"See Mom, Dad is on our side already," Claudia gloated.

Dinner was over quickly and David told us his thoughts about a vacation. He explained that a lot of his clients took long summer sojourns at the shore or to their retreats in the mountains, and nothing much got done in the advertising business in the summer. He also said that he had more than six weeks of vacation time coming to him, and it would be a good time to take it.

When the kids heard that they started hollering all at once, "Can we go to a ranch?" "No, no, Disneyland!" "How about where they make movies, etc.?" I looked at David and realized it was a fait d'acompli; we were going out west!

From that time on we started preparing for the trip. One of the first things to do was contact AAA to get a triptic made out. David specified a beginning route that would include a northern Michigan stop where he had to attend a client meeting. It happened to be held at a shabby chic resort in Harbor Springs. It was the kind of place that wealthy families visited in summers past, but by then was noticeably on its last legs, so to speak. It was trying so hard to hold onto its exclusive reputation while the paint peeled onto the ground. But we will cover that later.

Organizing a six-week trip for a family of five is no easy task. The first problem was how to carry luggage when the kids took over the back of the wagon. Most of the time the seats would be down and they would be sprawled on the flat surface with their games and books, and other junk. When we realized that situation, David bought a five-foot case made to fit on the Ford country squire roof rack. It was also a couple of feet high. It was meant to carry all of our suitcases. Each person was to be responsible for his own suitcase. Little Stephy had a little pink suitcase for her treasures, but not her clothes, and that was a huge problem. We had to decide how long we could go without visiting a Laundromat. As it turned out, we took way too many outfits for everyone.

The day before we were to begin our journey, Dean broke out in a rash and we had to get in to see our pediatrician. It was some kind of contact dermatitis and we got a prescription filled. Claudia wanted to have her best friend Laura sleep over, and I said it wasn't possible since we had to leave too early in the morning. She sulked the rest of the day. Stephy was busy gathering up about 50 Barbie dolls to squeeze into her little case, and I knew I would have to eliminate half of them while she slept. David came home late from the office with an armload of folders.

"What's all that about?" I asked.

"I just want to do a little research on a new company we're going after."

"I thought you were going to take it easy and forget work this time," I said.

"Well, six weeks is a long time and it doesn't hurt to keep the old brain functioning," he said with a smile. I was too tired to protest.

After dinner David started loading the suitcases into the monster box on the car roof. It was no easy job. I cleaned the refrigerator out except for the juice and milk we needed for breakfast. We had just enough bread left for everyone's toast. I had already laid out clothes for the morning. Everything seemed in order and I decided to call it a day. David soon came upstairs and was sound asleep before I counted my first Barbie doll. We all awakened early and I made breakfast. It didn't take long before we were on the way. When we were a block away I said, "You know, I think I left the back burner on low."

David turned to me and crabbily said "That's too *%VS#@! bad. I'm not going back." And so we began our wild and wooly trip out west.

We managed to arrive at the aforementioned Harbor Springs in time for dinner. It was beautiful countryside, but the hotel was as we expected; old, genteel surroundings with some old and some young employees. It didn't much matter to me or David what the place looked like. He sought out his client and I sought out the rooms we'd booked so we could all freshen up for dinner. There was one interesting attraction on the grounds—an authentic caboose parked on tracks behind the main building. Immediately following dinner the kids went out back to inspect the train. Claudia was the least interested in the inspection, but she was recruited to watch her little sister. There was not much else to do, but we had to wait out the two days of David's meetings.

When we finally got on our way again, the weather got a bit blustery for summer, but I guess that was expected for northern Michigan. Our plan was to see the thousand islands, Sault St. Marie and the locks, and continue on to Mackinac Island.

When we got near the locks it was hard to see anything because of the weather, and the ferry to Mackinac was temporarily halted, so we never did get there. So much for educational visits.

Since this isn't supposed to be a travelogue, I won't bore you with every stopover, but you must hear about our week at Triangle X Ranch. This was the highpoint of the trip, I believe. None of us had ever been to Moose, Wyoming before, and the terrain was really startling. The Grand Teton Mountains are magnificent, especially at sunset. However, it was the real working ranch aspect that made the week special. The few guests that were accepted were treated like the family that owned the ranch. Each of us had our own horse for the week, and the kids learned how to groom and saddle their mounts. Each day the wranglers would take a small group up into the hills, mostly walking, but sometimes the older children and adults would be allowed to trot or canter. I like horses, but I often preferred to stay back and read a book. David, who always said he wanted to be a cowboy, really got into it. He became proficient enough to ride in the protective line of wranglers.

The evening before we left we were taken on a real cookout. People sat around a campfire and ate and sang songs. It was getting dark and I was concerned about our "baby" Stephanie, who had to ride back on her big horse "Flair" in the dark. She was put on her horse and I rode behind her, and one wrangler was in front of her and David to her side. We didn't worry about the older kids. We all tried to talk to her so she wouldn't be frightened of the dark, but she was not answering. Her two guides looked over in the almost faded light and saw that she was asleep! I panicked when we had to walk through a creek up to the horses knees and come out the other side very rapidly, but I shouldn't have worried. Good old "Flair" carried her through and she didn't even wake up. When we got to the ranch and dismounted, David carried her to our cabin. We managed to get her into her pajamas without completely waking her.

It was hard leaving the ranch, because everyone was so happy there. Claudia even met a sixteen-year-old boy from Cincinnati who became her pen pal. Two years later he even visited her. Dean just went his merry way, never taking off his madras hat until Disneyland. Except for the ranch and California, we didn't stay in one place very long. It was a real job to load and unload the suitcases from the carry-on atop the wagon every night. It was amazing that David kept his sanity with all the heavy lifting. As I look back, I wonder at our patience. Of course we were young parents then. No major problems to get us stressed out.

I think our offspring were getting a little spoiled though. When we got to Winnemucca, Nevada, we got into a strange motel that was unlike anything we had stayed in previously. There was one tiny room, and just beyond two more tiny rooms. There was also unusually ugly furniture. Stephanie walked through the door and promptly said, "This doesn't look like the Plaza," and we all broke up laughing. That remark helped get rid of some of our tension.

San Francisco was delightful. It was the first time I had been there. Since I was not yet an avid golfer, I did not care about stopping at Pebble Beach, but we did want to see Hearst Castle, as David and I studied his life at journalism school. We wanted to see how the yellow journalists lived. The morning we headed south, we all had a big breakfast outside of San Francisco. What a huge mistake! The winding roads above the coastline caused four of us to lose our breakfasts. Our driver was okay and just a bit green around the gills, as the saying goes. We managed to get a private tour of the Hearst grounds even though it wasn't open for the day yet. We were impressed.

We continued on to LA where we looked up friends and family. David had become friends with a former tennis star, Tony Trabert, whom he met when he was promoting sportswear at The May Co., which was one of David's good clients. Somehow Tony told David we could use his apartment while he was on the East Coast. It was in a nice neighborhood, but it was not a very homey place. David told me that Tony was in the process of a divorce and he had moved out of his house. That made sense, since the closets were filled with dozens of sport shirts for men and no women's clothing.

One funny thing happened though. Stephy was looking for some of her jacks that fell in the bedroom David and I were in, and she was reaching under our bed and pulled out a small leather case with the initials AA on it. "What did I find, Mommy?" she asked.

I unzipped an inch or two and quickly closed it. "Just an old case Mr. Trabert must have forgotten. Go play in the other room, honey. I want to take a rest," I sputtered. David walked in from the kitchen just as she left the room. "Guess what?" I said. "Your friend Tony must be having an affair with a stewardess. She left all her paraphernalia under the bed," I laughed.

"So what?" he said.

"That must be the reason for the divorce."

"Don't ever say anything to him."

"What do you think I am? Stupid? I just wanted to tell you that it was a good thing I was in the room when Steph found the case or she would now be asking you what all the stuff was."

"Okay, okay I got the message," he growled.

We happened to hit LA during the Watts riots, and it was very scary for the kids to see army vehicles driving up and down the highways. The National Guard was out in full force. We decided to take off for Anaheim earlier than planned. Soon Dean and Stephy became attached to their Mickey Mouse hats, and the little one tried sleeping in hers. The second half of the trip took us to Scottsdale, Taos, and Santa Fe, and the amazing Grand Canyon, where I watched my mad man and his two older children go to the bottom on mules that made hairpin turns. As they moved farther away, Stephanie and I put our quarters in the big telescope and made each other nervous watching the rest of our family.

All of the rest of the trip was rather unexciting. We did show the kids Columbia, Missouri, and the University of Missouri Journalism School where we met. We didn't buy anything special along the way, nor did we indulge in any extravagant entertainment, except for Disneyland. What we did acquire was a husband and a father with a beard! He decided he liked the red beard and never wanted to shave it again. "You are nuts if you think you can get away with that at the agency," I teased. And of course, I was right. It only took a few days after we returned home that he bowed to his client's dirty looks. That's it for vacations and freedom of expression in the good old 60s!

Oh yes! I should mention I was the first one out of the wagon when we arrived home: I got my own house key out and ran into the kitchen. The electric Calrod burner was still on simmer. I gulped as I turned it off. The angel was on one of our shoulders, that's for sure.

David tested his associates on their tolerance for his post vacation goatee.

Stephanie and her Dad at the Snake River 1965.

Chapter 25

David considered entertaining his clients a major part of his advertising work. He preferred including wives and significant others in any form of entertainment We took people out for dinner at our club later on, but in his early years as an ad executive he suggested we have parties at home. We always mixed personal friends with business associates so conversation could float in any direction. We didn't need excuses like national holidays, but we did use birthdays and anniversaries. David also liked to come up with parties that had original themes.

One of our first parties was a surprise party for David's 40th birthday. He did not have anything to do with it, and he was really surprised. I scripted an invitation in rhyme asking the guests to wear casual clothes and bring a blanket to sit on for a special picnic honoring David. The gimmick was a new service by the best hamburger restaurant in town that brought a service wagon into your backyard. Everyone was told to park in the schoolyard across the street so there were no cars visible.

On the day of the party, I told David I had made plans to take the kids swimming at a friend's pool. That was a big event in those days, because very few people built pools in northern cities. It was a perfect way to keep David away from home, as he liked to sit around in the sun. I also arranged with another friend to be at the house with a bartender and canapé server. She was instructed to call our pool hostess as if to chat, but she was really signaling that everyone was arriving at home and in the house having their first drinks. I immediately got up and said I thought it was time to get home, and got the children into dry clothes. David was so happy lounging in the sun; it was a shame to leave. We finally left and I called out to my friend, "See you Tuesday, and thanks for the swim."

We got home in about 15 minutes, and all was quiet as we drove up our long driveway. We opened the garage door with the remote and were making the turn into the garage when we spotted Paul Wilcox coming out of the French doors to the yard.

"What the hell?" David exploded and stopped the car and got out. "Paul, what is going on?" he said, and then everyone started coming out back with their blankets calling: "Surprise!" and the fun began. The yard was soon filled with picnickers who didn't have a clue how they were getting dinner. After about an hour of cocktails, we heard some loud bells ringing and in came the Mawby hamburger wagon. No one had seen this before, and they all cheered. Our guests were able to specify the way they wanted the burger cooked and choose their side orders.

As the sun went down, everyone drifted back inside where some of the agency friends set up a mic and read silly offerings for the birthday boy. They also brought gifts that encouraged lots of comments. The guest list included bankers, tycoons, bosses, relatives, and good old friends. The unusual mix of people somehow put everyone at the same level. From then on we used the same formula for all our parties. Diversity works.

We usually entertained someone privately at least once a month. The fun parties were not as frequent, as they took some planning and some extra money. It was wonderful that David had such rapport with printing companies, because they were always eager to print the invitations that he or I dreamed up.

During the big tennis boom in the sixties, Cleveland had yet to build many indoor courts. When people wanted to play in the winter in the eastern suburbs, they played at the Old Cavalry Armory that was converted into tennis courts when the horses were no longer there. The members of the elite Skating Club were given access to the courts in some kind of deal, but since it was government property, anyone could pay to play there. One day when our children were having a lesson from the tennis pro there, we asked him to check whether we could rent the armory for a private party. He checked it out and told us we could have the place for a hundred dollars, payable to the city. David took it from there. He designed an elaborate invitation with a picture of a tennis ball under the lettering: "First Annual Cleveland Open." Inside was an RSVP card asking whether you were a player or spectator. It was such an exciting invitation (at least for our Midwestern town) that most everyone accepted.

When the invitations started coming back I had to get the players listed to the pro, who then started the pairings. At that point David was too busy to do any party planning. I felt like the Perle Mesta of Shaker Heights. There was really a lot to do. I got the best caterer in town, who really did "cater" to the social elite of the city and was hired for all their charity events. Then there were people like us who brought a lot of future customers into his realm. He and I decided on a simple menu that was elegantly presented. Two kinds of bisques, lobster and tomato, served in huge sterling bowls, salad fixings, and hors d'oeuvres. After all, it wasn't healthy to eat too much while engaging in a strenuous activity! The funny part is the food table had to be set up in front of a huge cannon that could not be moved from the armory. We couldn't do too much with the décor, but it didn't seem to matter. The tennis players wanted the winners' tennis outfits, and they played hard. David did make sure that the players got to their matches and were in decent shape to play. Oh, I did forget that spiked punch was also served.

Soon after our event, David was asked if he would be interested in starting an indoor/outdoor tennis facility, and of course he said yes. This turned out to be one of our better deals. We put down only $500 and waited over a year until the place was built. We were charter members, and were not assessed the $3,000 that new members had to pay. We spent many enjoyable hours there until our golf club decided to build indoor courts. We had to leave the Cleveland Racquet Club, and it was sad.

I'll tell you about some other parties as we move along in the "Big Career." I still have about 40 years to cover in these mad men tales. Even though David changed direction in his work, he still had the mindset of an advertising man. Whatever it was, it seemed to work. It was one big disappointment that changed his direction. I don't think a lesser man could have withstood it.

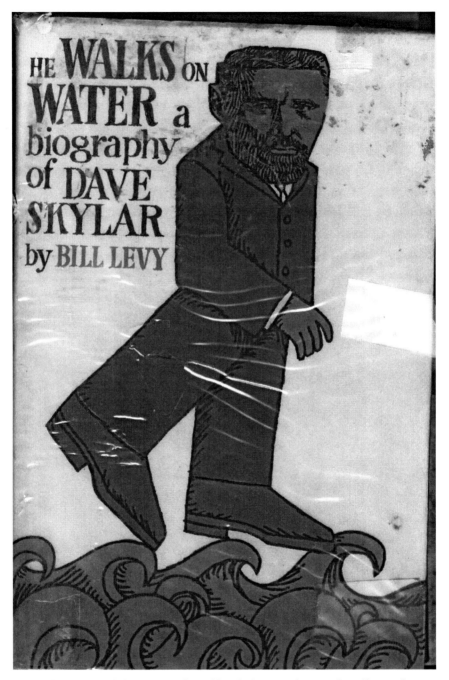

Bill Levy pasted this to a cardboard book that David put on his office wall.

ABOUT   * * SURPRISE PARTY * * SURPRISE PARTY * *

FOR RELEASE   AFTER JULY 11th - 'TIL THEN IT'S A SECRET

FOR FURTHER
INFORMATION   Mrs. Marilyn Skylar -- WY 1-1354
CONTACT   2863 Montgomery Road

* * FLASH * * FLASH * * FLASH * * FLASH * * FLASH * * FLASH * * FLASH * * FLASH * * FLASH * *

ON BECOMING FORTY

Surprise Big Dave Skylar?
He's dumb as those foxes,
That sold the poor Eskimos
Those great big iceboxes.

On July Eleventh,
He'll be edgy and sore,
Sad and retrospective,
A boy wonder no more.

He'll never suspect that
His friends might all rally,
He'll be down in the dumps,
With no million to tally.

So please come at five o'clock sharp,
And do try to prepare,
An ad or commercial,
'Bout the life of this square.

Wear comfortable sport clothes,
This picnic's a grasser,
To honor the New World's,
Greatest Living Gasser.

R.S.V.P.
        Mrs. Marilyn Skylar, WY 1-1354   Please Park
        2863 Montgomery Road   at Malvern School.

- 30 -

Invitation to David's surprise 40th birthday party.

Chapter 26

*A*fter two decades at the ad agency, David believed he had it all. And he did. He was recognized by the community's business elite, and he had a busy social life as well. I know, because we went to so many parties, both charitable and personal, that sometimes it just felt great to stay home and read or watch TV. He thought that his last promotion to executive vice president was a real milestone in his career. After the acquisition of the New York agency, he was traveling all the time. The responsibilities kept increasing, and so were his expectations. He was a member of the company's board of directors when Charlie Farran announced he was planning to become chairman and open the slot for president. A date was set for the next big meeting, which would decide on a new president. Most of the agency's employees believed that Skylar was Charlie's logical successor, since they'd worked together for so many years, first as mentor and student, and next as equal advisors to one another.

The day of the board meeting was bright, but chilly. Winter was just a few weeks away. David put on a handsome tweed suit from his client Barney's, because it included a vest. He never wore a really warm wool coat, but always an Aquascutum raincoat with the lining removed. It must have been a carry-over from the Air Force days. He decided to drive downtown that day, as he had some people to see in the western suburbs. All the way downtown he wondered what the outcome of the election would be at the meeting.

The board was to meet at ten, so he had some time to write a few memos and make some urgent phone calls. He left his office and was met by a few "Good Lucks" from some friends on the way. When he got to the boardroom most of the members were already seated. Soon everyone had arrived and the meeting began. After a few items on the agenda were disposed of, the secretary announced that two people had been proposed for the office of president, and David was one of them. The other was a man that was barely known in the agency, and who had just been brought in as creative director a few months before. He was asked to come into the meeting to be told of his nomination. After he arrived and was informed of the honor, both he and David were sent out of the room while the voting took place. I do not know if David, as a member, was allowed to have a vote.

After a long wait in another office, the two men were sent for and they solemnly walked into the boardroom. Charlie, as outgoing president said, "Congratulations Jim," and the others joined in. Jim Johnston became president of Griswold-Eshleman after a few short months. He then said, "And David, I would like you to become vice-chairman of the board."

David simply said, "Thanks, but no thanks," shook Jim Johnston's hand, waited for the adjournment of the meeting, and went straight to his office where he wrote his resignation letter in long hand. Miss Young took the letter to her desk to type and she had tears in her eyes. This couldn't be happening. Soon the whole office was in shock. Everyone felt as if they were deceived in some way. Nobody knew how they could respond to this stranger who had come into their midst and expected loyalty. As Joe Sallay, one of David's old agency friends put it years later, "It was so sudden, like *bang*, who is this guy and how can we work for him?"

Everybody walked around for days in a funk. Then began the speculation. Was David passed over because he was Jewish? Who voted against him? The whole advertising community seemed to go along with this theory. There didn't seem to be any other reason. Even David was beginning to accept this as fact.

We believe that Charlie Farran was on David's side. He was very upset when he received the resignation. Somehow it didn't occur to him that it would happen. In the few weeks until he left, he and David still collaborated on some work in progress. The company employees gave David a going-away party complete with a very creative autobiographical book which everyone in the agency signed. It was good medicine to help cure his first major disappointment. In the short period of time before he left the agency, David negotiated a plan in which he would start a new phase of his career as a newspaperman; not just a reporter or editor, but a publisher. After all, that was the field in which he was trained. He was ready for the change. He was 44years old.

Chapter 27

$\mathcal{W}$hen Charlie Farran found David's resignation on his desk he was really surprised, or maybe he only feigned surprise. He certainly knew David well enough to know he was not the type to take second prize. Although a vice chairmanship could up his salary, it would still take away any authority he had previously. I believe even now that Charlie was not the "bad guy" that kept David from the presidency of the agency.

Now the packing up began. There were calls to his clients explaining his new ventures, and generally getting his act together until the planned notice was over. All the time he was working on a unique proposal to his friend, Howard Metzenbaum. Howard and "Bud" Rand had just recently purchased two west side, Cleveland weekly papers that were not doing well. They thought that politically Metzenbaum would become more known in the community, as he wanted to run for the U.S. Senate. He had been in the Ohio legislature earlier. Meanwhile, Harry Volk, who started with one weekly in 1946, had begun to acquire a few other papers in the six years he'd worked the suburbs. David talked to Howard about the possibility of buying Volk's papers and combining them with the two he already owned. He explained his idea of circling the city; his concept of the "doughnut round the hole," which could bring old-fashioned community journalism back with modern technology.

There were many other towns that had small newspapers, and David envisioned gathering them all under one corporate umbrella.

Mr. Metzenbaum and his partner in the small papers they owned liked the idea, and it was up to David to first negotiate with Harry Volk. It took a bit of time, but the negotiations ended well. Volk's papers could be had for two million dollars. At that point David put in his share and joined Rand and Metzenbaum with the remainder of the money, and started Com-Corp Communications Corporation, Inc. In a few short months David was once more working in print journalism, only as a CEO instead of a reporter. His new title was president and publisher. Howard was chairman of the board. Although each paper had its own shop, the need for a main headquarters was an immediate necessity. Some space was found in the heart of downtown in a small building which housed a non-profit charity on the first floor and a fabulous furrier on the third. Sandwiched in between was the new kid in town: ComCorp.

To start, David put in a couple of desks, some telephones, and of course, Blanche Young. It didn't take much persuasion on her part to follow her young (not so young anymore) boss in his new career. It was a temporary set-up and very austere, but plans were already being executed in remodeling a huge one-story factory in the Cleveland Flats into the latest newspaper facility in the area.

The first few weeks were quite hectic. A complete staff had to be hired before any changes were made on the papers. First, Bob Chism was hired from Price Waterhouse to be the numbers man. A very young man named Steve Lebby was hired to be a national advertising salesman, along with a rep from the radio station WERE who would work part time. Soon came Gerald Gordon and Jerry Grilly. The new building was coming along nicely. David put Gordon in charge of the construction changes, as he worked well with union people.

David had consulted with many people as to the specific needs that they had. He almost single-handedly designed the spaces for each department. Then came the ordering of the equipment. This company was to be the first, local, completely computerized publisher. All ads, as well as news copy, were to be printed on computers. Then I was called in, since I had been freelancing in the design field, to pick out wall colors and carpeting, and some of the lighting fixtures. The whole place was to be carpeted, and that was a lot of carpet! I also got to work on David's office. It was huge and I had to somehow warm up the room a little. His furnishings were very eclectic. He insisted on using his five-foot roll-top desk that he had acquired almost 20 years before from the old Standard Drug buyout sale. He used a Herman Miller office chair with it. We found a perfect small couch and matching chair, and a coffee table for the center of the room. At the far end I put a contemporary pedestal table with four stainless steel, upholstered Miller chairs. The insanely wonderful thing that brought it altogether was a yellow, tweedy shag carpet that was a super bargain.

David never questioned me on my choices, but as I look back I wonder how I got away with it. It worked though. I think everyone wanted to take their shoes off when they entered the room. After David put up his ego wall and his butterfly collection, I gave him the perfect office warming present. I managed to buy a six-by-six foot painting that was featured on the Cleveland May Show catalogue cover. Suddenly the office was home away from home. Of course, he never stayed in it for very long. Publishing was just like advertising—it kept one always on the go. Now David had to visit all the papers and keep everything running smoothly.

Robert Chism was the banking type, and he was the best numbers guy David had ever come across. His Plain Dealer recruit, Gerry Gordon, was in charge of circulation, as that was the type of job he had before. This young man was a little on the strange side. To look at him one would never know he had a

Ph.D. in some esoteric discipline. He looked and talked like a hood, as I remember. He was totally different from Bob or the other new recruit, Jerry Grilly, who became one of the west side editors. Gordon did an excellent job, but would often disappear for a couple of days when he was needed, and no one could find him.

There was a tremendous amount of organization going on when the silent partner, Mr. Rand, decided to start acting like he was supposed to give orders and interject his ideas into day-to-day planning. He was not considered working management. Indeed, he knew nothing about the newspaper business and was just feeding his ego by hanging around. Since Howard was busy being "political," he had no idea that Rand was causing a disruption. Rand also thought he should be treasurer, but the SEC nixed that idea when a red flag went up on his name. He apparently had a bad business reputation. David soon told Metzenbaum, and it was agreed that Rand would take off for one million dollars. The fledgling company had to borrow the money from Metzenbaum, but they finally got rid of the distraction. All this took place after only one month of business under the new name, and the company had yet to move into the large quarters.

The day finally arrived, and all the corporate personnel were happily ensconced in their new quarters. Chism became treasurer and Grilly, who was editor of the *Parma Post*, was relieved of that job and became controller. There were other changes of personnel as well. Now the real business had to begin. More weeklies were brought into the fold, and it was time to start working on the owners' original plan to go public.

At that point there were 17 weeklies, now called suburban newspapers, under one jurisdiction. They surrounded the city of Cleveland and were starting to be taken seriously by the daily papers, who were losing ground on the classified advertising for one thing. The fact that suburban journalism became a new concept with ComCorp's founding also gave the company new prestige. Other weeklies in various states approached management, but only one was singled out at the time. That paper was the *Polk County Shopper* in Lakeland, Florida, that looked like a money maker. ComCorp made a deal to acquire it, and Jerry Grilly was sent down to run it. Everything was in place to start the public offering. The search began for underwriters. There was so much to do.

David with Byron Krantz and other key people in the ComCorp stock offering.

David carefully arranged his butterfly collection on his new office wall.

Chapter 28

    *E*veryone and his brother was giving David suggestions for underwriting firms to undertake ComCorp's stock offering. He met with several people until he finally chose the proper group for a publishing IPO. It was also approved by Bob Burger of Price Waterhouse, who had been an associate of Bob Chism. The firm chosen was located on the far west side of Cleveland, and not so well known by David's east side chums. Also, there were many more west and southwest papers in the new chain than on the east side. Whatever the reasons, work began immediately on the prospectus. It was a major job, and it was urgent that it got started.

    Since this publishing company was probably introducing a new sector to the stock market, it did stir up a lot of interest. There was a lot of local curiosity about ComCorp, but the underwriters wanted much more. David called me one afternoon and said, "Get packed! We have to go to London tomorrow evening." I was stunned. I couldn't imagine how to leave my three children at such short notice. Although the two oldest were almost young adults, there was still our ten-year-old to feed and watch.

    Another problem I had to share with David during that phone call: "I took Dean to the doctor this morning and it looks like he has Mono," I wailed.

"Are you kidding? What do we need to do for him? Can he be at home? What's the deal?"

"Well, he has to stay in bed and eat good meals, and there is no medicine," I told him.

"Can we get a nurse or sitter to stay at the house? We won't be gone more than a week, if that," he persisted. "Just try or I have to go without you."

There was one possibility. Claudia still had a couple of weeks until she had to return to school for her sophomore year. Stephy was at a local day camp, and Dean had to stay in bed and could not go driving around. Maybe Claudia could supervise the household! The more I thought about it the more feasible the idea became. I went upstairs to check on Dean, but he was asleep. I waited for Claudia to get back from the mall and told her about the trip, and asked whether she could handle the situation.

"Mom, it's as easy as pie (one of her usual expressions). I can cook and bake lots of good stuff, and Dean can't go anywhere, so what's the big deal? Besides, Steph is never a problem. Yeah, you must go with Daddy. You'll have fun."

When David got home all the plans were in order. I made sure that my sisters would check in on odd days, and a few friends were on call in case of a problem. David agreed that the kids were too old for a babysitter and the matter was settled. We packed our bags and went grocery shopping so the cupboards would be filled for the coming week. There was also the full freezer in the garage.

The next day David went into the office for a few hours, and then came home to pick me up to go to the airport. We parked in long-term parking and waited for our plane. In those days we had to go to New York to get an overseas flight. Even though I had been in England two years before, I was still looking forward to the trip. Just before our flight was called, I went to the phone to say goodbye one more time and see how the patient was doing. I was assured that nothing had changed since we left, so I boarded the plane quite happily.

As usual, David took out his yellow pad and started writing. When I peered over his shoulder it looked like he was writing a presentation for a client. I thought, *What goes around comes around.* The publishing business is just like the advertising business. Actually, he was preparing remarks to be given to the British brokers he was to see. One perfect Brit was recommended to him who headed up some large group of investors. He sounded perfect to me, as he had already arranged for our hotel and cabled that a car would be sent to Heathrow to take us there. I had always read about Claridges! After he finished his notes, David put his seat back, got a blanket from the flight attendant, and went to sleep for the rest of the flight. I tried to follow suit, but it is much harder for me to relax, as I dread every air pocket or unusual sound that might occur. David woke up in enough time to wash up before we landed.

We looked around for a man with our name on a card, but we didn't see anybody. So much for perfect Brits! We did see a chauffeur next to a Rolls Royce with a cap that said "Claridges." David asked him if he could take us to the hotel. He turned around looking for someone, and then said, "Yes sir, I believe I can. I was told that Mr. Onassis was to be on your flight, but apparently I got the wrong information." He gathered up our luggage and held the car door for us, and off we went. My husband and I grinned at each other like silly kids. We were the VIPs of the day. David did offer a tip, but it was rejected, and it made us realize how gauche the attempt to pay must have been.

When we walked through the lobby of the grand old hotel it brought to mind every literary character you have ever read about. It was so old fashioned, though elegant; you wondered what all the fuss was about. Today I guess it's called "shabby chic." We got to our room and I, for one, needed a nap. David made some preliminary calls to find out our schedule and we hit the sack. When we awoke we watched the news and found out Onassis had been mugged in Central Park, but was okay. He just missed his flight.

That afternoon we decided to join the interesting people at tea in the lobby. We'd had tea at other hotels, but never like this. We sat at a tiny table where sweets and tea were served by attentive waiters while we scanned the room for celebrities. We wouldn't have known one if we saw one then. Just looking at the murals of long-ago famous patrons was enough for us "hicks" from Ohio.

Later we walked around the area and since we had no commitments yet, we went to a simple restaurant that turned out to be the newest chic spot to be seen. There we saw our first celebrity, Michael Caine, who had dinner right across from us. I flipped. David paid no attention. As I recall the restaurant was called Mr. Chow's. We saw no one else until we were leaving the hotel the next day. Getting out of the very same Rolls that we engaged the day before was little Ari Onassis. He was not a person of beauty! It troubled me to think that Jackie needed so much wealth that she married this man.

The meetings were to begin that day for the first investor group. I saw David off in a cab and I wandered around shopping and stopping for refreshments when needed. I discovered Harrods again, and a remarkable place called Marks and Spencer. Little did I know it was like a Sears store, but with many more exciting products. From that day on anybody that I knew was going to London I would have them buy me underwear. It was the best. I managed to find my girls clothes at various boutiques, but I hadn't found anything for Dean yet.

I was exhausted when I got back to the room, and found David propped up in bed reading all the English newspapers. "Where you been?" he asked "I've been back for an hour and a half at least."

"I had a ball shopping," I told him, "and I may never shop again." With that remark I remember I went to soak my feet in the bidet. A real class act!

That night we were invited to the home of the broker's mother. He gave us directions to the "flat" at Cadagon Square. His mother was married to the head "honcho" of Shell Oil in Great Britain. It was no ordinary flat. We took a private elevator up to her floor and exited into a foyer the size of a room. Lining three walls were lighted cabinets which held art pieces of all shapes of cloisonné. I later learned it was the largest collection of its type in Great Britain and Europe. The very British young broker greeted us and started to introduce us to his mother, stepfather, and an international potpourri of diners. That was just the beginning.

The dining room seemed a bit crowded, but that was probably because the original Queen Ann table and a dozen chairs were quite large, as well as beautiful. When everyone was seated I looked around and noted the fabulous buffet on one wall with a gold framed Monet hung above it. In fact, every wall was filled with various paintings of old masters or impressionists. Later when I went to the powder room there was a magnificent Degas over the commode. These people were for real.

The food courses were served by three young Indian girls. I tried to take a little of everything served, but since I was, and still am, a weird and picky eater, I knew I was just going to move the food around on my plate and probably starve for a plain steak. It was difficult enough trying to keep conversing with the gentlemen on either side of me. Naturally, I was separated from my husband. He was lucky to have a charming woman from S. Africa who spoke English next to him. It was just the luck of the draw. The evening passed quickly and we were quite exhilarated by the attention. We also learned a lot about how real old wealth lives.

The next day when David finished two more presentations, we took off for Portabello Market. We had discovered it on our previous trip and couldn't wait to find little treasures to take home. The pièce de résistance was a special gift for Dean: a bright red uniform jacket with brass buttons and gold epaulets that must have been a band member's outfit. It was just the funky kind of thing our son would wear to school.

The last time we were in London it was for the opening of an HCA hotel. That, too, was a great experience. The general manager of the hotel also had a private dinner party for us and a VP of the company. Then, too, the guests were all very international. There was even a Princess Hohenlohe that impressed me greatly. I can't speak for David, as he doesn't impress easily. Whenever work ended on a Thursday in England, we decide to take the weekend in another country. The first time we went to Paris and stayed at the Plaza Athénée. A couple who were HCA investors from Johannesburg were going there and arranged the accommodations for us. Wow. We had a suite that was completely done in red velvet. That was a red hot weekend! On the second trip we could not spend too much of the new company's money, and we decided to go to Copenhagen. We stayed in a hotel room that had bunk beds and seemed like a compartment on a train. We didn't mind, since we had never been there before. This time we bought original designer chairs and fabrics, and a couple of tables, as we were redecorating our second floor at home. We also found a perfect gift for our daughter, the nursemaid, which she still has today: a silver necklace from George Jensen. Getting home after the long flight felt wonderful. We found Dean on the mend and even praising his sister's good cooking. Now the preparations for the IPO began in full swing.

Chapter 29

$\mathcal{A}$fter our brief trip to London, the work on the stock debut escalated. The PR was, of course, always up to David. He spread the word through all of the many organizations he was affiliated with, as well as the tons of friends and acquaintances he had made since he came to Cleveland in 1949. It seemed as if everyone was ready to buy a few shares of this communications company. It was decided that shares would go on the market at $12 dollars. That was considered fairly cheap in those days, and not many people dealt in so-called penny stocks back then. There were no computers and no day traders. The market didn't fluctuate as often as it does today. The IPO was "blue skied" in Ohio, and so the games began.

The initial offering proved to be successful, and now other issues had to be assessed. New advertisers were always necessary to keep the profits flowing. More salesmen were put on the road to tell the story of this wonderful concept of the "doughnut around the hole." The neighborhoods that an advertiser wanted to pinpoint were so much easier done with the selection of ComCorp's local newspapers. Most good-sized businesses were eager to advertise, but there were a few holdouts that no one could convince of the benefits of the new concept. A few years later David dealt with them in an unusual way.

There still remained the chore of relocating some of the weeklies into larger quarters. Some of the eastern suburban papers were combined into a large building in Chagrin Falls, Ohio, a charming, older, gentle community that seemed to draw people to its main street where you could find interesting shops, as well as large ice cream parlors and restaurants. And, of course, there were really falls to look at!

The building chosen had to be remodeled to fit the business, and it took some time to get the job done. The company hired some excellent private carpenters who followed the prescribed plans sketched casually by David and put into final form by an architect friend. I was able to take advantage of these skills. It's a tale within a tale.

As somewhat of an antique shopper, I stumbled onto a piece of furniture I coveted in the worst way. The only problem was that it was in pieces in the back room of a small shop. I had walked into the store and asked the proprietor if he had any French armoires. I showed him a picture of what I wanted from a magazine. He told me that he had acquired one, but it was in bad shape and he had taken it apart to analyze it. He was rather reluctant for me to see it, but I talked him into it. I went back to his storage room and I saw the armoire parts lying in a pile on the floor. I knew they would be perfect if restored. I told the man sadly that I wouldn't know how to put it together, and asked him to call me if he ever got around to doing the work.

That night I told David of my find and he told his super salesman, Steve Lebby, about it. Between the two of them they devised a scheme to buy the broken furniture parts. Steve drove a vintage Bentley at the time, and he was a big guy with a silver tongue. He went to see the antique dealer a few days later dressed in a suit with a string tie and a 10-gallon hat. "Howdy, sir. I'm a dealer in Dallas just come up here to scout a few new pieces for my clients," he drawled. "Seems all the ladies back home are lookin' for these big closets called armoires. Do you have any?"

The owner glanced out the front window and saw the unusual Bentley parked in front, and answered the big "Texan."

"Well, it may not be of interest to you, but I have a partial armoire in my back room," he said.

Steve pretended to not understand. He looked over at the store owner and asked innocently, "What's that mean, exactly?" The shopkeeper walked him back to the rear storage room and showed him the cabinet parts. Steve asked him if he thought they could be made into something, and the man said indeed they could and would be very valuable. He said since the parts were in pretty good shape he could probably sell them for around $1,500. Steve examined the sections again and said he would be interested in a purchase, but the price was too high. He took out a fake business card with only a name on it and scribbled his local phone number. "I'll be in town till Thursday if you decide to lower the price to say $350 or so," and he started walking toward the exit. When he was about to open the door, the owner called him back.

"Since it's almost Christmas, I suppose I could lower the price to $500," he said. Steve told him he would only go to $400 and removed a wad of $100 bills from his pocket. The man's eyes bulged when he saw the cash, and promptly sealed the deal just the way Steve asked it to be. He realized he could get rid of some less-than-desirable inventory with the end of the year coming up. The big guy from Dallas said he would send a truck the next day to pick it all up. The carpenters working at the new building had an unmarked van, and they brought the furniture parts out to Chagrin Falls where they used their spare time to reconstruct the armoire for the "boss" at very reasonable rates. These men turned out to be real craftsmen, as the finished product was magnificent and a true 17th century French product. As for Steve, he was very excited that his acting did so well. The fact that David gave him exactly $400 in cash was also a plus.

Getting back to the stock offering in January 1970, it should be noted that the company went public with gross revenues of approximately $2,500,000 and net losses of several thousand dollars. From 1970 to 1977, David led ComCorp to a respected position in the community with revenues of over $7,000,000, and pretax profits of over $700,000. All the newspapers were redesigned, other properties were acquired, and a top management team was built. *Sun Newspapers* became known across the country as the best weekly newspapers in the business. They had, at this point, circulation of over 250,000, and constantly won prizes for their excellence and performance.

In the beginning, though, the monies raised had to pay off two of the original weeklies owners who needed $500,000 each for ending their life's work. It really didn't end it though. David kept one of the men on in sales on a small salary, and the other as a consultant on one of his original papers. Rand and Metzenbaum, the new guys in the deal besides David, took stock for their ownership. It didn't take long until the young corporation was in perfect sync with advertisers, neighbors, and of course its local politicians. David saw the growth escalate and he was quite pleased. He also got free reign from the original big-money man, Metzenbaum, who was still looking to become some government official. In time that happened.

A pleasant CEO pose.

Chapter 30

*A*fter all the fanfare of the stock offering, it was business as usual for David. He carried through all his beliefs about getting to the advertisers in a personal way. It was not uncommon to see him stopping in at a local men's clothing store or a small boutique in a local shopping center along with one of his salesmen. He chatted with the proprietors, and always purchased some small item like a tie or a bracelet for one of his daughters. He made friends easily, and never perceived himself to be in a loftier position than his customers. Sometimes he even arranged a dinner date with a client where I went along to keep the wife company. That wasn't always such a good idea. Some of the wives were not "my cup of tea." I remember one who put a price tag on everything she talked about!

As David performed the mundane tasks of publisher, he also kept up his community relationships. He joined more boards of non-profits that needed his expertise. By 1972 he was a board member of USO, educational TV station WVIZ, The Montefiore Home, National Conference of Christians and Jews, Jewish Community Federation, Greater Cleveland Growth Association, Diabetes Association of Greater Cleveland, Jewish Convalescent and Rehabilitation Center, the Health Fund of Greater Cleveland, Citizen's League of Greater Cleveland, Cleveland Zoological Society, United Cerebral Palsy Association of Cuyahoga County, Greater Cleveland Council of Boy Scouts of America, Cleveland Institute of Art, and the Better Business Bureau. In addition, he served on the savings bond division of the US Treasury Department and was honored with the "Liberty Bell" award, the division's highest recognition for work in connection with promotion and sale of savings bonds. He also continued the United Appeal and Heart Fund work.

With all of the above, one might think he didn't have any time for enjoyable pastimes. Somehow he managed to have more good times than most of his peers. He played tennis and golf a few times a week, often using the golf course camaraderie to promote his business. He took advantage of opportunities to view other venues that might become ComCorp properties. And then there was the occasional trip offered by a vendor that wanted his business. The most unusual trip that I recall was to Quebec City during the Bon Homme festival. The newsprint manufacturer that ComCorp dealt with wanted to "thank" its customers. Now the shoe was on the other foot, and we accepted the invitation. This was a new experience for us, and it was a very, very cold one! I can't ever remember being that cold since.

We flew to Montreal and caught a cab to the railroad station. When we got there we found that a special passenger car was attached just for customers of the paper company. When we boarded we saw that we were joining a wild bunch. There were very few women in the group, and there was a lot of booze flowing. As the train got rolling there was a lot of singing and jovial talk. That was just the beginning of the long weekend. As the train pulled into the station we noted a large bus with the paper company name on it was parked next to the tracks. We gathered our baggage and stepped out into a dazzling world of swirling snowflakes so big they looked like pieces of Kleenex flying around. The wheels of the bus were hardly visible in the accumulation on the ground. Although we had normal height boots, they were not adequate for the situation. So much for the written clothing instructions we had been sent. We managed to get on the bus along with our fellow passengers, and soon we were slowly moving along to our hotel. I don't believe I had ever seen so much of the white stuff before. We kept looking out of the windows, which were barely clear, when a magnificent castle rose up in front of us. With all of its lights blazing, the Chateau Frontenac was a stunning sight and a welcome one. It was really cold. We couldn't wait to get inside. As we drove up the hill to the front entrance, I first understood what the travel people meant when they called the hotel "magical."

Our host had people at the registration desk to greet us and give us small keepsake packages, along with itineraries for all the planned events. At that point I know I just wanted to run over to the big fireplace that was going at full speed. No chance for that, as we were given our keys and whisked away to a magnificent room with windows overlooking the St. Lawrence River. Our luggage followed. Luckily there was no event planned for that evening, so we called for room service and crashed under the European style duvet. The next morning David took a phone call which suggested we all meet for breakfast and event number one, which turned out to be a walking tour of the city's winter highlights.

After a huge breakfast we donned our ski clothes and started a very difficult trek through the snow sidewalks with our guide from the paper company. It seemed that storekeepers are reluctant to clear the walkways until the blizzards are over. Somehow we got to our first destination and marveled at the creativity involved. We saw these marvelous ice sculptures, but overshadowing them was the Bon Homme Ice Palace that was truly a remarkable work of art. Apparently the construction of this palace dated back to the mid-50s when Carnival first started. We were told that at night there were shows of light and sound, and fireworks that didn't even melt one of the 5,000 blocks of ice it took to build the palace. As we marveled at the ice art we still noted that the snow kept coming down. People crowded the streets as if it were a summer day. There was so much going on everywhere that we began to understand why the carnival was called the Mardi Gras in the snow. It was still too cold for us.

I didn't want to appear ungrateful, but I asked the guide if we could head back to the hotel. I got a "look" from David, but I knew that he really wanted to do the same. As we neared the chateau I noticed a huge Quonset hut nearby. When I inquired as to its use, I was told that it held a few tennis courts. I perked up. Was it possible we could play in the middle of all this snow? Yes it was, our guide said, and we could rent rackets and buy balls in the hotel shop. But first there was lunch in the grille, so we ate again. We did a lot of that. After lunch we went to our room to read and have a nap. Something about cold weather makes one groggy. When we awoke it was almost time for a cocktail party that preceded a big dinner. We dressed in our best finery and went downstairs for a perfectly beautiful evening. It was nice being the client for a change.

The next morning the big bus was waiting to take us to the factory where we had a full morning's tour of the facilities. We saw how the paper was made and put on those huge rolls for shipment. I don't remember the terminology, but it was interesting to see. David asked a lot of questions, but I didn't have a clue what they were about.

That afternoon we actually played tennis. I remember the heaters mounted on the joists of the hut everywhere you looked, but I'll be damned if I remember what the surface was on the courts or what kind of shoes I wore to play. I don't think we took tennis shoes to a snow belt. It was a lot of fun and a nice change from the first activities. That night we were told to dress warmly and meet the bus at six. We were in for another surprise. There was no bus, but a parade of horse-drawn sleighs filled with hay, no less, and we had to climb up on one and grab a blanket that was offered. I hadn't been on a hayride, let alone a snow sleigh, since my high school days. I needed a boost getting on. I remember hot cups of cocoa and coffee, but I cannot remember where we had dinner that night. Somewhere I seem to see a barn lurking, but that is as far as I can go. David had never experienced an evening like this; it wasn't the norm in the Bronx.

The next day we were on our own and we wandered around the city; there were so many shops and exciting displays, and international tourists to gawk at. At night there was another event for which I was not exactly prepared. Toboggan competitions! It was not something I was trained to do in my life. As I recall I was put between a driver and someone behind me, and we went zooming down this steep hill, and I held on for dear life, as they say. David was on a different toboggan and I hardly got to see him all night. I hated walking back up the hill each time. Although I was dressed in two sweaters, a warm-up suit and a ski jacket, I was cold! I don't think my team won whatever the race was.

Our final day was mostly indoors. I am not sure what building we were in, but we watched the famous International Canoe Race. Crews had been practicing for weeks before Carnival, and it was the big event of our visit. All sorts of groups send out their crews for the big day. The idea is to go from free water to the ice flows, carry the canoes to the next patch of water and start all over. It is a very strenuous type of competition on the river, which is mostly frozen at the time of carnival—the end of January until almost the middle of February. It is nice to watch from a window in a warm and cozy room. All sort of bets were taken and it was a lot of fun.

That night we dressed in dinner clothes again and attended a sumptuous small banquet at another venue. I was able to wear my new mink coat (yes, I did mention the furrier above ComCorp's first office!), and I felt like a lady again without all the heavy winter apparel I had worn all week.

We caught the same train to Montreal the next morning, and from there the plane to Cleveland. It was truly a great experience. ComCorp got bigger and bigger, and bought more and more paper from that nice company in Quebec City. Darn, I just can't recall its name, but I'm sure I wrote a glowing thank you note. Too bad they don't make paper from palm trees.

David with Curtis Lee Smith (President of the Cleveland Chamber of Commerce, admiring an award they received.

David at the annual Browns luncheon September 8, 1972. L to R: Jack Walton, President of Penton Publishing, Robert Miller, Cleveland Trust VP, Art Modell, owner of the Cleveland Browns and Louis B Seltzer, Editor of the Cleveland Press.

David on the bus to Quebec City from Montreal.

Chapter 31

About a year after ComCorp started, it was already time to expand. David carefully sorted through various small newspapers that were up for grabs and settled on the *Polk County Shopper*. After much negotiation it was purchased for about $500,000. In today's inflated figures it would be ten times as costly. David felt that it was a very good deal, and he persuaded young Gerald Grilly to move to Lakeland, Florida, to be general manager. Grilly soon changed the shopper to a good, local, weekly newspaper and the classifieds, including the legal advertising, made it a strong competitor of the daily *Lakeland Ledger*.

The owner of the *Ledger* was the *New York Times,* no less. They were not too happy with the *Polk County Shopper* and started looking for ways to cut the little weekly down. Their efforts culminated in starting a new weekly with 66,000 circulation and predatory pricing practices, among other "dirty tricks," which began to hurt the *Shopper*. When David saw what was going on he conferred with Grilly and they hired a high-powered local lawyer, and sued the *New York Times* regional and national company in an anti-trust suit that was well documented with the competitive pricing and all. Com-Corp wasn't sure they could win against the giant publisher, but they thought they could shake them up a little.

After much legal haranguing, ComCorp won the case! The settlement they received paid for all the legal fees. But the best outcome of all, the new weekly started by the *Times* ultimately folded. The *Shopper* became even more profitable.

David continued to look for other viable properties, but his partner was giving off vibes that he might eventually get back into politics, and might want to sell out. David had to tread carefully at this point.

In 1974, Governor Jack Gilligan of Ohio appointed Metzenbaum to finish the senate term of William Saxbe, who was to become Attorney-General of the United States. It was while he was in this temporary position that the big strike of the daily newspapers occurred in Cleveland. Metzenbaum attempted to run for the senate on his own again, but lost to Glenn in the primary. This period was tough for David, as he was not sure if he should look for new acquisitions or new buyers.

David with Joe Sallay - conducting business with Society National executives.

Chapter 32

*A*few years after ComCorp became a powerful addition to the media structure in Ohio, an event occurred that gave the company an additional boost in income as well as prestige. The Cleveland Newspaper Guild struck the daily *Plain Dealer*. At 6:00 a.m. on November 1, 1974, a picket line was set up at the plant. The printers union and the stereotypers attempted to cross the line, but were met with much violent protests. The other unions, like the mailers and pressmen, didn't even try. It was an extremely unstable situation. Management tried to get the non-striking unions to work, but they became more frightened to cross the lines and so the strike was intensified. For a few days the *Cleveland Press* printed some of its rival's sections, but then it, too, declared a shut down. The city no longer had a daily voice. It was strange to see such personalities as the society editor, the church editor, the business editor, and even the gossip columnists taking their turns in the picket lines holding up placards.

This lack of news didn't last long, however. David made a deal with the local Teamsters to deliver papers daily that all the *Sun Newspapers* could produce. Their reporters were not members of the Newspaper Guild, since they voted against joining in 1971. *Sun* employees had all the perks they wanted and didn't need union support. The teamsters in the area at that time were led by a tough man named Tony De Palma. He liked the deal that David came up with to give his men the work they needed, plus certain bonuses over time. Somehow they even used the same trucks used for the PD delivery.

When the *Center City News* had to be supplemented, David took the phone calls from striking reporters who needed to get some work. In a few days the temporary daily *Sun* had a staff comparable in size to the *New York Times*. The papers were, in fact, as "fat" as the *Sunday Times* every single day. ComCorp made many friends, but lost a few personal ones.

One story must be told. I think I mentioned casually before that I would tell you about one of the big advertisers in Cleveland that never advertised in the *Sun* papers. Now, when the whole city was clamoring for some advertising space, this advertiser insisted on getting a large share of space. David, for the first time, pulled rank and would not allow his people to accept ads from Forest City. First and foremost, loyal *Sun* advertisers were given ad space. After all, they had been supportive of the young company since its inception. They deserved the right to advertise!

The CEO of Forest City, Sam Miller thought otherwise. He insisted on a meeting with David. When he had a chance, David went to see him. He explained the situation and the limited space available, and told him that his customers came first. He was as amiable as he could be, and was not prepared for the tirade that followed. David simply got up and walked off. That was not the end of it. Mr. Miller went to Howard Metzenbaum to complain. Subsequently, the Senator called David, who explained the situation all over again. In the end, Forest City was given some space with the promise that he would become a regular advertiser. Big joke! When the strike did end he never advertised, nor did he say thanks. He was a real obnoxious person.

Each day of the strike brought new and interesting problems. At one point it was feared that the newsprint would run out. David got to the suppliers and they overnighted a double supply. One problem was the *Sun Newspaper* carriers. Some of the little boys found it difficult to carry the heavy daily papers. Somehow the papers got delivered. Maybe the parents helped.

Each day of the strike, David had lunch with the drivers instead of going out to a restaurant. They had set up a barbecue in the parking lot, and the smells of Italian sausage and other ethnic foods drifted into the offices every time a door was opened. David couldn't resist and joined the men eating out in the cold. He made some good friends that way, too. He was always honest with these men, and they trusted him completely. It was almost as if he had formed some kind of special team.

The large department stores at the time had always taken small ads in the suburban papers, but now planned full-page usage. It was a lucrative time for ComCorp, and they took advantage of it. Nobody knew, though, how long this bonanza would last. Meanwhile, the *Sun* papers had given anybody who needed one a job. No one went hungry. With all the court suits going on there still were no completed negotiations. Everyone took the attitude that this could go on forever, even though they knew the bubble could burst at any time. After a month of exciting business, ComCorp started talking about a possible Sunday edition. That was a ticklish idea, because it meant that new deals would have to be made and the paper would have to include many more sections. Besides, every day brought new rumors about an end to the strike. When nothing had happened after two more weeks, David decided to have a party for all the reporters, staff, drivers and the suppliers, as well as the company that had been printing the papers. All the loyal advertisers were also invited. It was to be held in a new restaurant in Little Italy that had a large upstairs space for private parties. All the calls were made to the invitees and the party was set for Friday night, December 20th. Rumors were flying hot and heavy that the "lucky strike" would soon be over.

Everyone who was invited showed up, as well as a few friends that we included in the festivities. There were speeches by David and others in management, then speeches by some of the reporters that were able to work during the strike, and even the drivers made an effort to give their thanks to the company. During the evening the negotiation stories were called in by "friends." It looked as if the end had come. David hoped he could have one more day, as Saturday's paper was all ready to roll and he didn't want to waste it. He sat tight lipped when the news came in. But just then the Teamster leader got up and said, "We better stop drinking and eating, and catch a few winks, because we have a paper to deliver tomorrow." David broke out in a big grin and everyone cheered as the drivers got up and left the party. They stuck with ComCorp till the end, and the *Plain Dealer* had to wait a day for their services. Hey, being a good guy didn't hurt.

Some of the Teamster leaders that got him through the operating jobs during the daily newspaper strike were really characters. When they liked someone or actually put their trust in someone, they would protect you for life. That certainly was the case when the "man" also known as Tony De Palma met David Skylar. Maybe because David treated him as a friend instead of an opponent, like others in the business. He and some of his sidekicks invited us to all sorts of events.

One time we had to drive 50 miles to the wedding of the daughter of his vice president of the local chapter. After the wedding we then drove another 10 miles further for the huge reception in some hall. We were in a gigantic room with strangers, except for De Palma and a few others that guarded him. At one point David was just making conversation when he remarked about De Palma's pinkie ring. It was a handmade filigree casing with a two-and-a-half dollar gold piece in the mounting. He took it off and said, "Here, try it on. Ain't it a beauty?" David agreed that it was, and started removing it from his finger. De Palma pushed it back and said, "Keep it. It's yours."

After several protests that fell on deaf ears, my husband had to take the ring and pretend to be overwhelmed. David didn't wear his wedding band for more than a year, let alone a fancy pinkie ring. He learned fast that it isn't smart to refuse a gift from a tough guy.

There were many stories about this very small Teamster leader. When David turned fifty years old we had an open house for all his friends. We invited Tony De. Halfway through the afternoon I glanced out the window and saw him marching up the front walk flanked by two giant bodyguards. At least they looked giant, as he seemed to be only about five feet, two inches tall. I met him at the door and he thrust a package at me as David walked to the door to greet him. "I brought you a present. Open it right now," he growled in his natural voice. Other gifts were piled on a foyer table unopened, as was the custom. David did as he was asked and found a carefully wrapped tree of life done in some metal, with semi-precious stones as leaves. Attached to the branches were fifty dollar bills somehow tied on. We were astounded, and then Tony came up with some of his eager pronouncements. "Dis tree is worth more den de money." After thanking him profusely, we ushered him into the buffet in the dining room where he and his guards spent the rest of their visit standing in the corner. I didn't mind, since some of my snobby friends were giving me the eye as if to ask who these guys were.

When Tony De Palma died, David went to the wake. In the hall he saw some of the tough guys talking about the departed. David heard one remark: "Bedda him den me." He tried to slip in and offer his condolences to Mrs. De Palma, and leave quickly. That was not to be. She grabbed David's hand and motioned him to sit next to her facing the casket. She obviously considered her husband's friend important and wanted to continue the friendship. It was a long hour until David could break away. Somehow others much higher up the Teamster ladder approached him soon after. That may be the tale of tales yet to come.

Chapter 33

 ven as David was busy as head of ComCorp, it became his turn to be president of the Cleveland Advertising Club. It doesn't seem possible, but I don't believe there were many women members back in 1971. I knew of a few very talented women in the day, but as I recently looked at a monthly news edition of the group from October 1971, there was no mention of any woman in the masthead except the editor. No woman could have tolerated the annual Ad Club outing, which took over six hours for the golfer participants. And then the dinner and prizes. It was definitely a "man thing."

I don't think the ad members of the day gave much thought to changing the system. I am sure there was no restriction against women. They didn't want to join it seems. But as usual, David had more important plans for the club than to include women in the mainstream. Early in October of the previously mentioned year, he called together representatives from advertising agencies, the graphic arts industry, media people, and industry leaders, to discuss plans for a federation of advertising and related groups. I would like to quote David in his presentation that day, because it was the beginning of a certain awareness of the industry's problems to come in the future. Here are some of his quotes:

"We have asked you here today because we feel our industry, the advertising, communications, graphic arts industry, stands unprepared to face the assault waves which have been launched at us from many sources. We, today, are being probed, investigated, reviewed, prodded, urged, threatened, and often jabbed by a whole host of people, government agencies, and consumer advocates ranging from Nader to Nixon."

After stressing more issues against the industry, David went on to say, "The Federal government is talking about hearings in advertising; the state is talking about taxing advertising; and some hysterical consumer advocates are talking about outlawing advertising."

Additional quotations that I found important should be noted. He went on to say "Advertising is not alone in this assault. As never before the free press is in serious jeopardy. All of us in journalism smiled with pride when the *New York Times* published the Pentagon Papers, but I remind you that for one week the Federal government challenged and stopped the publication of these papers and the validity of the First Amendment.

"The Congress also got into this act by almost forcing CBS president Frank Stanton to release his "outtakes," the edited material from his famous TV special on the Pentagon. And now our vice president, with the apparent consent of the White House, continues to harangue and discredit the free press in the nation."(ED. Note. Ha! If they only knew then who would be discredited next!)

David's speech to the local big whigs seemed to be convincing. It was eventually agreed that all the segments of the industry would get together and form a new federation based on five proposals. The first one was the gathering which was already taking place. The second was fundraising from 100 companies who would each contribute 100 dollars to the cause of organizing plans to "fight for our rights." Thirdly, an ad hoc committee would be formed to work out specific programs along with the Ad Club representative, and the last two items on the agenda would form committees from all groups involved to set up programs to enhance those of all the smaller groups, and also set up another working committee from all the groups for long-range planning.

The plan was well received, and it formed the most relevant part of his time in office. The year heading the Ad Club was bridging the gap between his agency experience and his newspaper publishing. But once an ad man always an ad man. He never stopped dreaming up ideas, and especially now for some of the smaller retailers that advertised in his weekly papers. It didn't seem strange to David that he could come up with a slogan for a little haberdashery to put in their ads, as well as editing the column size of his papers. The small advertisers were important to the *Sun Newspapers*, second only to the classifieds that were overwhelmingly profitable.

That first year after David started the company he also continued his civic pursuits. That was the year that we became the first husband and wife chairs of the Heart Fund. I got to the first meeting downtown in a hotel before David. Other dignitaries were already there awaiting the new chairmen. I sat down next to Louis Seltzer, who was the longtime editor of the *Cleveland Press*, and he greeted me warmly. He was half my size, but he still scared me because he was my first boss when I became a copy boy. A few minutes after I arrived, in walked my other half. He greeted me with a peck on the lips and got down to business. While everybody was in deep discussion, Mr. Seltzer passed me a note written on a small piece of paper. I have it still today, framed on my nightstand. It read "The Skylars - Somehow I gain the vague impression that you two are very much that way about each other - LBS." The word *that* is underlined. I guess it showed back then, what was still is!

June 26, 1972--Annual Meeting
"Now you have the opportunity to serve your industry and pay for all those lunches
for the next 12 months, talk to Beier every damn day, sign all of Sandy's checks
(none of which are made out to you), and listen to all the complaints. But look on
the bright side, next year at this time you can turn over the gavel to some other
poor sucker."

David turns over gavel of Ad Club presidency to Robert Miller.

Chapter 34

About seven months after the newspaper strike, David received an unusual call from someone he knew of, but had never met. Jackie Presser, the newly elected vice president of the Teamsters called to ask him for a favor. David was unsure how he had been chosen to help him. The conversation went something like this. "We've never met, but I understand through our senator that you know a lot of people in the Cleveland establishment," Presser began.

"I'm not exactly understanding where this conversation is going," David responded.

"There isn't much to understand. I just want to meet some of the elite WASP businessmen in the area and Howard thinks you are the man to introduce me," Presser said.

David was thoughtful for a second, and then said, "Mr. Presser, I think I have an idea. Do you play golf?"

"Yeah, I do when I get the chance," he answered. "What do you have in mind?"

"I might be able to set up a golf game with some friends at Society National and one of their clients. I'll get back to you," David said.

That is how the most bizarre golf game ever took place in Cleveland. Unfortunately, we have no photo documentation, as this was to be an almost secret event. As David described it to me afterwards, it was both comic and ironic to witness. First, the club chosen was the Pepper Pike Club, an exclusive male only private setting for business elite of Christian faith. The banker and important businessman both belonged. When I heard the description of the game, I couldn't get it out of my head. As David told me, "The first cart that went out held the businessman with Presser. He was sort of pushed to the edge of the cart, as Presser, who was over 450 pounds at the time, needed a lot of room. Then I came along with Jim, followed by a cart with Presser's two bodyguards, and another cart holding two caddies. It was quite an entourage that caused the few golfers out to raise eyebrows. Imagine, two Jewish people as guests at the same time! And one of them a union leader," David laughed.

Dinner followed the golf game and I was never apprised of what was discussed. I know that very few people knew of this meeting. I guess Presser needed to educate himself about the thoughts of the so-called Cleveland elite. As an aside, I want to tell you that the club was not only religiously prejudiced, but it also made wives wait outside if they had to pick up their husbands. This was 1975!

I just recently found out that Jackie Presser had also discussed a relationship between the Teamsters and ComCorp. I will include in its entirety a secret letter that I found in David's files. Nobody I spoke to who had been at the company at that time knew anything about this. Here it is:

the communications corporation

July 28, 1975

Mr. Jackie Presser
1870 E. 19 Street
Cleveland, Ohio 44114

Dear Jackie:

I've spent considerable time reflecting on the questions you raised at dinner the other night.

In the summer of 1969, after I left the advertising agency business, I spent several weeks preparing a plan and program which in August of that year became the basis on which we formed ComCorp.

What you have asked me to do in this report is to come up with the second phase program to continue to propel ComCorp while at the same time helping to promulgate the Teamster concept. You've asked "can the two ideas be married?" What will be the benefits to each, to both, to the public? How will Dave Skylar fit into this new concept?

Permit me to ramble just a bit. I'd like to discuss a number of facets of this subject and give you sufficient data and background to make your own opinions. I will not discuss the legalistic or financial aspects of a possible marriage. Others are more expert than I in these fields.

First some general background on the Press and the Establishment.

Idealistically, the U.S. Constitution protects the press from governmental control. This is in fact only partially true, because historically the press has been owned by the power elites. Who are these power elites? They are the scions of the establishment, big businessmen, political brokers, senators, congressmen, etc. Over 40 members of congress own large portions of the media that serve their constituency, Taft in Cincinnati, Johnson of Texas, Hobby of Texas, and many more. How did this all happen when Thomas Jefferson proclaimed that if he had a choice between government or newspaper he would choose the latter.

It came about because the press was, and is, the most effective vehicle to influence people. Those who had resources and sought to influence -- took control of the press.

133

-2-

We must remember that in our first 100 years we were an agrarian nation. The farmer's vote was crucial as they were the majority of the population. The newspaper lobbyists influenced the writing of postal regulations. They did this to keep more newspapers from entering the market place, not because they feared competition for the advertising dollar, but, because they didn't want political candidates or parties to have a vehicle for influence. That is why the requirements for obtaining a second class permit were so stringent then and are today. The second class permit is in reality a government subsidy. It permits newspapers to mail their papers at a considerably lower price than normal mail. (Sun Papers have these permits.)

In other words, the newspaper lobby kept others out of the industry by using government as a manipulator. At this point in our history most newspapers or periodicals were delivered by mail because the population was rural.

When the nation began to move from a rural to an industrial economy, the elites also began to expand their control over the press. . . . Hearst, Scripps, Howard, Hanna, Field, McCormick, and many more. Mark Hanna, the maker of presidents, was also the same Mark Hanna whose family owned both the Cleveland Plain Dealer and Cleveland News. His blood relative is still the publisher of the Plain Dealer, even though it now has an absentee owner.

Who were the first to publicly attack the unions as being socialistic and radical? It was, and is, the press, which was, and is, controlled by the same group of people that controlled most of the means of production. The Hanna family also owned mining and steel manufacturing companies. And thus, the Plain Dealer was a leader in the media, attacking unions and any other group that threatened the establishment.

Those who were at the core of the power structure, in many cases, directly or indirectly controlled the press. Nobody seemed to mind when I. F. Freiberger was both Chairman of the Board of Cleveland Trust and Chairman of the Board of the Forest City Publishing Company, which owned the Plain Dealer.

The establishment has long ago learned that economic power is important, but not nearly as effective as when you can combine economic power with community pressure power. Those that control the press have great power over the thinking habits and the life styles of large groups of people.

Have you ever thought why the Forest City Publishing Company allowed the Plain Dealer to make less than 3% on a dollar for years, when the interest rate was 4-1/2%? Simply because the Plain Dealer belonged to the power structure and it was not designed to make money itself. It was designed to enhance the position of those who owned it, to use for more important goals. If unions were a threat to other industries, the press was use to smear them. Stated simply, power begets privilege, and this begets prestige and those that own the press know this.

What better example can I give about the way the elites operate the press than to review the recent interview the Plain Dealer ran with you. It was positive press -- but it apparently caused a reaction. Because on July 22, 1975 the Plain Dealer printed a story about an informer who said that William Presser received kid glove treatment by the government. The text really was vague and meaningless, it was an unfair story. But how many people just read the headline and became more negative toward the Pressers, labor, and especially the Teamsters?

The New York Times Syndicate sends out hundreds of articles to their subscribers, the Plain Dealer among them. About 10 to 15% of this volume is used by the paper. How come this story was one of those used?

Was the second story appearing in the Plain Dealer a coincidence? Perhaps -- but I doubt it. The Plain Dealer gives and the Plain Dealer takes away.

Should this kind of power rest only in the hands of the elites? Those who would close out of their own business and social sphere the Pressers, Metzenbaums, and others.

Actually this situation is getting worse. Fewer and fewer newspapers are today independent. Almost every major city newspaper is today owned by a chain--Knight-Ridder, Gannett, Newhouse, Media General, etc., etc. These large chains have portrayed themselves as owners who don't tamper with editorial policy on a local level. There is absolutely no truth in this statement. As the economic squeeze continues, these chains have taken over more and more of the day-to-day operations of their newspapers. The local editors have little, if any, power -- except to make minor decisions -- on a local level.

Think down the road and imagine what will happen if the chains decide that labor and/or the Teamsters are to be "put in their place". What defense would you have?

It won't be done by a frontal attack across the bargaining table. That one they know they can't win.

It will be done by the force of public opinion -- effectively molded by the press and implemented by Congress and the legislative bodies.

There isn't an industry in the country that is presently strong enough to take on the Teamsters -- nor is there a great hue and cry to do so. The Teamsters have good friends in the White House as well as well as the State Houses in this country. But, it was not always so, and it may change again.

You know that in the past newspapers have been very effectively used by the likes of Louis Seltzer, Newhouse, Hearst, Tom Vail, and others to put into office those who were responsive to their whims. And who maintained close contact with these editors and publishers while they were in office.

Although ComCorp and Sun Newspapers are small by comparison to the Press and Plain Dealer, everybody from the Governor on down keep in constant touch with us on all sorts of matters.

-4-

A marriage of the Teamsters and ComCorp could bring an initial negative press.
Certainly, the media would say the unions should not be allowed to own media,
it's a privilege of big business, they would claim.

You have told us that the Plain Dealer has already indicated their concern about
you moving into the media field. And although Vail said he would be helpful, you
can anticipate some initial negatives.

In reality, it is what you can do economically for the newspapers that creates the
real threat to the Press and Plain Dealer. Under public ownership we have not been
able to expand as rapidly as we would like. You have the capacity and resources
to substantially increase the volume, which in turn does two things. First, it will
increase profits, but equally important -- more ads mean more news hole. This
means more opportunity to do the kind of job, editorially, which is not now being
done in this area.

The two major chains who own Cleveland's newspapers would quickly realize that
they would have to "accomodate" the ComCorp-Teamsters marriage because it pre-
sents an economic threat to them.

Teamsters could own and operate "small" newspapers in every state in the union,
and thus become a formidable watchdog over the press. The First Amendment works
on occasion -- but power works more effectively. The press rarely, if ever, attacks
their peers. When last did the Plain Dealer attack the Press -- but look what they do
to TV, radio, outdoors, etc., etc.

Now let's discuss Community Journalism and the Teamsters.

When we put ComCorp together I wrote some thoughst on what we were going to be
and what we would stand for.

I said then, and it's more true today, that ComCorp is a communications utility.
As the designation "communications utility" implies, it's primary purpose is to provide
public service. But make no mistake, it also is a profit-making organization and,
in order to succeed, we must serve yhe public, giving them something they need
and want.

We are restoring journalism to people in the communities where they live, borrowing
the people-to-people relationship from the past, but presenting it with the most
modern technology and relevant content possible.

This group of newspapers is not a newspaper chain; in fact, it could be called a
newspaper non-chain. Each paper reflects it's own community with it's own editorial
policy.

We have no quarrel with massive mass media, per se. It serves a magnificent function
in it's sweep across the nation and the world -- and into outer space -- scanning the
Big Picture.

But in the process over the years, it has desensitized the news, neglecting the little things that are still so important to us.

Through the marvels of modern communication, Americans have become so know-ledgeable, so technologically oriented, so overwhelmed with profound concepts, that even very real issues such as marijuana and the Pill seem commonplace. We accept death and violence routinely; we are even a bit blase -- after a brief awe-struck interlude -- about a man on the moon.

We need to return to basic unsophisticated facts of living. As never before in our nation's history, there is a desparate need to treat people as people, not as statistics or labeled categories.

It has been said that a person gets his name in the newspaper three times in his life, when he is born, when he marries, and when he dies. For the average person who is not necessarily newsworthy, even these three press clippings are not assured today in most metropolitan areas.

Our ambition is to multiply these three news items many times for every reader! We want the community to know about individual's promotions, wedding anniversaries, college careers, awards, activities and opinions on community affairs. We want every reader to know we care and their neighbors care.

That may sound old-fashioned, but if it is we're convinced that an entirely new kind of journalism has emerged from old fashioned "people coverage". Not the quaint county weekly style, but a vital and relevant reflection of the character and dimen-sions of each particular community.

We certainly have not lost sight of the Big Picture. But the Big Picture, like a half-tone photo, is made up of many hundred small dots. We're bringing into fine focus each community's segment of dots, so our readers will better appreciate their own position in the Big Picture.

Our concept is simple. Unfortunately, simple things are often not easy.

It's hard to dig back beyond today's journalism -- so highly scientific, computerized, analyzed, cateforized and too often desensitized -- to retrieve the nugget that is the foundation of our policy of public service.

In a way, we are traveling back from Metropolis to smalltown journalism, where most of the surviving big-time newspapers began and flourished in the past two centuries.

Somewhere along the way, as metropolitan journalism grew to its present stature and scope, it began to struggle and anguish to find consensus; it couldn't make up its mind whether to tell readers all it believed they should know or to condes-cendingly include only copy that it believed an "average" reader at the 12-year-old level could understand. It worried about the mythical "little old lady in Dubuque" and "the Kansas City milkman" trying to fit them into a homogeneous mass.

ComCorp's area of public service is to pay attention to people's real needs, real interests and real attitudes; to provide them with information relevant to their daily lives; to preserve the importance of each individual in his own right.

I believe this kind of journalism fits into your thinking of building a better image for the Teamsters. We could emphasize the hundreds of little things your people do and the total impact would be far greater than one or two major splashes by the leadership.

We have been ready to move into Parma on a daily basis, as well as to operate twice weekly throughout the county. But we recognize that each venture could cost us up to $500,000 during the initial stages. As a public company we would not be in a position to impact our earnings as far as the banks and our shareholders are concerned.

I have told you once before and will repeat the fact that if we could crack a dozen accounts we would not only enhance our paper, but we could make sufficient profits to finance our expansion.

I have no hesitation or reservations in saying to you that you have the where-withall to make any expansion of ComCorp almost instantly possible.

Now, let's review areas of growth and expansion.

Expansion in Greater Cleveland

Euclid -- this group of newspapers is owned by Harry Stone. Because of personality problems, negotiations have broken down to acquire this group. We currently have a detente with Mr. Stone. We represent these papers for regional sales purposes.

These papers could be acquired bor between $300,000 to $600,000. We would merge these into Sun Newspapers -- do their composition and printing.

Expansion in Ohio

The ComCorp concept could be applied to other cities in the state. Dayton, Columbus, Toledo, Cincinnati, etc. all have good weekly community newspapers, many of which are for sale, for very modest figures. We could expand the Teamster influence throughout the state via this vehicle.

Expansion outside of Ohio

For the past several years ComCorp has had the opportunity to acquire several similar community newspaper operations in such cities as Minneapolis, Seattle, Denver, Miami. Just last week we visited publishers in Houston.

Should the Teamsters acquire ComCorp in Ohio, we would suggest that other Teamster Joint Councils in other cities finance the acquisitions of these newspaper operations.

-7-

ComCrop could supply the management services and be the holding company unbrella to operate these companies for the benefit of the local Joint Council. For example, your equivalent group in Texas could participate in the purchase of the Houston papers. We could apply the same techniques as we suggest in Ohio for the ongoing management.

If this is conceivalbe, that under the ComCorp banner, the Teamsters could form a national newspaper non-chain -- all tied together, yet owned and managed for the benefit of the local council.

Multi-Weekly Operations

Our current operation has the capacity in production, sales and editorial to produce two complete papers each week. We have studied a Saturday/Sunday publication for some time and are convinced that one could be successful for Sun Newspapers. The following steps would need to be taken:

1. Sales and market reaearch project. We should determine the best publication date. Preliminary studies indicate the the Sunday Plain Dealer is vulnerable and another Sunday paper could be sold in Cuyahoga County. Our paper would have 300,000 circulation -- be zoned east and west, not go into the city of out of the county.

2. Acquire the UPI sports and photo wires -- during the recent newspaper strike we began negotiations with UPI to acquire wire service coverage. This would be necessary to cover late sports and features. We would also use the KNI (Knight Newspaper) wire service.

3. Arrange printing facilities. To compete with the Plain Dealer it would be necessary to handle late breaking sports. This calls for a late closing. Therefore, a large press capacity is needed. This is available in Dover/ New Philadelphia, and other cities. It is also possible to print this paper at the Cleveland Press under a contract printing arrangement. The presses at Western Press could be had for the moving costs. These could be moved to a new location and handle this.

4. Set up a distribution system. This is the least difficult of the problems. We would have to decide on paid by subscription, or voluntary pay. We would want to compete for the preprint business now carried by the Plain Dealer.

Go Daily in Parma Area

Parma is now the ninth largest city in Ohio. Canton is tenth and supports a rather large, influential paper. This area will support a samll local daily newspaper. To compete, a wire service would be required. To succeed, this must be a fully paid newspaper and we would have to have 25,000 circulation.

-8-

Now, what about David Skylar?   Last week, when I celebrated my 50th birthday, I made the comment that I've been a remarkably lucky man. After the army and school, I've had two major jobs -- first a 20 year career in advertising, and then ComCorp. In the advertising business, I went from 3rd assistant to the mail room clerk to Executive Vice President of a major advertising agency. I helped build this company from $6 million to over $40 million during this period. The ComCorp record, is, in my opinion, equally impressive.

I now feel I am in a unique position to combine my intimate knowledge of the media with my years of experience in advertising and public relations into a third career.

I intend to continue to run ComCorp -- and would be willing to sign a five year contract, to back this position. As ComCorp leaves the pioneering stage of it's growth and enters more and more into the consolidation stages, I could devote part of my time to other activities. I think I could make a significant contribution to you and the Teamster movement in the next five years. As my background indicates, I have moved with ease in various important areas. I could continue to do this on behalf of the labor movement in general, the Teamsters in particular and Jackie Presser as my focus.

Should the Teamsters consummate a deal with ComCorp, I would expect to renew my contract for five years, or whatever time span you would request. In return, I would expect a comfortable salary, plus normal benefits, plus some incentive plan based on a mutually agreed upon formula.

Thank you for reading this far. I will be at your office at 10:30 a.m. Tuesday, prepared to answer any questions you may have.

Sincerely

President

David Skylar/c

That recently found memo to Presser makes me realize how naïve I was about David's business. The memo itself brings up a lot of "what ifs" and second guesses pertaining to the motives of the Teamsters over forty years ago. Would they have injected the funds into newspapers that had to close when the economy soured, or technology stole all the subscribers? Would there have been a larger middle class face to front pages across the country? We cannot possibly know what the outcome would have been.

One thing I know for sure is nothing was done about Presser's dream. I did find a one liner from Senator Metzenbaum at the end of a letter to David which simply said, "The fat man's father said 'no'."

It seems to me that right around that time David was called to Washington to observe Jackie's new Public Relations department. When he came home he told me he was offered the job of Vice President in charge of Public Relations for the union as Presser was to become President.

I looked at my husband and with much disdain in my voice I said, "You take that job and I'm out of here." With the amount of money he was being offered it was a risky thing to say. Thank goodness, I made the cut.

Chapter 35

$\mathcal{M}$y attempts to tell David's story on an exact timeline is too difficult, as so much happened during his days as CEO of ComCorp. One event was especially exciting for him. It started when he got a call from Washington from one of his stringers. Yes, even weekly newspapers have the good sense to put some government stories in their news mix. The reporter said that he'd heard President Ford would be stopping somewhere in Ohio for a speech, but the location wasn't decided yet. "When is the trip supposed to be?" David asked.

"I think in about 10 days or two weeks. I'll find out for sure," the young man answered.

"Don't bother. I'll take care of it. I think I know who to call. I will get back to you if I need anything else, and thanks a lot." David smiled to himself when he hung up the phone. The big *Sun Newspaper* promotion of Good Neighbor Awards was scheduled for that time period. If he could get the president to come to Cleveland…

And so he began to make inquiries. After a few calls he got through to the public relations staff at the White House and said it would be a perfect venue for President Ford to address the Good Neighbors in Cleveland. "Also, you might be able to come up with some neighborly gesture of his own when he lived in Grand Rapids, Michigan. We could make a special award for him. What do you think?" David asked.

"Not bad, not bad," came the answer. "I'll take it up with the bosses right away."

It was just about 24 hours before David got an okay from Washington. Then began the specific date planning and procedural stuff for an appearance by the president. When the White House didn't come up with a story of a good deed, David dug out a story himself. He called the mayor of Grand Rapids, Michigan, and found out that President Ford had indeed been very helpful to someone. The award was made up as a surprise for the president, and everyone was running around with smiles of great satisfaction to think they had pulled off this coup.

The secret service came to town to check out the hotel and the environs. It was decided that the banquet should be held at the airport hotel so that Air Force One would be nearby for a quick exit. The hotel was not really that well equipped for large crowds, and the small ballroom had to hold tables for the award winners as well as a huge roped in area for the media. I sat at a table in front of the dais with others from our company, but my husband said I could not meet the president because of protocol, and I was rather miffed at the time. David did ask a few of his best friends who had to stand on the sidelines. One of his friends, Dr. Ed Eigner, just told me recently not to forget what David said when he stood up to welcome everyone. This is what he said after his greeting:

"I have always wished to say two things in my life. First, 'Stop the Presses!' And secondly, 'Ladies and gentleman, the President of the United States.'" After a great round of applause the president moved into the podium center. The following speech was delightful in as much as it contained no politicking!

"Thank you very much, David, Governor Rhodes, Mayor Perk, distinguished guests, and ladies and gentlemen. It really is a great honor and a very high privilege to congratulate the Good Neighbors selected in 46 suburban neighborhoods in the Greater Cleveland area; to congratulate not only the winners, but the families as well, and your distinguished mayors and your community leaders.

"I commend David, the 17 *Sun Newspapers*, as very good neighbors for providing the recognition to all of you for bringing a ray of sunshine into the lives of others. It is a wonderful occasion and I am honored to be here. My understanding is that none of the winners of the Good Neighbor awards sought the nomination. (laughter) In politics you have to do that. But no politics were involved in your selection. Nevertheless, you won the popular vote and all of the electoral votes in each and every one of your communities. Believe me, as I understand it there was no apathy on behalf of each and every one of you. I recall the many good neighbors that Betty and I had in communities where we lived. Of course, Grand Rapids was our home, but our four children were brought up in Alexandria, Virginia. And good neighbors in both places were essential and just wonderful, as far as our young family was concerned, in Betty's and my married life. The spirit in both those communities, I know firsthand, is still alive, but it is also alive here in Ohio. But more importantly it is still alive throughout the United States.

"Our traditional values in this great country just haven't gone out of style. As individuals, I understand that you noticed that snow needed to be shoveled off the sidewalks of some elderly neighbors; that hot meals were required by people stricken with illness; that a blind person needed a ride to a shopping center; that neighborhood teenagers needed help with their schoolwork; if someone was away, their pets needed some food; that a disabled veteran and a new neighbor needed friendship; and you didn't refer them to some government office, whether it was local, state or federal, for assistance. You responded as a human being to another human being, and I think that's what makes America work. It always has. It is what America really is all about: neighborliness, kindness, homes, families, religious values... all adding up to that special quality of what we proudly call Americanism.

"As I look around this room tonight, it is obvious to me that Americanism has not died; Americanism is alive; it is well. It is living from Cleveland to Rocky River; to Parma and North Royalton; to Richmond Heights to Shaker Heights; to Garfield Heights... Gosh, I can't think of all the other communities (laughter), but they are all great communities in this great State of Ohio, and it is similar in all the communities throughout the United States. And I am proud to say that as long as I am president, I will do all I possibly can to keep that spirit alive."

At that point David stood up to present President Ford with a national Good Neighbor award. The president said, "Thank you very much, David," and went on to comment about the person he helped who nominated him.

"I could make quite a speech about John Collins even before he nominated me. (laughter) You might be curious. He is 90-something now. He was the mayor of East Grand Rapids countless years, and he was a very hardworking, dedicated, religious man. He worked for—some of you may have used their product—the Bissell Carpet Sweeper company for years and years. I mean years."

The president went on to say that Mr. Collins was such a stalwart individual that he walked six miles to and from his job for 50 years, and until his doctor and his family told him he should not hold office or work at his job any longer. "But John is the kind of person who really ought to get this award, and I am honored that he would think that highly of me. But I accept the award and I say this sincerely on behalf of all the American people, because I travel around this wonderful country where we live, that we are all good neighbors with one another. We're without being disagreeable, we can work to keep America working." (At the time I don't think any of us paid too much attention to the last jumble of words. It was the president for heaven's sake!

He ended the speech calling for all good neighbors to carry out the teachings of our forefathers and of the past 200 years, and make our own history for our children and grandchildren to carry out. He said that was our mission and our responsibility to continue to make the dreams of our forefathers into reality.

He thanked the audience, then the dignitaries on the dais, and he was whisked out of the ballroom, followed, of course, by dozen of members of the press. After that it was anticlimactic. The awards were given out and speeches were made, and the event ended on a wistful note. Nothing like this had ever occurred before. It didn't matter what was said, or the political party he was in, it still was the President of the United States that came to call. Looking back I believe it was something of a coup for David. He made many new friends that night, and I believe he really felt humbled.

President Gerald Ford holds up Good Neighbor Award presented
by David on behalf of Sun Newspapers.

Chapter 36

avid worked hard at whatever he set out to do, but he also liked to relax a lot and take short vacations. When Steve Lebby, his super salesman, told him that his new wife, Ellyn, was a travel agent, he perked up. "What kind of trips does she do?" David asked.

"Right now she is working on something special for our belated honeymoon. Want to come with us?" Steve laughingly asked.

"You're kidding me. Go on your honeymoon with you? That's taking our business relationship a little too far. Hey, but where are you going anyway?" he added.

"Ah ha! Gotcha! We are planning on taking the first Caribbean cruise on the new QE2. Ellyn got us a super deal."

"Could she get us a deal, too? We could almost be your parents. Well, at least an uncle and aunt," David remarked. "You know, it's not a bad idea. We've got an anniversary coming up and..."

"This could be a lot of fun. I'll see what Ellyn can arrange," Steve said as he went back to his office.

The next day when David arrived at work there was a note on his desk. "Chaperones get the same discounts as newlywed travel agents. Itinerary forthcoming."

David smiled to himself and wondered when the exact cruise was to begin. He wanted to clear his calendar. Just before quitting time Steve knocked and stuck his head in the door. "Got a minute?"

"Sure, sure. Are we all set for the trip?" David asked

"Yep. Ellyn made a sweet deal and we are now on the ship's first Caribbean cruise. We catch it in New York and do we ever go to the best ports. It will be 10 days of pure luxury. Can't wait," said Steve excitedly. "I heard the ship is just about fully booked, too. I'm not sure of the exact date though. Right after New Year's I think."

"Okay, get me all the particulars so I can show MJ. She likes to plan for sitters and outfits, and all that stuff. And thank Ellyn for all her help," he called to Steve, who was going out the door.

David pulled his swivel chair in closer to the roll-top desk and got back to work. He never left when his employees did, since he spent so much time out of the office that papers piled up on his desk daily.

The above discussion took place in late November. The New Year was just around the corner. After the usual quiet celebration at the club, we went home to pack our bags for the cruise. In those days it was still mandatory to attend formal nights on the ship at least twice during the trip. There were no extra charges for bags on the airplanes, so we could take as many outfits as we wished. I guess I took much more than I needed. Since I did most of the packing for both of us, I snuck in some of David's clothes that he would never have thought to pack. He was a real fashion plate in public, but at home he dressed like a ditch digger sometimes. Let me give you an example.

One day we drove the kids to a movie at Shaker Square. I interrupted David's yard work to tell him we were ready to go. "Aren't you going to change your clothes?" I asked.

He responded, "What for? We're only going to shop a while and then pick up the kids after the show." I didn't feel like arguing about it and off we went.

We dropped the moviegoers off and drove around the square looking for a place to park. David happened to find a spot in front of a store called Bunce Bros. where he somehow had never been a patron. "Hey, let's go in. I could use some lightweight suits," he said. When we walked in the store no one came over immediately and David busied himself going through the racks until he found a suit he liked. He called a very haughty gentleman clerk over and said, "Do you have this in a 44?"

The clerk gave David the once over and said, "I'm not sure. I'll find out. You know that suit sells for $275." David said he knew while he wondered at the man's arrogance. When the man returned with the correct size, David took it and went into a dressing room. When he came out he was holding up the pants that were too big.

"Can you please fit these pants for me, and I'd like to buy the same suit in charcoal and blue," he said. The clerk was dumfounded when David pulled out his Gold American Express card. When we left the store, which was Cleveland's answer to New York's Brooks Bros., David said, "I just don't understand such stupidity. How did he know what I could afford or not afford?"

I looked at him and smiled when I said, "Honey, you are looking like one fine garbage collector. He thought you might contaminate the store."

David looked down at his torn khakis and laughed. "Okay, I got the point. Let's go grocery shopping."

The morning we were leaving, we got the news that there had been a fire in the galley of the QE2. It was not a serious problem and would not interfere with the ship's schedule. However, when we got to New York we found that over half the bookings for the Caribbean cruise had been canceled. That meant the ship would sail with more crewmembers than passengers. We wondered whether it was safe to embark. Ellyn was able to get inside information that all was well, and the people that cancelled were unduly alarmed. It turned out to be a super deal for the remaining travelers. Every time we turned around there were stewards at our beck and call.

Right from the very first day we were treated royally. We were not in the highest class, but the dining room we were assigned was beautiful and quite large. When we went to our assigned table there were three waiters just for us. David and Steve ordered smoked salmon with capers, while Ellyn and I had more mundane appetizers; shrimp cocktail for her and tomato juice for me. Then the "boys" ordered strip steaks for all of us. Before I had eaten half of mine, Steve ordered another for himself! He was a growing boy after all! Even David with his huge appetite could not keep up with Steve. Then one of the waiters insisted on doing the "flaming bananas foster" dessert. I passed on that and had a fudge sundae. After the first night with all the food and great service, David called the closest server around and set the groundwork for the rest of the trip.

"When you see us coming into the dining room I want you to have double martinis in hand for Mr. Lebby and myself. And simultaneously, your associate should have the smoked salmon ready for us. This will be your main focus for the rest of the trip," he said with authority.

"Yes sir, we will do that, sir," the young man answered. And true to his word, every single night when we walked in the orders were on their way to the table. It really gave them something to do, because half the dining room was empty. As I look back, this was the best cruise of all that we have taken over the years, and it was all due to the amazing service which came about because of a small fire.

This cruise really had great stops, none of which were on any subsequent cruises. One special port was Caracas, Venezuela. I was glad we came in by ship when I later heard that planes had to fly in between buildings to get to the airport. It turned out that Ellyn had distant cousins there in the jewelry business. I must admit that we wasted half a day looking for the store, but it was worth it. We felt we should at least buy a few little things there, as the cousins were so nice. I bought a necklace with semi-precious stone charms on it and a few other gifts.

Then we found a cab to get back to the ship. In San Juan we left the Lebbys alone and went to a casino. It was more foreign than the one on the ship, and much more frightening. One felt as if a whole band of ex-patriot mobsters were breathing down one's neck. We were the last people returning to the ship. We must have been breaking even if we stayed so long.

One day as the ship was in open water going back to New York, Steve, who was always ready for some fun, asked David if he wanted to do a commercial. "What are you talking about?" David asked.

"I was talking to a guy and he asked me if I knew anyone who could be convincing on camera for American Express, and I told him about you," Steve said.

"Why me? What about you?" David asked.

"Well, you have an American Express card and I don't, and you would be more legitimate," he laughed.

Just then a young man came up to them and Steve introduced him to David. After a few words of direction, he had David lean against the railing of the ship saying these words as best as I remember them: "The American Express card is good everywhere on a cruise except at the gaming tables." It was very convincing, especially with the wind blowing his hair around and the sun shining brightly. And so it came to pass that David was showing up on TV for the duration of the "real people" campaign. Believe it or not, he actually got residuals. Nothing much, but he sure was noticed by friends around the country.

The last evening of the trip, while we were gorging ourselves as if we would never eat again, Steve excused himself and came back a few minutes later with a silver champagne bucket filled with a bottle of bubbly, and he presented it to us. It was engraved with our 25th anniversary date and signed by all our friends at ComCorp. Steve remembered David's off-hand remark back in November. He was like that. He was always very thoughtful and made you feel special. I will never forget that special trip with our young friends.

Chapter 37

In the summer of 1976, David was doing a lot of traveling. He and his partner, Howard Metzenbaum, the on again / off again senator from Ohio, had just sold ComCorp to a midwestern company called Booth Newspapers out of Michigan. Howard had put his shares in a blind trust just prior to that sale, as he was running again for the senate. David had not wanted to stay in the company as an owner, but he did condescend to staying on as president for one more year.

During that summer David was setting up more acquisitions for Booth and was constantly on the go. In July he was in Philadelphia on business for two days. When he got home on Friday night he was very tired, and went to sleep early. The next morning he had his usual tennis game, but stopped playing in the middle of a set thinking he had pulled a muscle in his side. When he got home it really started hurting. He called his old friend Dr. Leo Walzer, who said he was just going out and would drop by to check him. When he was examining him, he asked me to run out to the nearby drug store to get some special heating pad. When I returned home there was no one there. I was wondering what happened when I saw a brief note by the doctor saying they went for an x-ray.

I immediately drove to Suburban Hospital, which Dr. Walzer headed, and found David already getting into a private room. Things were different in those days, and a little influence by the head of the medical staff didn't hurt. After the x-rays were read it was obviously not a pulled muscle. The x-rays showed pneumonia. Dr. Walzer was known as an incredible diagnostician. Within the next 24 hours all hell broke loose. David's fever started climbing. He was coughing and in great pain. That night I spent on a bench in the hall outside his hospital room. For the first time I realized that my husband was anything other than invulnerable.

After about five days of normal tests and medication, I was beginning to feel that he was getting better. I had gotten the kids in from various places and we all cheered him on, but it was false hope. The next day as I came for my daylong visit, I saw a flashing light at his door and people running in and out of his room. I was panicky. It was Code Blue and I didn't know what had happened, and I couldn't get into the room to find out. Eventually, I was told they had to get into his lungs somehow through his back. I can't say exactly what transpired, but I think a lung had collapsed. From then on it was touch and go. At one point he slept on a refrigerated bed because his fever was so high. All sorts of specialists were called in, and they all were concerned that normal treatments were not working well. Finally, after three weeks some new medications were working. David was feeling much better and was talking normally again. I forgot to mention that at one point he was causing a riot in the hospital. He was insisting that he have a phone by his bed and when he was not allowed to have one, he started yelling that he would have his own people wire up the room. I can't begin to tell you all the demands he was making. We chalked it up to his delirium. So, yes, we were happy that he was on the mend.

Meanwhile, Metzenbaum, who was to finally get legitimately elected to the senate in a few more months, had taken out a million dollar policy on David, which didn't thrill me too much. He also called in specialists from other cities to help with new diagnoses. But as I said, the situation improved, and after five weeks David was home, thirty pounds lighter and rarin' to go. I finally convinced him to take it easy for a few more days when he was at home. He was eating more substantial food and sleeping better in his own bed.

We found out later, months later actually, that David had Legionnaire's Disease. He had stayed at the same hotel that held the American Legion convention, the Belden Stratford in Philadelphia. Gradually David's strength was returning, but I insisted that he work only half days for a while. One word from me and he did what he wanted to do anyway. I was lucky to slow him down for even a short time. As he got back into the daily routine, he did manage to stay in town. That was as good as it got as far as slowing him down went.

A few days after he returned to work he got a call from Common Pleas Court Judge John J. Carney, who appointed him foreman of the Cuyahoga County Grand Jury. In a newspaper interview (not his paper!) he made some interesting remarks. It just didn't sound like him as I look back, but he must have prepared well for the interview. The following is from the news clipping.

"I've always been fascinated by philosopher Reinhold Niebuhr's concept that man's capacity for justice makes democracy possible, while at the same time his inclination to injustice makes democracy necessary. To my mind, the grand jury system fortifies man's capacity for dispensing justice and safeguards against inclinations to injustice. It truly represents democracy in action, and I am honored and eager to serve as foreman," Skylar said.

It started as a new experience for David and ended up as a real eye-opener for him. There were to be two grand juries running simultaneously, the other foreman being the wife of a prominent newspaper owner in other parts of the state. But the hard-core crimes went to David's jury. I'm not sure why. He would come home at night just wiped out after hearing of all the brutality and sick crimes that were committed. There were other types of crimes that were more political and fraudulent in nature. One prominent government official had been rumored to be crooked for years. David's grand jury got him indicted finally. He had been asking for contributions from his employees "for a special flower fund" for donations which would be used for partying and his own interests. The indictment brought big headlines in the daily papers. There was also the indictment of Robert Steele for the murder of his wife.

Another very serious charge was brought against a prominent surgeon. Apparently, he was billing for services that some other doctor actually performed. Several patients complained that he never showed up to take care of them, but billed them just the same. It was the beginning of "double billing" scams in the area. The funny part of this story is that this surgeon was a member of the racquet club where David was a chartered member. One of David's friends from the club said the talk was that David "better not get hemorrhoids or the like in this town." When he did run into the guy at the club, they silently glared at each other. But justice was served again. When the four-month term ended, David was asked to stay on to complete more indictments.

Then, as now, there were too many guns and too many killings. When he finally ended his service he wrote an in-depth report on the deplorable situation in the county, and suggested ways to remedy the huge problems. This time he submitted the report to the daily papers, but really played up the problems in his own *Sun Newspapers* where the story got down to the grass-roots, to all the communities in the county. I will try to give you some of his suggestions as quoted in the media. They are as relevant today as they were forty odd years ago.

As a whole, David felt that the grand jury serves as an extremely important part of the judicial system. He felt that it just needed a few alterations to improve its value. First, he believed that there should be a three-man investigative team made up of professionals that would act as an arm of the grand jury fulltime. He felt that these extra staff members would facilitate procedures. Second, he noted that the drug laws in Ohio at that time were not working, and they needed to be changed immediately. About half of all cases brought before the grand jury were drug related, and the law was making it more difficult for lawmen, prosecutors, chemists, judges, and other professionals to make a case.

Finally, David had to comment on the use of guns in the county. He called Cleveland "an armed camp" in his report. And he maintained that gun sales and registration laws had not helped. Calling guns a political issue, he said that the only way around it was to "save the public from itself" by changing the law to make carrying a concealed weapon a major crime. "Let's bypass the politics of the issue and make carrying a concealed weapon so tough people will think twice about carrying a weapon," he wrote.

There were many more observations and suggestions in the final report, but his remarks during the interview were especially interesting. He commented that "...this is not an appointment that you take for show business purposes. Anyone who takes a grand jury appointment had better be convinced that it is a commitment of the highest order, and be certain to fulfill it. For four months I think I worked 15 hours a day, two or three days a week. But it's one of those things I think happens to work. I was very impressed with it.

"In looking back it was one of the most illuminating experiences of my life, and at the same time one of the most frightening."

In typical fashion, David threw a dinner party for his jurors when their term ended. I know for a fact that he was hugely affected by the cases he worked on. He laughed when he said he worked harder on the jury than he did at his own job, and for "...ten dollars per diem, which only paid for part of the parking garage."

Chapter 38

For several months after his grand jury experience, David tried to find ways to improve the system. Some ideas were discussed among the judicial parties, but not too much was implemented. He went back to his job and since it was going to be his last year at ComCorp, he wanted to leave with a good record. Now that the company had new owners, he had to follow somebody else's orders to some extent. Luckily, Booth knew all about him and gave him lots of leeway. They were happy that he decided to stay on for another year after the buyout. He kept up all the community activities and participated in golf events that the suburbs often arranged for their elected officials and friends. They were usually "wild and wooly" events.

The best example I can recall was the Parma City Open. That was the suburb's main party of the year. It was golf "under the influence," if you will. Each hole that was played had a temporary table set up for drinks and snacks—mostly drinks, and not only soft ones! From what I heard later, some of the guys had brought extra shirts because they knew in advance that they had to run in the clubhouse and stick their heads under the shower to try to snap out of the stupor. David did not bring an extra shirt, but he went in and stuck his head under a faucet. He snapped out of it alright, and ended up winning the whole tournament. He wasn't trying very hard to win, as he wanted the Parma people to get the honor. However, they were all miserable golfers and more tanked up than he, so it happened. By the time the dinner was served and all the prizes were awarded, Skylar was in as bad a shape as the rest of them. He also had the longest way home. Parma to Shaker Heights is a good 45-minute drive. He strapped the almost three-foot high trophy into the passenger seat and proceeded home at about 35 miles an hour. When he finally got home, he woke me to show me his splendid award. Sorry, but I cannot write my response in this epistle.

Nobody had a clue that Booth would flip its ownership of ComCorp so quickly, but it did. This time to the Post Corporation, which was better known in the newspaper business. It had many properties, including *Parade* magazine, which was inserted in most big daily papers. This time David did not agree with the policies of the new owners and decided to leave his position. He didn't want to think of what would happen to his concept under the new management. It was agreed to let him leave before the end of the year.

Then came the onset of friends and acquaintances that turned to David for his expertise. It was lunch downtown at the Commerce Club or in a quiet corner of the men's grille at Oakwood Club, or even at a booth at McDonald's. It didn't matter where he took on these business problems; they became his challenges and he was happy to offer solutions to them. Besides, one of the macho remarks my husband always repeated was, "I married for better or worse, but not for lunch."

One day I got his attention while shaving. "Well, whose problem are you going to solve today?" I asked casually.

"What's that supposed to mean?" he answered sarcastically.

"It means that you are blind to the fact that all these people are coming out of the woodwork asking you to give them advice when they know damn well it would cost them plenty if they went to a PR or ad agency. Isn't it about time to start charging for your knowledge?" I said.

He looked at me with a face half covered in shaving cream and muttered, "Maybe you're right." I knew I was right. He was 51 years old and retired. We had a lot of years ahead of us. Some income would be nice. Soon after our discussion, Skypro, Inc. was started. It was to remain as a company for the next 30 years, even when other companies were formed. Skylar Professional Services covered a lot of business deals as well. There were several of those, mostly investments that went downhill, but that is part of the game when one is looking for action.

In 1978, David got a different kind of action. He was appointed civilian aide to the Secretary of the Army, in this case Clifton Alexander, the first black to hold the position. David took his new appointment very seriously. He acted as a conduit from the Fifth Army Command to the Secretary, and made innumerable trips to Army camps when the secretary was not available. The very first trip was to Washington to get acquainted. I got to be part of that one, and several more. After all, he was given the temporary rank of lieutenant general. I loved being a general's wife!

Buddies stand with the winner of the Parma City Open.

Chapter 39

$\mathcal{T}$he very first trip that David made to Washington was actually an introduction of the civilian aides to the Secretary of the Army, who was also new to the position. It was a new way of life for David; none of the pomp and fancy uniforms were de rigueur when he was in the Air Corps. But this was the Army in peacetime, and it was glorious to observe.

For starters the venue where we were assigned was a little on the seedy side. It didn't fit with the rest of the meeting. I assumed the Army didn't wish to be perceived as blatantly extravagant. Maybe I expected too much. As I recall, it was a small hotel in Arlington. For some reason I think of it as being a one-story building, but I wasn't feeling well when I got there, so my recollections could be all wrong. The morning that we left I had awakened with a terrible pain in my shoulder and David had to take me to the doctor on the way to the airport. I wasn't about to be left behind on such an important occasion! It turned out I had my first case of bursitis. The doctor gave me a shot and put my arm in a sling, gave me some sample pain killers and sent us on our way.

That evening there was a formal dinner and I was a mess. David had to meet before dinner with some Fifth Army people, and he helped me undress and put a plastic cleaning bag over my arm so I could shower. I wasn't sure I was going to make it to the ballroom. I somehow got most of my clothes on, but it was difficult when it came to my dress. I was really in trouble. The zipper was in the back. I knew all the men were in a meeting, and I decided to be brazen and knock on the door across the hall. A very sweet older lady opened it and I asked if she could help me finish dressing. I'll never forget how kind she was. "Come on in, honey, you poor dear," she said. "Are you in much pain?" I assured her that my pills were working fine, but I just couldn't get to the zipper. She helped me finish dressing and I thanked her. I told her my name and that David was the new aide from Ohio for the fifth district. She then told me her name and I tried hard not to say OMG. It was Mrs. Westmoreland.

I thanked her profusely and started back across the hall to get my purse and leave for the ballroom. She told me to wait a second and she would go with me. I was amazed at her friendliness, but I was thrilled at the same time. When we walked into the ballroom we saw all the men milling about. Most were in dress uniforms, but many were in civilian tuxedos. When David came to greet me he had no idea who the lady was next to me until he saw General Westmoreland heading in our direction. By the look on his face he probably thought I had done something wrong, but he was reassured when he saw the smiles on our faces. Since I remembered the evening so well, I can't understand why I did not note the general's clothing. I knew he had retired in 1972 after he was called home from his command in Vietnam, so maybe he was still allowed to wear his uniform. I think he was a speaker that night, though I don't know what he spoke about.

My main thoughts of the evening centered on the "cute" general in his uniform that looked like a bellhop's at the Plaza. He didn't have a wife with him. David said later that women always go for the men in uniform. He should know. He had a ball in the service those many years ago. It was hard to dance with my arm in a sling, so I caught David's eye to begin saying his goodbyes. I know he was exhausted also.

From that evening on he took this new voluntary job seriously. He was outfitted with fatigues, heavy parkas and combat boots. They looked so strange next to his black patent Gucci loafers in his closet. This new voluntary position definitely fit into his normal lifestyle, flying here and there wherever he was needed.

On March 2, 1978, David and two other civilian aides, Bill Bentley of Oklahoma and William Vernon, Jr. of Iowa, got their first taste of Army pageantry. They had to attend an honors ceremony at the Fifth Army Quadrangle at Fort Sam Houston, Texas. I did not go there, but chose instead to meet our friends in Dallas until David could join us. From the photo of the event I could tell that my husband found this ceremony quite meaningful.

From then on it was intermittent visits to Army camps and National Guard units. David was treated just like any two-star general, which was the temporary ranking given to him by the Army. About two miles down the road from our home there was some sort of a National Guard set-up with a helipad. When David had to go anywhere in Ohio, or get to a big airport, he was picked up by a helicopter. I used to drive him over and watch him take off before I left for home.

One Thursday he found out he had to make an inspection on the coming Saturday. He wasn't too happy about it, as his 16-man golf group played early in the morning. He decided to have a little fun despite the situation. Usually when the group met they all put their golf balls into a hat to see who drew whom as partners. David called a couple of the guys and said he would drop his ball at approximately 8:00 a.m., and to watch for it.

He nicely ordered the pilot to fly the other way so he could see his friends down below. He did not tell him what he planned to do until he took a ball out of his pocket. The pilot called out, "No sir, you can't drop a missile out of this aircraft!" They were already over the first tee and the guys were waving and laughing, and holding up their golf balls. David waved back, shook his head and laughed.

Not every trip he was called to take was for public relations counseling. Sometimes he had to observe, as well as participate, in actual Army maneuvers. He admitted to me afterwards that it was a bit scary. Remember, he had been in the Air Force with no mud or ground snipers to worry about. Even though there was no live ammo, it was a harrowing experience to a man unaccustomed to such chaos. Along with the big brass from the Fifth Army there were some foreign gentlemen observing our war games. One of the men was very quiet and was never included in any discussions. David noticed he was very sullen, but since it wasn't David's game he didn't get involved introducing himself. Nobody else introduced him either. Finally, one officer said, "Oh, he is an Israeli who was invited to observe our maneuvers."

When it came time to leave, David saw an Army staff car arrive to pick up the Israeli. When he shook hands with everyone he still had a dour look on his face. David felt sorry for him, because he was basically ignored during the whole presentation. When he shook his hand he said the word "Shalom" to him, and the man smiled for the first time and said in return, "Shalom Aleichem." David realized the American brass didn't know what to say to a "Jew." He felt that someone could have done a little research to make this foreign guest feel comfortable. David had no idea who the man was. When he got home he picked up his newly arrived *Time* magazine and recognized the man on the cover. It was Ariel Sharon! He flipped.

David in fatigues with the Ohio National Guard in an early stint as civilian aide to the Secretary of the Army.

David and other aides at swearing in ceremony in San Antonio.

Explaining some PR issues to the troop in South Carolina.

Every Saturday morning David's golf group put their balls in a hat in order
to find their partners for the day. Then the bets began.
Show here are Dr. Edwin Eigner and Rabbi Daniel Silver.

A happier time. Sadly, half of David's long time golf group are no longer with us.

Chapter 40

$\mathcal{I}$n the fall of 1978, the civilian aides opted to have their annual meeting in the "gastronomical paradise" of New Orleans. We were excited about the trip for two reasons. We had never been there before and by chance, our daughter Stephanie had just begun her freshman year at Tulane. It was a perfect time to get her settled into her dorm. David had to attend meetings, but he was beginning to use some of the clout of a temporary general to get some chores done for his daughter.

Since we didn't have a car, he arranged for an Army vehicle to take me around to the stores. Stephy needed a new bike for her campus transportation, and we searched the ads in the Picayune immediately. We found a wonderful bike with a great price was being featured at a Western Auto store. We got to the store and the deal was fine, except the bike was not assembled. The second lieutenant driver told us not to worry. He took the box with all the parts back to the Army base and put it all together. He then took it to the Tulane dorm where the recipient was delighted to get her gift so soon. She was beginning to like her dad's new-found prestige. The part she was not so delighted with was her invitation by the post commander to attend the gala dinner of the Army brass and the aides. The staff arranged for her to be escorted by a young lieutenant. She said that she didn't have anything to wear, but I managed to find a silk skirt of mine that had an elastic waist. When she put it on it didn't need to stretch, and a silk top covered the waistband. I gave her some pearls to wear and she looked quite lovely. She came into the back room at Antoine's looking like she visited the place regularly. She also learned about the protocol of the various services that night. Several officers of the Navy, the Marines and the various Air Forces were also invited.

There was an unusual interval of toasting. It started with a low-level officer toasting his captain. The captain then toasted the general in command of the local base. He in turn toasted the Secretary of the Army. Secretary Alexander toasted "our supreme commander, the President of the United States," and then we all sat and drank our wine. It was an impressionable evening for us, and especially for our daughter. When I spoke to her recently I asked what impressed her the most as an eighteen-year-old at her first big banquet.

"You know, Mom, I was sort of overwhelmed by the protocol and the serious toasting to the higher ups and the various services, but what really impressed me was the signal to all the waiters to take the covers off the entrees at the same time. That really was cool!" And we thought having an escort in full dress uniform would have been her fondest memory.

We did the usual tourist excursions for the remainder of the trip, never thinking we would be visiting the city in the near future. The civilian aides went to another yearly gathering the following October. It was at a place the exact opposite of New Orleans—Ft. Sill, Oklahoma—but steeped in even more protocol. I would like to share a formal letter I received prior to the event. I showed it to David when it arrived, and he just grunted. "Do I have to go along with all this goody-goody lady stuff, honey?" I asked him while scanning the final page of the letter.

"I think once you get there you can choose whatever you think you should do. Just remember that we are their guests and we have to maintain a positive attitude. This is the Army, after all. You remember the fondness for regulations and stuff. Just relax," he said as he looked through the other mail.

So I read the letter again:

Dear Mrs. Skylar: During the Fifth Army Civilian Aide Conference at Fort Sill, I shall be your tour escort for the ladies' separate activities. The attached itinerary reflects our plan, for both the separate activities and for the evening social events. The first social activity of the conference will take place Wednesday evening, November 7th at 7:00p.m. at the Ft. Sill Officers Club. Transportation will be provided, leaving the Montego Bay Motor Hotel at 6:45 p.m. and returning at the end of the evening. This is a black-tie event and I recommend a long dress or a formal cocktail dress. The following evening we shall dine casually at the Ft. Sill Polo Club. Friday, the last evening social will be at the Ft. Sill Officers Club again and a cocktail (long or short) dress will be appropriate; the gentlemen will wear business suits. We expect brisk fall temperatures, however, Lawton has unpredictable weather during this season. The ladies' itinerary contains joint sessions with the gentlemen and some separate visits. For all the daytime activities, casual clothes will be fine. We shall do a bit of walking, so comfortable shoes are certainly recommended. A sweater, shawl or light jacket should be sufficient day and night. You may wish to bring along a scarf Friday afternoon, as we shall visit a training area to observe an artillery firing demonstration.

Mrs. Bentley, the wife of the Civilian Aide for Oklahoma, is a resident of Lawton and she will be hostess for the ladies' luncheon Thursday. There is no luncheon planned for Friday, as we are meeting at 12:45 p.m. However, we shall have some refreshment at the Sherman House just before the special Retreat Ceremony. Mrs. Merritt, the wife of the commander, Ft. Sill and Commandant of the US Army Field Artillery Center, will be our hostess at the Sherman House.

I look forward to seeing you upon your arrival at the Montego Bay Motor Hotel. A brochure containing the schedule for the ladies and a list of all the participants of the conference will be distributed at that time. I shall be delighted to discuss the ladies' activities with you personally any time. Please call me at the Public Affairs Office, Fifth U.S. Army (512) 2212402/4742, if you have any questions. Have a good trip to Lawton. Sincerely, Madeleine Petrillo CPT,GS,USAR Community Relations Public Affairs Office.

But the best part of the letter was handwritten below the above. Capt. Petrillo said: *P.S. I really look forward to seeing you again. This trip will not resemble last year's. Lawton is rural and steeped in Indian culture. I was there last week and its very pretty territory, albeit remote.* There were no truer words spoken. I can only recall snippets of our time in Lawton. I remember the formal I wore the first night only, because we were photographed. I also remember the silk ribbon dress I wore another night, because it was the first and last time I wore it. I also remember how proud I was of David as he stood so straight and tall at the flag ceremony. But I think what I remember most was the afternoon David got us a ride to the best cowboy boot store in town, where we each bought authentic "work" boots that we have till this day.

The civilian aide period of David's life was quite important to him. He learned so much about the workings of the Army and its secrets when he attended the National War College as an insider. He, in turn, taught many public information people a lot to help them with promotion and recruiting. I was not as gung-ho about all the protocol and all his helicopter flying to various bases, but he was just doing another one of his jobs—only this time he was doing it as a general. What's not to like?

The first Fifth Army gathering in New Orleans.

David and Stephanie at high school graduation 1978.

Greeting the host at Civilian Aide gathering in Ft. Sill, OK.

Chapter 41

During the hectic period of all the Army travels, David was still working on various deals. I happily went along with whatever he did, as it didn't interrupt my activities unless we had to go out of town. I had found the house of my dreams right next door to my dear friend Holly Arvanites, who had moved to Shaker Heights when her husband became president of the May Company.

I told Holly at the time that I would love to meet the elderly owner some day when she sat out on her terrace having her 5:00 p.m. martini during good weather. When the opportunity arose, I told the woman that I loved her house and if she ever planned on moving to a smaller place to let me know. I really never even thought she knew what I was talking about. I just forgot about the whole idea. Then one day in 1979, after my friend had moved to Texas, the phone rang and a strange voice asked to speak to Mr. or Mrs. Skylar. It was the son of the dear elderly lady that had been Holly's next-door neighbor. I took the call.

"This is John Sealer (name changed to protect the memory). My mother passed away yesterday and she had asked me to call you awhile back. Are you still interested in buying her home?" he inquired in a very businesslike manner.

"Oh my, I'm so sorry for your loss, and yes we are definitely interested," I said firmly, although I hadn't discussed the possibility with my husband for at least a year.

"Can you meet me at the end of the week? I would like to make a deal as soon as possible," he said. When I hung up I wondered what I had just implemented.

When David got home that night I told him of the conversation. He didn't bat an eye and just asked me if I had ever been inside that house, and I told him only on the first floor. "Do you really want this house, babe?" he asked, "because if you do, I will negotiate with Sealer and see what happens."

"Oh yes, it's a dream. It is a little gem. Well, it is a little smaller than our house...fewer bedrooms, but bigger downstairs and right on the Canterbury Golf Course."

"Okay, okay relax. I'll take care of it." Whenever David used that expression I knew we were going to move on it. By the end of the week David and our attorney met the son and his attorney on the beautiful brick terrace of the French-style house. The price was quite reasonable, and much lower than we expected. David took out a bridge loan until we sold our home, and we ended up in good shape. There was not much difference between the prices, which was amazing. The refurbishing was not a big deal: Mostly paint and wallpaper, and some new appliances were all that was needed. The house was only fourteen years old, while our present house was fifty. It was the deal of our financial lives. When we had to sell it ten years later, it went for two and three-fourths the original price.

While I busied myself with decorating plans for the new house, David had been working on another deal. He had gotten a call out of the blue from the president of Cox Enterprises out of Atlanta asking him if he would like to head up their entities in New Orleans. This time David wasn't so sure he wanted to work for anybody anymore, so he decided he might consider it, but on his terms. As he settled himself in on his flight to Atlanta, he wrote down a list of perks he wanted. It was really an impossibly outlandish list. His requirements not only included a huge salary, but a three-day week, a country club membership, all commuting expenses in first-class seats, travel costs for me, and hotel accommodations until he got more permanent quarters. He put the list in his pocket wondering what the meeting would bring. It was almost as if he was chiding Cox for even calling him.

It turned out the president agreed to all the demands, and David found himself having to go to work for someone again. He was going to start running Cox's weeklies as suburban papers, just as he did in Ohio. His reputation was just too good. When he got home he told me he couldn't believe how much they wanted him. He was to start work in about three weeks.

Everything doesn't stay rosy for long, though. We had become snowbirds in 1977 when David was working for himself, and commuting weekly to Florida. I stayed down south after Stephanie started college, so there was no need for me to go back and forth so often. In 1979, I was watching David shave as he was getting ready for his trip up north and happened to see a little pink pimple on his back. It didn't really look so ominous, but being an attentive wife I told him to see the dermatologist when he got home. Actually, I made him promise to do so. This was a Tuesday and he flew to Cleveland, did some work, saw the doctor on Wednesday, and came back to Florida on Friday afternoon.

As we were having dinner that night the phone rang. I answered and when the doctor asked for David, I had a strange feeling in my chest. I knew something was wrong. And so it proved to be. The doctor said he had to return immediately, because the biopsy he took of that little pink pimple was malignant. We left Sunday together. On Monday we went to the doctor's office when he told us the news in person: the biopsy showed a Melanoma lesion. He had to have immediate surgery. The dermatologist asked us if we had a preference for a surgeon, and we gave him the name of Dr. Thornton that members of my family had used. It turned out he was head of surgery at University Hospital in Cleveland. The plan was to get David admitted that day to get all the pretests done prior to surgery on Wednesday.

The surgery was performed, but not completely by Dr. Thornton. We found out later that one of his staff did the work with Dr. Thornton coming in and out of the operating room to supervise. It was not a perfect operation. The area excised was about the size of a large steak, and reached all the way down to the muscle in his shoulder. All the nodes under his right arm also had to be removed. The trickiest part was grafting skin over the wound, and the young surgeon apparently did not have a lot of experience. It was a very difficult procedure. After a few days David left the hospital, but had to return a few times for more grafts and treatments for infections.

David was not aware of all this trouble. He could not see his shoulder. He did realize that the time was coming up for him to report to work in New Orleans. When he did get down there, the dressing still had to be changed daily. He had Stephanie there, and she started to perform the task, but she had classes to attend and he found some head housekeeper at the Pontchartrain to do it. He did not want the people at work to know of his problem. After a few weeks of commuting to Cleveland, the doctors said the wound was healing okay, but they wanted to do another procedure on him. This was a real surprise. They decided to remove some of his bone marrow and freeze it in case the need for it would arise in the future. This was a painful procedure, but they drugged him enough that he got through it fine. His frozen cache was number 112. Twenty-five years later when it might have been used, nobody was aware of its existence. All of the above is considered health crisis number two in David's life. There will be several more, but they never held him back from finding more exciting jobs to do.

Chapter 42

This new job that David accepted turned out to be a real eye opener. The job itself was just more of the same ideas and promotions that he had experienced in the past. The real excitement was the City of New Orleans with its diverse parishes and unusual citizens. But I won't get into that just yet. First, let me take you into the new world of corporate management.

Cox Enterprises and its many components was a whole new situation for David. He had always been on the outside instructing the companies in ways of the advertising or public relations methods. Now he was on the inside learning how the executives really handled their lives. These people were certainly among the most industrious and generous people he had ever met. Money was no object to them. After a few short months, David and I were invited to join the top executives on a trip to Hawaii for the American Newspaper Publishers Association (ANPA). I couldn't believe it! "This is really amazing," I said to David over the phone. "You have only been there a couple of months and you must have done something special."

"No, I have only started tearing things apart and organizing the departments and the employees. Nothing special about it. I don't get it either, especially since we are in the midst of such change. Hell, I'm all for a little R and R anyway," he laughed.

"Fine with me. What is the timetable and where do we leave from?"

"I'll be back in Florida on Friday as usual, and we are to fly to Atlanta and meet the group there. I'll get all the dope later today," he said.

When I got home from golf that afternoon the mail had already arrived, so I sat down in the den to go through it before I did anything else. In the pile of all the junk there was an envelope of expensive stationery addressed to us in "wedding invitation" script. It was an invitation to a private cocktail party from Barbara Cox Anthony at her home. Holy Cow! (My usual exclamation of the day) She was one of the wealthiest women in the world. I couldn't wait to tell David that night. This was a new dimension of my brush with business workings.

On our flight to Atlanta we mused about who would be going on this little trip. David figured that some of the editors and cable managers would be asked. Can you imagine our surprise when the president of Cox newspapers, Chuck Glover, and his wife; one of the editors of the *Atlanta Journal* and his wife; the chairman of the board of Cox Enterprises, Garner Anthony; and an elderly, charming gentleman (whose name I will try to recall later) were there. A light lunch was set up in a private room at the airport. I never knew there were such rooms. Our bags were whisked away when we arrived, so all we had to do was lunch and leisurely board the plane to Hawaii. It was first class all the way. I decided that Cox was the greatest company in the USA! I seem to remember spending the night in Los Angeles, because certain members of the party decided it was too exhausting to fly all the way to Hawaii. I also remember a sumptuous dinner at Chasen's where a last-minute call got us in immediately. Loved that upscale corporate life.

Somewhere along the way, David mentioned to Garner Anthony that I had been having some back problems and wasn't sure I was going to make the trip. By the time we were ready to leave, however, all my pains had disappeared. Mr. Anthony took David's conversation to heart. He said he had some help for me in mind, and after we got to Honolulu he would take care of my problem. When we got off the plane, Mrs. Glover said she was going to the restroom. That seemed like a good idea. A very normal idea, indeed. Chuck Glover sort of took me aside and asked if I would watch over his wife. I wasn't sure what he meant, and then it dawned on me that she had some sort of mild dementia. Nobody had heard of Alzheimer's in those days, and as I look back she could have been suffering from something similar at a young age. Everything was okay in the restroom and I came out of there slightly puzzled.

I was further impressed when individual cars were awaiting our group. We were whisked away to what was then called the Kahala Hilton. Our room was in one of the villas that opened onto the golf course. I remember watching televised pro tournaments from that venue. After unpacking we still had time for a nap. David decided to look over the agenda for the conference, but I was slightly jetlagged and fell asleep. When I woke up I saw he had finally fallen asleep. Then it was hurried showers and dressing for dinner. I knew we had to stay with the Cox group, since we were considered representatives of the publisher. That first night our group was able to dine independent of any agenda. The next day, April 21, 1980, was the start of the conference. The big story was that Ferdinand Marcos had been invited to speak at the AP main luncheon. The local Filipino newspaper called for a boycott of the conference and insisted on mass protests. The ANPA was just one of three groups that extended the invitation. Marcos was eager to improve his reputation. He was just one of a number of government and diplomatic leaders invited to the conference.

Those who issued the invitation to Marcos claimed he was invited for his interest, not for his political philosophy. The fact remained, though, that the ANPA had provided a forum for a discredited dictator, and not without some U.S. involvement. The protests were loud and clear. I honestly wasn't aware of the nuances of that Marcos trip to the U.S. after eight years. I had my own issues.

Garner Anthony was true to his word; he wanted to help me with my back pain. Hey, I couldn't protest. He was, after all, chairman of the board and married to one of the wealthiest women in the world. Who was I to deny his help, even though I felt great at that point? He called us first thing in the morning and said he would pick us up after breakfast to go see the most amazing therapist in the Hawaiian Islands. Since I was not familiar then or now with the highway system in Honolulu, I can only say that we drove along sleek highways for over 45 minutes. We had no idea what to expect. Finally, we pulled up in front of a slightly rundown, ranch-type house with an unkempt patch of grass and lots of bushes. Mr. Anthony rang the doorbell and a wizened Chinese man opened the door with a big smile on his face. I was feeling a little jittery at this point. He had me lie down on a mattress covered with a flowery cover, as I recall, and when I did so, I noticed the satin case in his hand with rows and rows of needles. I looked at David as if to say, *What have you done to me?*

Then it began—needles in my spine, then needles on my toes, my knees, my fingers. You name the place—I had the works. All the while David and Garner were having tea and cookies. When my ordeal was over, I called out, "It's your turn, David. I want you to enjoy the experience."

"Yes Dave, you'll feel great," Garner insisted. So my big-mouth husband got the needles, too. I got the last laugh. All the way home the big boss was expounding on the joys of acupuncture and his many sessions with the Chinese "therapist." David wholeheartedly agreed over and over again.

Though we had been to Hawaii before when we took *Sun Newspaper* readers on a tour, we had never experienced the luxurious treatment that we received from the Cox people. There was nothing but the finest for them, and they extended their generosity to us. The Louisiana suburban papers that David ran were just a "tiny drop in the bucket" of Cox entities. Even the kindly older gentleman, who shall still remain nameless out of necessity, was fawning over us like some long-lost children. One day he insisted that I walk with him to a department store he wanted me to see. I think David went to some seminar. When we got to the store he asked me if I wanted to get anything, and I told him I didn't need anything at the moment. He steered me over to the costume jewelry counter and told the saleslady he wanted her to bring out this necklace that he saw in the case. He explained that it was made of special seeds that were native to Hawaii, and he thought I should have it as a souvenir! The seeds were brown and there were several strands of them, and I tried really hard to tell him I couldn't accept such a special gift, but he insisted. I had no idea what it cost, but it was definitely not pretty. He had it put in a jewelry box and tied with a ribbon, and handed it to me beaming with joy at his generosity. When we walked back to the hotel I thanked him excessively. I should have picked out something I could actually wear, but it was what it was. When I showed David the necklace he was as surprised as I was that I needed such a souvenir. Needless to say, I never wore the ugly thing. Mr. No-name was still a sweet man. I will always remember his gesture.

The most exciting part of the trip was the cocktail party at the Anthony's. The home was in Diamond Head and it was gorgeous. Actually, for billionaires it was rather low key. It was not like the mansions that you see today. Walking out the back door to the rather small yard that went to the edge of the mountain, you could see all of Honolulu. It was spectacular. On the whole, I would say it was a very nice house. The one thing that set it apart from the ordinary was the original French Impressionist painting hung outside on the walls of the lanai. I kept thinking, *Are these paintings specially treated to withstand moisture, or when they are ruined are they thrown away?* That issue has stayed in my mind for over 32 years. Rich or poor, it's nice to have money, or so the old saying goes. The highpoint of the evening, after all, was meeting the famous people of journalistic fame. Just shaking Katherine Graham's hand was probably the highlight of the trip. All the biggest publishers were at that party, but meeting her was the living end for me. I think even David, the unimpressionable, was excited to meet these top guns.

After a couple of luaus and a round of golf, we left Honolulu on a very sad day. President Carter's plan to free the hostages in Iran had failed because of malfunctioning helicopters and other factors, and the country was in turmoil. Carter was blamed for poor handling of the situation and never got over it.

We found a flight that went directly from Honolulu to Dallas, which was much better than spending time in L.A. When we got on the plane there were several TV newsmen on it as well, as they had been covering the ANPA conference. They were all anxious to get back to cover the big crisis. From Dallas we flew back to New Orleans. We had just rented an apartment there, and I needed to start decorating it so David could move out of his hotel room. At first I wasn't so keen about having a third residence, but I got over it. My big problem was that I never knew where that big package of M&M's was!

Mr. and Mrs. Garner Anthony

request the pleasure of your company

Sunday, the twentieth of April

six thirty until eight thirty

3944 Noela Place

Cocktails

Our invitation to a very exclusive cocktail party in Honolulu during the ANPA convention.

Chapter 43

*A*fter our five-day junket to Honolulu, it was hard to get back to reality. David was still in the midst of reorganizing newspapers and putting the right personnel in the best situations for their various talents. He also had to buy a lot of new equipment. One of the biggest purchases was an immense press so the papers could be printed in-house. Meanwhile, I was trying to get the apartment in order. As soon as we got back to town we ordered two bedsprings and a king-size mattress so we could get out of the hotel. At the same time we bought some inexpensive dishes and silverware, some towels and sheets, and a few pieces of furniture at stores that advertised with the *West Bank Guide*. Some of the furniture was so ugly we would end up buying accessories like baskets and candlesticks so we wouldn't be judged too particular and have our advertisers give up on us. We had already bought a huge, Marimekko, beige and white sectional that was to be shipped the week we got to town. Other rugs and chairs from Cleveland that we didn't need in the new house were also on the way. It was going to be a charming little apartment for David to use whenever he was in town. Stephanie loved it. She used to bring her laundry over, as it was equipped with a washer and dryer, and she didn't need to use her precious quarters.

The fascinating personality of the city really got to David. He went out of his way to meet the clichéd movers and shakers, some of whom took him under their wings and showed him the New Orleans that tourists never see. Even some of his employees enjoyed showing him around. One evening when I was in Florida, he was going to meet one of his assistants for a casual seafood dinner at a neighborhood restaurant on the West Bank. It was supposed to be a favorite dining spot. He got to the restaurant a few minutes before the young man arrived. He could hardly find a place to park. *Hmm*, he thought, *this must really be good food*, and his mouth was watering for the shrimp he envisioned. He walked in the door and only one or two tables were occupied. Just then his assistant arrived, and David looked at him quizzically. "The parking lot is overflowing, but there is nobody here. What gives?" he asked.

"Let's sit down and have a beer and some oysters, and I'll explain everything," he said.

"I'm starving, Bob. Get a waiter, please."

"Okay, okay, see that door marked restrooms? Come on… I'll take you through," and he got up from his chair and signaled David to follow him. When they went in they followed a long hallway to the loud hum of voices in another room at the end of the hall. When they walked in there were dozens of people standing or sitting around all forms of gaming equipment. David was amazed to see a few police officers among the crowds.

"I'll be damned. Isn't gaming still illegal here?" he said.

"It is supposed to be," Bob answered, "but nobody gives a hoot in this town. This is just one little example. This town is loaded with places like this," he chuckled. "So, you want to play?"

"Are you kidding? It's dinner time. Let's go back and eat!" That was the first eye opener, but not the last, for the new guy in town. Some of the people I may mention in this story may still be alive. But even if they are, some of their actions or utterances were uncalled for at the time, and I have no guilt in exposing them.

I'll give you an example. In the few times I went out socially with David's new friends, only once did the wives join the party. I finally realized that New Orleans men thought "mama" should stay home at night with the kids. These men had an attitude toward women that was strange, if not old world. David wondered about it also, but continued to bring me along to drinks, food, or big events, because it was what we always did. I began to think of myself as a big faux pas!

One evening we went to meet his friend John Mamoulides, who was the district attorney in Jefferson Parish, which included the West Bank where David worked. John, in turn, brought along a friend whose last name was Perez. I cannot remember whether it was Chalin or Leander; both brothers were powerful members of one of the most strongly entrenched political families in Louisiana. After the male conversation waned a bit, the Perez guy turned to me and asked in the thickest of southern accents, "Well, how do you like our fair city?"

"I'm not too sure at this point. There is so much crime here, and so many murders..." I trailed off.

"That's no problem. We'll get you a gun and you will be safe," John casually mentioned.

"A gun? John, are you kidding? I would never touch one of those things. Why, what if I used it and killed somebody that was going after my purse. I could go to jail for life, and there would be no witnesses or proof it was self-defense. Oh, never!" I exclaimed, really upset.

Mr. Perez smiled at me in a funny way and said in that maddening accent, "Maarlin, if you killed a n....., we'd give you a medal!"

Whoa, that was a little frightening to me, and I realized then how bigoted these people were. I wasn't so keen on meeting many more of the new Skylar friends.

Shortly after that dinner, David was asked to meet the Perez brothers on their own turf. It seemed that after decades of the family dynasty's dictatorship of Plaquemines Parish, their power was beginning to corrode. At that time Leander was district attorney and Cholin was president of the parish. In 1980, political opponents were making serious inroads in the local elections. I'm not sure of the reason, but they wanted to talk to a newspaper man they heard had a public relations and advertising background. David agreed to go down to their parish, which seemed like going to the end of the world, but he was curious about the area. He was driving an old boat of a Chevy convertible, which he had obtained from a former employee in Cleveland just to keep in New Orleans.

As he approached the area it seemed like there were very few lights anywhere, and no streetlights in view. He came to a small overpass or bridge and heard a siren behind him, and saw a bright light shining on his car. He stopped and a patrol car pulled up, and a big burly cop got out and asked David for his license and where he was going. David gave him his creds and said he was looking for Chalin's house. The cop asked him to get out of his car and patted him down. He then got on his car phone and called Perez. When he was told the "guest" was legitimate, he changed his attitude and offered to lead him to the house. David followed him through many dark streets and was relieved to finally arrive at a very large, but ordinary home. He thanked the cop and rang the bell. Chalin Perez answered the door himself. I cannot tell you how the political discussion went, but later David told me they listened to his advice. He did tell me that the place was furnished with magnificent antiques standing side by side with junk tables and lamps from Kmart. When it came time for him to leave, Chalin called the patrol car to escort David out, as if it were possible for him to snoop around the parish in the dark.

When he got back to the apartment he was visibly shaken by the experience. As it turned out, by 1982 a nine-member council of parishes sued the Perez brothers, whom they believed secretly profited from the parish-owned oil royalties that were valued at millions of dollars. Eventually, they had to turn back all their lands to the parish.

David had, at about the same time, met an outspoken Chinese sheriff named Harry Lee. He was elected sheriff of Jefferson Parish just when David hit town. Harry Lee was the son of a laundry man who became a well-known restaurateur. Harry was a fine student and went on to LSU to get a degree in chemistry. He ran the restaurant for his father and got a law degree at the same time. He was a successful magistrate before he was elected to his sheriff's position. He was not a newcomer like David, but he was new to this job. When the two men met, they became pals immediately. One day David told Harry about his illegal treatment upon entering Plaquamines Parish.

Two days later a package arrived at the *Guide* office. When David opened it he found a shiny deputy sheriff badge encased in a black leather folder. A note read: *Dave, just show 'em this next time. Harry.*

It was a great souvenir, however it couldn't help in some other New Orleans' situations that would come about later. In just a couple of years so much happened.

Chapter 44

*I*t is important to note that Cox had purchased the *Guide* newspapers about a year or so before David was recruited by Charles Glover, who was president at the time of Cox Enterprises. They were little more than shoppers with 99% local ads and a few paragraphs of canned news. There was much speculation about when Cox was going to do something about its new acquisitions.

The *East Bank Guide*, the *Orleans Guide*, the *St. Tammany Guide*, the *St. Bernard Guide*, as well as the *West Bank Guide* had a terrible image problem. When Joe Howard, the general manager of the papers, first picked David up at the airport he knew things were going to be different. He later said in an interview for a story, "In the 45 minutes it took to drive to Gretna, I knew things would never be the same again. I found out that Skylar had been in and out of New Orleans a half a dozen times before we met. He already knew about the business community, the politics, and the competition. He was ready for action."

I think the best way to describe David's tenure in Louisiana is to copiously quote an underground weekly newspaper called *Figaro*. A young man named William Metcalf, Jr. was the publisher. In 1981, after a year and a half of behind-the-scenes repositioning of the *Guide*, David allowed himself to be interviewed by Metcalf. He never thought much about it until *Figaro* came out with David's face on the cover touting the lead story: "Who is This Man?" It was a bit embarrassing, but the article told it like it was at the time. For the next few pages I may quote the article. After all, it really captured the situation better than my memory could do.

"Skylar spent another three months driving through the neighborhoods. 'He didn't waste much time,' said one of the *Guide* editors. 'He came in late July and by November we were already endorsing candidates. For 20 years the *Guide* had never taken sides, because we didn't want to make anybody mad. We shied away from controversy completely. But in September,' commented another editor, 'we got a memo for setting up private meetings to discuss local politics. He wanted to know who was behind all the candidates, who put up the money, and who was calling the shots. When we made endorsements in October, we surprised a lot of people.'

"Most surprised were the politicians, who certainly didn't expect another medium to spar with. 'It is so much improved, so much more professional,' said Terry Gee, Algiers' state representative. 'I love it. I think Skylar is doing a good job. He's good for the area; we need more people like him.'

"'Skylar's turned the newspapers around,' said Jefferson Parish Councilman Butch Ward. 'The man is a very capable individual, a very bright individual,' Representative Ron Faucheux, a political public relations man says. 'The new *Guide Newspapers* show improvement and a growing awareness of the importance of localized news coverage, especially in New Orleans East.'"

David had a style of management all his own. Although he carried the title of publisher, he acted like a managing editor. Each time the papers came out he would go over them carefully, and then call a meeting of the editors. It was not to change opinions or ideas, but only to question writing methods or syntax. He constantly wrote memos to all the editors and reporters.

"Skylar changed the face and guts of the newspapers, bringing every aspect of the operation under his style. He moved into the Pontchartrain Hotel, leaving his wife in Florida; after a 12-hour day at the office he'd have dinner sent up from the Caribbean Room and would work until bedtime writing memos and planning. 'We made more changes in a few weeks than we'd ever thought possible,' says Joe Howard, the general manager, 'but he was here to rebuild a newspaper and a company.'

"The rebuilding gives us an insight into the future plans the *Guide Newspapers* may have. A 40,000 sq. ft. building was constructed on Belle Chasse Highway, and in it were installed over $2million in new presses, computers, cameras and other equipment, all of it highly advanced and clearly capable of handling more than any weekly newspaper could keep it busy with. The press is second in size to the *Times-Picayune* and can run an entire issue of any of the *Guide* papers from scratch in just a few hours. The *Guide* now has a lot of surplus capacity."

The big question at the time was whether the *Guide* would go daily.

"'I'd be kidding you if I said we weren't thinking about increasing our frequency,' responds Skylar. 'We've done our research and some planning, and nothing has been firmed up. And nothing will be for a while. I wouldn't call this the best economy to make such a big move.'

"'Starting a daily newspaper is like giving birth to a hippopotamus,' he continued. 'It takes time and if it isn't done right, it can be mighty painful. We're moving very slowly, and I sure as hell don't want to get the *Times-Picayune* all nervous.'"

According to the *Figaro* article, the *Times-Picayune* already had been fighting back; it had gotten a toehold into the West Bank, and only a little more successful in East Jefferson Parish. It had pulled a page from the *Guide's* book, by giving all non-subscribers free issues of two new advertisers that it called the *East and West Advertisers*, that were broadsheets with a bunch of short copy culled from the daily *Picayune*. They set rates comparable to the *Guide*. The *T-P* also tried zoning into the outlying areas where they would run a couple of pages of local news to the different zones, but it didn't really get into community doings like the *Guides*.

One home furnishing store owner called David the brightest marketer he had ever met. "He has more comprehension of this market than any newspaperman I had ever dealt with. He knows the nuts and bolts of marketing." According to Bill Metcalf, "Never before has the *Times-Picayune* courted the advertisers as they have been doing lately. We hear of half-price sales, two for ones, and all sorts of other unheard-of marketing moves by the *T-P*."

David was quoted as saying he had heard about the new tactics of the *T-P*, but as long as nothing illegal was done it was not a problem, but if there was anything clearly illegal he would call them on it. "Cox did not come into New Orleans to get pushed around, and the *T-P* people know this," said Skylar.

"I'm always hearing this crap about cutting into their market," Skylar continued. "They don't own the market; they serve it as we do. Those guys are smart enough to know that the days of rolling over this town are over; the new breed of politicians and businessmen are no longer intimidated by the press as the old-timers were.

"Look at Jefferson Parish. For years it was the *T-P's* whipping boy. They never talked so much about scandals or corruption in their own back yard. The West Bank, according to them, is where everyone hung out. Even today their coverage of St. Bernard and Plaquamines' parishes is uneven," he said.

"The *Times-Picayune* is a hell of a product for 35 cents on Sunday. It's one of the best buys in the country. But the real pros in the business do not rate their editorial package too highly. They seem to be concerned with what the good old boys think, and they play a lot of unnecessary games."

Figaro claimed that for all his bravado, David hedged his bets and set his goals in another direction. He said that the *Guides* were really not competitors of the *T-P*. He said that they were good at presenting the news of the world, the country and the state. "The *Guides'* interest is mostly in the neighbor-hoods," he explained. "We never covered the assassination attempt on President Reagan," he said. "We would have if one of the secret service men had been from Gretna or St. Tam-many."

David explained in the article that there was not even com-petition for the advertising dollar. "We have never gotten too many ads from the big department stores. It's hard to break tra-dition. There are only three reasons for an advertiser to buy media: reach, frequency and saturation. The *T-P* has got us beat on the first two reasons. But we have definitely got them beat on the third. We deliver papers to 50% of all households in our area, which is everywhere but the inner city. It's my old concept of the doughnut around the hole again that I used so success-fully in Ohio," he claimed.

"The reason the *T-P* is looking at us is because up until recently they had the only game in town. Technology raised its lovely head, and small companies like our predecessors could start papers without investing millions of dollars. It was only recently that the *T-P* came kicking and screaming into the 20thcentury. When it combined the two dailies in New Orleans, they pulled the usual arrogant trick of not dropping any features of the two papers. They bought everything they could just to make sure that no other start-up paper could get any features or other services. The syndicates went along with the tactics because they didn't want to clash with big users, and Newhouse was a very big user.

"So consequently," Skylar said, "we don't have the depart-ments and features that we could use. However, we put out about 200,000 papers a week and fill them all with our own features produced by our own staff, but those we lack can make the papers seem light to some people.

"When we took over, the papers were no more than shop-pers, and in 18 months we have added hard news and commu-nity interest. Ask anybody what we have accomplished. Hey, I was the midwife for this birth of our operation, and I believe she is beautiful," Skylar beamed.

The *T-P* had made quite an issue of the fact that the *Guide* and other operations like *Figaro* were given away free, and people didn't bother reading them. That issue has never been proved. David felt that if you pick up a free paper and take it into your home, it gives you the chance to read what the advertiser is offering. The local advertisers were all jumping on the *Guides'* bandwagon because of the great saturation.

At the time David hinted that the free concept might change. He said if and when they decided to come out more frequently, they might have paid subscriptions. At that point in time they had voluntary payment of one dollar a month, which the carriers collected whenever they could. There was a little ad on the front page encouraging people to shell out the buck.

David told the interviewer he thought New Orleans was a great place to live, since there was a lot of action; it was a fun town. But from a business point of view, he said he was disappointed. It bothered him, he said, that cities like Nashville, Houston and Atlanta had passed up New Orleans. "There is too much fun and not enough desire here," he said. "In lots of cities you can find at least a dozen men and women across all segments of the population who can get things done. Here there are many leaders, but no superstars, and that's what they need here.

"I am amazed at the intensity of the political races here, though," he continued. "There are connections built on connections. I admit that I don't know much about Orleans Parish, as I have been concentrating on Jefferson, Plaqumines and other areas first. I admire the new breed who are running the show. In Jefferson, I think John Mamoulides is sharp, honest and dedicated. He's tough and he does his homework." (ed. note. This observation did not hold up in later months)

He named several of this new emerging breed of politicians in other parishes, and said some of them were changing things for the better. He went on to say that he didn't actually know who was honest and who wasn't, but he felt that if the media did its job of investigating, most politicians would stay on the clean side. "If we focus the glare of publicity on the political arena, there won't be any shadowy deals," Skylar said.

"We've begun to discover some junk with our investigative reporters, and we wrote some interesting stories. Sometime back we got involved with a big story and called in some of the top Cox reporters to help us. With our parent organization we can get the real pros to investigate with their numerous resources."

When asked if this meant the *Guides* were changing their focus on only local issues, David replied, "Certainly not. It means that we want to present a total product. We're even covering Baton Rouge now. We filter out the thousands of news stories and try to present our readers with materiel they won't see on the six o'clock news on TV."

Figaro's interviewer editorialized that David Skylar was no shrinking violet. "In fact, his job does great things for his ego; however, as was mentioned previously, he would not consent to any interviews during his first year and a half in town. He even stayed in the background at the groundbreaking of the new building. But everything that he does seemed to have a purpose.

"'We've got no secrets,' he says, 'and I'd invite the *Times-Picayune* to see our plant if I thought they'd come, not that they don't know what we are doing here anyway. I felt it's important for me right now to talk. I want to be a good citizen, and that means that people have to know me and trust me. I'm the new guy on the stage, and maybe the spotlight has to be on me, but this is the Cox show not the Skylar show. If we do well it's because of the commitment our people have made up and down the line.'"

The interviewer commented that it was quite a commitment. Four million dollars had already gone into the young growing operation. It looked as if a daily newspaper was in the not-to-distant future. As an example, if you looked into the classified department of the *Guides* you would see three modular desks with six positions each, filling about half the floor space. At each position was a computer terminal through which the operator took classifieds from the phone and entered them directly into the typesetting computers upstairs. This was obviously not weekly newspaper technology.

"Expanding a newspaper is a lot like sending a rocket into space," said Skylar. "It's risky and expensive, and takes a lot of planning and work. And everything in the environment or marketplace has to be right before the launch. In space talk they look for the right 'window,' the right time when all systems are 'go.' We're looking for the right window to push this thing through," he concluded. "If we miss a chance this summer, we may try again next spring."

During David's tenure, Cox people were true to their usual technique of leaving their publishers to do their own thing. Once a month the top brass would fly in and meet David for a shrimp dinner at Pascal Manale's famous restaurant. They rarely had any input on the operation. David would have the monthly figures drawn up and presented to them, and they were happy with what they saw, and then they flew back to Atlanta. Sometimes they never even visited the plant.

There is still so much extracurricular activity in which David indulged while in New Orleans. Some of it caused a huge financial problem in the years to come—and I mean huge!

David graced the cover of the alternative newspaper, Figaro, in New Orleans.

Chapter 45

I cannot remember at which times I was in Ohio or Florida or Louisiana, and when David commuted to those sites or when we traveled together. The couple of years with three households were all jumbled together. I believe I preferred my luxurious mini chateau in Cleveland during the summer golfing season, and the townhouse in Florida during the winter. It wasn't as though I had any responsibilities; Stephanie was at Tulane, and Dean and Claudia were married. I probably should have stayed in the New Orleans apartment more. David also liked to play our north and south golf courses. He didn't have to leave New Orleans just to hit the links; true to their word, Cox got us a membership to Timberlane Country Club, the first and only private club on the West Bank. Robert Trent Jones designed a very difficult course that wound through a plush new neighborhood of homes.

We went to a new member dinner where we were introduced, along with others, and that was the extent of our social endeavors in Gretna. I did, however, join the Ladies Golf Association, which gave me one more place to compete. It was important to be a part of the community that David served, even if he didn't have time to play. The people were a little different on the West Bank. I guess the older families lived in Metairie or near the university, and didn't mingle with those across the river.

Just recently I googled 1750 St. Charles, the apartment complex where we rented in 1980. It is now a condominium and had some penthouse unit listed for a million plus. I was amazed at its longevity and exclusivity. When David first rented the one bedroom and den unit, he befriended the owner of the building, who was divorced and also lived there. He came from an old New Orleans family that seemed to have a monopoly on wholesale linens in the city. Of course, we took advantage of the deal to outfit the apartment. There were no discount linen stores in those days.

It was especially exciting to live along the parade routes. We could stand right outside our building and throw and catch all the beads we could handle. One time when some of David's political friends were marching with one of the krewes, they invited us to walk with them, which was a lot of fun for Ohio hicks like us. We ended up at a special grandstand almost two miles away, and had to walk back home with sore feet.

There wasn't much to do when David was working except play golf and shop a little, but on weekends we went to the flea market held at the edge of the French Quarter. That was when my husband noticed a man with interesting carvings. All of a sudden he became a collector. These carvings were made in Indonesia, and as far as we knew they were authentic. Every week David would find the guy who sold them to see whether any new ones had arrived. Soon the collection of small painted figurines were joined by interesting centerpieces and large animal carvings. I was happy that my workaholic husband had found a new hobby. Weekends were also the best chance we had to see our daughter.

Before we moved to the apartment, she had already driven her jeep down from Cleveland. She left the hardtop back home for me to sell. David told me that when she came to see him at the Pontchartrain, the doormen would always leave it at the curb and watch it for her. They knew her name and she knew theirs. She never had to worry about her jeep getting stolen. She would often pick her father up to go out to dinner. She usually made the recommendations, since she had been in New Orleans longer.

One evening she said she would like to try a restaurant she'd heard had Mexican food, so off they went. When they walked in they did not see any female customers, and at first didn't give it any thought. They started to get some funny looks and then it dawned on David what was going on. He explained to Stephanie that this Mexican restaurant was a gay enclave, and wondered if she felt uncomfortable and wanted to leave. To his surprise she wanted to stay. They ate their dinner at a table in the middle of the room with numerous eyes upon them.

I had a similar experience with a lot of men, but they were macho men. David got the invitation to fish in the Grand Isle tournament and he was to attend the banquet beforehand. Naturally, since I was in town, he took me along. To our dismay, when we walked into this huge hall filled with tables of registrants in the tournament, there was a stage of some sort with some speakers. The secretary of the organization was a woman. She was the only one in the group of several hundred men. Nobody warned David of this. I felt like sinking into the floor. My husband just told me to ignore the situation, and after a quick bite we left with our heads high.

One of the "good ole boys " that befriended David had a printing business, I believe. He was divorced and quite wealthy, as well as connected politically. His brother-in-law held some office in Jefferson Parish. When David and I were invited to his home for dinner, I was anxious to see the inside of a large Metairie home as his was supposed to be. When we arrived we were greeted by this gentleman and his lady friend, and we had a very pleasant steak dinner that the host prepared on the grill outside. We just sat and talked with the lady while he scooted in and out. A housekeeper had set up all the ingredients and set the table, and there wasn't much we could do to help.

After dinner he said he wanted to show us something special, and led us out the back door of his house. He hit a switch and night turned into day, showcasing an immense shooting range. Since I had never seen any range before, this was overwhelming. I couldn't imagine anyone in my home suburb of Shaker Heights, Ohio, ever having anything like it. About 75 to 100 feet in front of the gun racks there was a long shelter with mechanical animals running through it and in front of it whenever our host called out to his worker to turn them loose. Then he started insisting that I learn how to use a rifle.

He found what he said was perfect for me, placed it on my shoulder, and put my fingers on the trigger. I had a special glove, as I remember. I was terrified. David just looked on with an amused grin on his face, and started shooting the targets that ran so fast in front of him. When I pulled the trigger I almost fell over. I was told I would get used to it. After two more attempts to shoot a bear, I begged off. Guns don't appeal to me, and they seem to be a way of life for some of the Louisiana boys that never grew up.

David had a lot of adventures that I cannot verify, as I wasn't there, and as I have repeatedly mentioned, David cannot recall anything preceding 2004. However, I can verify that the so-called friends and business partners that he met in the "Big Easy" turned out to be "hazardous to his health." And I might add, hazardous to our net worth.

Chapter 46

The last story to come out of New Orleans is probably the most complicated. It is also the one of which I have the least knowledge. As I discussed previously, David became friendly with many of the power elite in the city. They proved to be unfriendly as time went on.

When David was living temporarily at the Pontchartrain, he noticed that right down the block there was an old storage building that was not in business any longer. It was in a great location, not far from the new apartments that were just built on St. Charles. He wondered how the old place could be converted into something beautiful, as well as useful.

One day he was having lunch with his new friend, John Mamoulides, and asked him about it. He said he would find out who owned it and he would get back to David about it. When John found out the owner of the OK Storage Company was willing to sell it, all the ideas and plans started. Since the Olympics were coming to New Orleans in a few years, they thought some upscale condominiums would be snapped up by corporations or sponsors. John, who was the district attorney of Jefferson Parish at the time, was seriously connected to the power element of the city. He gathered together several interested investors in the project. Besides himself, he recruited Judge Jacob Karno, Carl Eberts, Judge Wallace LeBrun, JR Investments, which was the front for Ruth Fertel and James

Queyrouze, and David, who was the only one from outside Louisiana.

When David left New Orleans in late 1981 or early 1982, he left the project in the hands of Mamoulides. Every so often he would get calls in Ohio saying that this plan or this idea was not working. There were also many calls for money to pay for architects and legal fees ad infinitum. When the original architect that David brought into the partnership bowed out (he was a Cleveland friend), the troubles seemed to escalate. It was decided to make the OK storage building into a nursing home. That seemed like a good venture, as the facility would be well accepted in the area. Since David had been long gone from New Orleans, he didn't know everything that went on with the project.

As I write this tale, I have done much research on the project. Most of the interesting and shocking material has come from the blogs of someone named Doug Handshoe, who publishes the *Slabbed Nation* on line. I don't know much about this gentleman, but he is a CPA (retired) who searches for the truth in politics in Louisiana and Mississippi. The information on the Ave. Partnership that David joined showed up in a scathing report on John Mamoulides, the former D.A. in Jefferson Parish. The report is probably accurate, but I cannot say for sure. Some of the information was given by anonymous respondents to the *Slabbed* original blog.

"The failure of the rest home project spawned at least 11 lawsuits seeking about $4 million in damages over unpaid bills and defaulted loans. Most of the money was never collected. Mamoulides and several others formed a real estate partnership in 1981.

"They subsequently purchased the old OK storage building at 1901 St. Charles Ave. in New Orleans, and several surrounding houses. The partners' first development idea, office condominiums, was nixed in 1985 when the office market started to turn sour. St. Charles Living Center was pitched as the first project of its kind in the New Orleans area, a 322-unit development that would offer several types of housing for senior citizens, ranging from self-sufficient apartments to traditional nursing home services. Over neighborhood objections, New Orleans City Council approved the proposal in 1986. Several pre-Civil War houses were torn down to make way for the project in 1987, but that was the last site work to take place. Mamoulides and his partners were never able to obtain financing for the venture.

"At one point, in an effort to seek approval for an $8.4million HUD loan, records suggest that three nursing homes put up for collateral already, were put up as collateral for another loan. That, and subsequent efforts to obtain HUD financing, fell through. One potential lender backed away after taking a look at the project in 1985,citing the partnership's lack of cash, failure to produce a marketing plan, and inflated profit projections.

"At least five vendors, including a local law firm, and two architectural and engineering companies, sued over unpaid bills totaling $450,000. Two of the vendors won judgments against the partnership totaling $143,000, while two others settled out of court. The partnership was also sued by two lenders over unpaid loans totaling $2.4million. Both lenders won judgments in the full amount of their claims. NOTEWORTHY: In 1990, longtime Mamoulides business associate Carl Eberts bailed the project out of one problem when he satisfied one of the two big judgments against the Ave. Partnership. Having done that, he then sued to collect from some of the partners. But Michael Berenson, an attorney for one of the partners, said in an interview that Eberts' 'selectively' collected from the group. There is no record in Orleans or Jefferson Parishes that Eberts sued Mamoulides.

"THE FALLOUT. First National Bank of Jefferson won a $1.7 million judgement against Mamoulides and his partners, but was never paid by any of the partners. The bank foreclosed on the six-story OK storage building in 1992. Though other proposals have since surfaced for the property—ranging from a welfare office to an Italian restaurant—the building remains vacant."

As I write this segment of David's career, I am getting angrier by the minute. If nobody paid anything to the banks and vendors, where did half our net worth at the time go? While all this was going on, David was already setting up a new marketing company, and for at least 15 years he had assumed his obligations were over. We did not expect what occurred next.

In the mid-nineties we were enjoying our new condo lifestyle, unencumbered by gardeners and snow plows. One day as we drove the long driveway out of our magnificent building on the way to a doctor's appointment, we were stopped at the security gate by a sheriff's car. We were wondering what had happened. We found out soon enough. We were told to pull over and open the window. A tough looking sheriff said we were to follow him downtown. We were told that David was under arrest for non-payment of a judgment out of New Orleans. He showed us the warrant and it was for $1,363,580! I have never seen David so shocked in my life. He remained calm on the outside, but I could tell he was seething! He finally prevailed upon the deputy that we were late for our appointment and we would talk to him afterwards. Would you believe he followed us all the way and sat down in the waiting room until we were through?

This was the first time the doctor discovered that David had atrial fibrillation. His heart was really pounding. But that episode was not the last of the problem.

Live in Uncomplicated Elegance

La Place on St. Charles

The deal that got away!

Mar/Co. 464-B — BARRETT BROTHERS, PUBLISHERS, SPRINGFIELD, OHIO

AFFIDAVIT, ORDER AND NOTICE OF GARNISHMENT OF PROPERTY OTHER THAN PERSONAL EARNINGS AND ANSWER OF GARNISHEE
(O.R.C. 2716.11, 12, 13)

THE STATE OF OHIO
COUNTY OF CUYAHOGA SS
FIRST NATIONAL BANK OF JEFFERSON PARISH
aka HIBERNIA NATIONAL BANK
NEW ORLEANS, LA 70112

ALLEN COUNTY COMMON PLEAS Court
LINA Ohio

_____ Judgment Creditor

vs.

Docket No. XXXXX Page XXXX
Case No. XXXXXXXXX

DAVID SKYLAR
5200 THREE VILLAGE DR., #3R
LYNDHURST, OH 44124 _____ Judgment Debtor

AFFIDAVIT

The undersigned, being first duly cautioned and sworn, affirmed according to law, says that I am the Judgment Creditor herein/Attorney or Agent for Judgment Creditor herein, and that said Judgment
(cross out one)

Creditor heretofore, to-wit, on the _____ day of _____, 19__, duly recovered a judgment before this Court against said Judgment Debtor David Skylar

AMOUNT NOW DUE $ 1,363,580.04

The affiant has good reason to believe and does believe that Allen Broadcasting Co. has property other than personal earnings of the Judgment Debtor that is not exempt under the laws of the State of Ohio or the United States.

DESCRIPTION OF PROPERTY Wages or dividends from Allen Broadcasting Co.,
1301 N. Cable Road
Lima, Ohio 45805

ATTORNEY FOR JUDGMENT CREDITOR
JOSEPH A. MAHONE
75 Public Square #525
Cleveland, Ohio 44113
(216) 621-3251

Sworn to and subscribed before me
7th day of August, 19 97.

NOTARY PUBLIC
EDWARD J. BERTONE, Attorney
NOTARY PUBLIC - STATE OF OHIO
Section 147.03 R.C.

SECTION A. COURT ORDER AND NOTICE OF GARNISHMENT

To Allen Broadcasting Co. _____ Garnishee

The Judgment Creditor in the above case has filed an affidavit, satisfactory to the undersigned, in the Allen County Common Pleas Court stating that you have money, property, or credits, other than personal earnings, in your hands or under your control that belong to the Judgment Debtor in this case, and that some of the money, property, or credits may not be exempt from execution or garnishment under the laws of the State of Ohio or the laws of The United States.

You are therefore ordered to complete section (B) of this form, return the completed original of this form, together with any amount shown due on it to the Allen County Common Pleas Court not later than _____. Deliver one completed copy of this form to the indicated Judgment Debtor. Keep the other copy of the form for your files.

The Total Probable Amount now due on this judgment, including interest and court costs, is $ 1,363,580.04

You also are ordered to hold safely anything of value that belongs to the indicated Judgment Debtor that has to be paid to the court, as determined under Section (B) of this form, but that is of such a nature that it cannot be so delivered, until further order of the court.

Witness my hand and the seal of this court this 19th day of Sept., 97.

_____ Judge

INSTRUCTIONS: To complete the back of this form: (1) tear stub off top. (2) reverse carbons. (3) continue typing or writing on the reverse side.

Chapter 47

*W*hen David chose to return to Cleveland, I was somewhat surprised. I guessed he was anxious to get back into the political scene after his many forays into campaigns for local Cleveland politicians. Then, too, he explained that Cox wanted him to move entirely to New Orleans, which he didn't want to do; apparently everybody was in agreement. I realize now that David felt he had done the job Cox wanted, which was to get the weeklies into shape for a daily run. The economy didn't allow for that at the time, though.

Working for Howard Metzenbaum was never easy. He made a deal with David to be campaign manager at what seemed to be a token salary of $50,000. The amount of money meant nothing to my husband as all he wanted to do was get his candidate elected. The story goes back a few years.

For several years Metzenbaum served as an Ohio state representative and senator. In 1970, he decided to run for the U.S. Senate seat of Stephen M. Young, his mentor and friend. He was able to defeat John Glenn in the primary, but was defeated by Robert Taft in the general election. He took a hiatus from politics and continued his former practice of legal consulting and investing in new companies, one of which was ComCorp, David's exciting idea.

As I mentioned previously in late 1973, when William Saxbe resigned to accept the nomination of U.S. Attorney

General, Governor Jack Gilligan appointed Metzenbaum to fill the remainder of Saxbe's term. Some months later he ran for the senate seat, but in a bitter primary he lost to Glenn, who went on to win in a landslide. In 1976, he ran again against Taft. This time he won, riding in on the coattails of President Carter. Metzenbaum had his son-in-law manage his campaign officially, as David was still winding up his contract with the Post Corporation. He did give some advice to Metzenbaum, but he was not always in agreement with the son-in-law.

In 1982, however, when David answered the call to manage the re-election campaign, he was in full charge. Although the opponent, State Senator Paul Pfeifer, was generally unknown, the Republican Party gave him full backing and promotion to try and beat Howard.

David traveled to towns all over Ohio with Metzenbaum to get his message across. Southern Ohio, particularly, was not very democratic. It was a tough fight to put across a northern Ohio candidate with the name of Metzenbaum.

In the past candidates had testimonials of some artists among their backers. David and Howard came up with the idea of a fundraiser that had never been done before. They arranged for over forty acclaimed artists to create an original work of art which could then be converted into a limited series of signed prints. These artists joined together to give the American people a chance to invest in their country by supporting the reelection of Howard Metzenbaum, and at the same time acquiring graphics and other important works.

Here is how the promotion was set up. A slick folder held various photos of the prints available. Each photo had a price listed at the bottom with the artist's name and biography, along with the number of the limited editions. No person could contribute more than one thousand dollars for the general election. A husband and wife could each contribute that amount, and then choose the art with the appraised equal value of the contribution. If the total amount contributed by a whole family equaled four thousand dollars, they could select art with the appraised value of five thousand dollars.

The promotion was a huge success. The art show of the originals traveled to all the major cities in the country. With names like Claes Oldenburg, Andy Warhol. Jim Dine, Frank Stella, and Robert Rauschenberg, to just name a few, who wouldn't take the opportunity to donate for a good candidate and get something so special in return? When the show came to Cleveland, Howard was now among his neighbors and friends. As David said to the *Plain Dealer* reporter covering the event, the gathering at Shaker Square was of very "heavy hitters." The campaign raised some big bucks with this promotion. Of course, as a campaign manager, David had to make his contribution as did I. We put in money from our kids also, and picked out a few nice prints.

Another fundraiser was set up for more of the grassroots contributors. At that time there was a huge theater in the round called Front Row in Cleveland. Every major entertainer was booked in there, and some musicals as well. The campaign came up with a Howard Metzenbaum night with the stars and it was some glittering evening. The ones I recall are Dinah Shore, Robin Williams, Harry Belafonte, and a very popular standup comedian whose name I don't remember. After a fantastic performance by each of these stars, we were invited back to have coffee and conversation at Howard's gorgeous penthouse. David had arranged for a private plane belonging to one of Howard's big givers to take Belafonte to his next appointment in the middle of the night. He was so engaged in conversation that he made his ride to the plane wait almost an hour. It was a most memorable occasion. The packed theater was made up of twenty-five dollar ticket holders. Despite the huge sums of money the Republican PACS gave to the Pfeifer campaign to stop the liberal senator who was against oil companies, and all the New Right stood for, it was in vain. Metzenbaum won the seat, which he held until he retired to let his son-in-law have a go at it.

I will never forget what happened the night of the big win. We stood at the back of the hotel auditorium and watched while Howard thanked all his old cronies and their brothers, but never mentioned the one guy who really bent over backwards to help him win: my husband, David Skylar. I turned and said something to David about the slight, and he replied, "No big deal. It's typical."

So life went on. Howard still called us most Sunday mornings at 7:00 a.m. when he was in town from Washington, and asked to speak to David. He wanted to be sure David would be available for tennis at the club that morning. My love would groan, get out of bed, and throw on his whites. Not many wanted to play with the senator; he wasn't very good at the game, but he always had enthusiasm!

I think Howard finally realized he had forgotten to thank his campaign manager. A few months later he gave David a few left-over prints from the art deal. Just recently I sold them at a profit.

Chapter 48

After the stint of campaign manager for Metzenbaum, David was able to go back to his consulting business again. He always enjoyed the freedom to "do his own thing." One day a young man called and asked if he would be interested in talking to him about a business proposition.

"I think my service business could meld very well with your consulting skills," Michael Jacobson explained. He told David he had been suggested by a friend who praised his marketing ability. How could Skylar refuse a meeting after that introduction?

For some reason, the two men met for lunch at the old Cleveland Stadium restaurant. David learned that Michael's service business was almost like a corporate concierge setup. He supplied his clients with gadgets, advertising specialties, gofers, ticket buying, tee shirts and the like; everything but advertising and public relations advice. He had some interesting clients as well. After much discussion an agreement was reached. They shook hands and David's creative processes began immediately.

He came up with a new name for the new company: ADPRO. The new partners began a search for suitable quarters. They found a small building that had just a few other occupants, and it was in a good location; equidistant to all parts of the city. When the sign went up it could be seen clearly from I-271, an important highway.

Work began on remodeling the space. It was the era of "greys and mauve" in the decorating field. Once the walls were painted and the quite plush, grey carpeting was laid, the new partners moved in. The desks and chairs, as well as conference room furniture, had not arrived yet. On day one there was an aluminum folding table and a half dozen folding chairs. Michael's secretary, Arlene, was the third member of the staff.

As the trio busied themselves bringing files and office equipment, the phone rang for the first time. Arlene quickly picked up the receiver and answered: "Adpro Incorporated," and the two men saw her face turn beet red. "The White House," she stammered, "for David," and she handed him the receiver. I have never found out who the caller was. It certainly wasn't the president, but at the time I wasn't apprised of the call, so I will never know. Just one more fact dislodged by an ischemic stroke.

Adpro had some of David's old clients added to Michael's. Revco, Stouffers, and Society National Bank, which became Key Bank. Sherwin-Williams was an old client from David's advertising days, and Sears Optical and dental divisions, plus Pearle Vision and Convenient Food Mart, were the most notable clients. The remainders were small businesses that wanted to be serviced by the new firm.

Sid Dworkin, who was part of the Revco startup twenty years before, was now chairman of the company. The president was Bill Edwards. Sid had come to rely on David's assistance in matters that he was not proficient, like speech writing and delivery.

One of those times Sid came to him and said, "Dave, we've got this big annual meeting coming up and you know how boring they can be. What can we do to get some excitement into it?"

"Don't worry about it. I've got an interesting idea for you that will knock their pants off," he said.

And so he followed through immediately and wrote a great speech that was primarily made up of questions and answers. After explaining how to deliver the speech, he began several days of rehearsals. He got the big guy to go over sentence after sentence with the right emphasis, both verbally and with gestures, until it came out perfectly. Michael told me recently that you could hear the sessions throughout the office, even with the door closed.

The big day came and the speech was a huge success. When Dworkin returned to Cleveland, he told the Adpro partners, "You guys were the best investment we ever made!" David also wrote Sid's speech when he spoke before the AMA on the safety of generic medicine. He was a good friend to David until his death.

David's partnership with Michael turned out very nicely. David was able to move freely, and once his consultations were made he could continue his charitable service in the city. He was often asked to speak to various business and social groups. He had written a lot of articles that he edited into speeches. No group was too small or too big to hear his speeches. The reason why he was in such demand was that he was always dedicated to his subject, and it showed.

We decided to take a vacation in the spring of 1985 after our daughter Stephanie's wedding. We spent two glorious weeks in Italy, and came home in the best of spirits. Unfortunately, it didn't last long. I found out after the usual tests that my suspicion was accurate. I had breast cancer. This time it was I who was rocking the boat. Luckily, I got into a national experimental group called NSABP, which was advocating lumpectomies, and my surgeon agreed. After the surgery I was given the random treatment of two years of chemotherapy with the initial series of radiation. Others in the program got only six months of chemotherapy. At the time I was upset that I drew the longer treatment. Now after twenty-eight years I am thankful that I got it.

David was his usual stoic self and saw me through the two years. One day when I had just completed my last treatment, he put down the travel section of the *Times* and said, "MJ, we are going to Tibet."

I looked across the king-size bed and said, "You are crazy! That's all we have to do now!"

"No, no, I mean it that would be Shangri La, where Ronald Coleman and whoever his leading lady was found happiness and started over. I'm going to check out a trip tomorrow." And so he did. Although I had quit smoking and gained fifty pounds, I made it through thirty days of China and Tibet. David was like a kid eating all the non-familiar food along the way. I carried mini cans of tuna, Lipton soup packs, Nestles cocoa, and cookies. We loved most of the trip, except the flight in an old Russian-made plane from Chengdu over the snow-capped Himalayas that looked too close for comfort——a cliché that had no substitute. Half the seatbelts were broken, and David's later joke about stewardesses saying, "Hold on tight," was almost true. We were happy to get home, though, and distributed the gifts to the children and the grandchildren.

I'm not sure of the date, but one of our best parties occurred in the latter days of the 80s. We had many obligations to fulfill, but we just felt like having a party anyway. I wanted to have a real French feeling, and had tables set up in the courtyard between the living room and the dining room. There were French doors on either side for guests to circulate for hors d'oeuvres and drinks. The tables were round with checkered tablecloths and candles. If I can brag a little, everything was perfect. After the delicious dessert was served there was a banging on the front gate, which had been closed for privacy. David pretended to be concerned, and stood up from his chair and opened the gate to a shabbily dressed women with a basket. He angrily said, "What do you want?"

By now the guests were a little curious, and then the woman said, "I want to tell your fortunes."

Then David let her in and introduced her as Basha. Of course we had clued her in with names and funny notes about many of the guests. She went around the courtyard and asked for certain names, and went over to them and recited their fortune, and gave them a piece of her voluminous clothing. She would sometimes sit on a gentleman's lap, to the consternation of his wife, and hug him a little. By the time she was finished with all the fortunes, she was down to a skimpy jeweled bra and low sarong-type outfit. Someone in the dark had turned on her portable music and the belly dancing began. It was a very special night. I think the magic came from the house itself. It was our very favorite home.

David and I in Venice.

Enjoying the elegance of the Peninsula Hotel in Hong Kong.

Chapter 49

$\mathcal{J}$ erred when I said in a recent chapter that I was covering the last story to come out of New Orleans. A bigger story came later. A big company sued a small one, and David was right in the middle of it.

Earlier in the eighties, David had continued his mentorship with Bill Metcalf, the young man who wanted to start a business paper when his *Figaro* paper ended. While David worked up north he kept in contact with Bill, who had put together a group of papers into one group which he called the New Orleans Publishing Group (NOPG). *CityBusiness* was the first paper in the group. When that was starting, David met Bill and one of his partners, Mark Hopp, in New York to discuss all the preliminary issues. He certainly knew his subject after starting ComCorp back in the day.

Bill and his partner took all the information back to the other partners in New Orleans, and they were on their way to a successful publishing company. As time went on they decided to sell one of their weeklies, the *Jefferson Parish Times and Democrat* to the *Times-Picayune*, and they called David down for his advice and counsel. According to a recent communication from Bill Metcalf, "David handled this key sale for us." It must have been a politicized event, because Bill went on to say how much David helped them with their relationships in Jefferson Parish;

probably through his friendship with John Mamoulides and Sheriff Harry Lee.

Later, the *Times-Picayune* sued NOPG and *CityBusiness* saying they had no legal right to carry the JPSO (Jefferson Parish Sheriff Office) legal notices. It was a big deal in New Orleans. I remember flying down for a few days as David was subpoenaed for a deposition in a large courtroom with a lot of lawyers. I went with him at the appointed time, but I was not allowed in the courtroom. He was really weary when I saw him coming out into the corridor for a lunch break.

Our contingent walked around the block to a new Smith and Wollensky. Bill was always a great host. I saw the guys put away huge steaks and wondered how they could make it through the afternoon session. We learned later that the lawsuit was not settled for a long time. Apparently, when it was over and *CityBusiness* won, it was a major event. Little guys aren't often victorious. David kept up his involvement, and he must have done something special, because Bill got him a Mercedes 3E as a reward for his services. It came equipped with a phone, and that was unusual in those days. At first he thought the phone was stupid, but when he had to make long jaunts to see clients in outlying towns, he found he could return phone calls that would otherwise have to wait until he was back in the office. He became a believer.

Something strange happened down the line in New Orleans. Out of the blue he got a call from the young publisher of the *Times–Picayune*, Ashton Phelps, Jr. He asked David if he would be a consultant to the paper. David and his company, Skypro, were perceived to be the experts on legal advertising. When he met with Phelps he was given a contract that was beneficial to him as well as the paper.

There were nine points in the agreement. The first point was his retention as an independent consultant "to render services to *T-P* on an advisory and consultative basis with respect to *T-P's* legal advertising business as directed by *T-P*. Skypro shall (a) provide the services of David Skylar ('Skylar') to fulfill its consulting obligation hereunder; (b) cause Skylar to report to T-P's publisher and/or his assignee on a regular basis; and (c) cause Skylar to perform these duties in connection with obtaining legal advertising contracts as T-P shall request."

It went on to discuss the consideration fee for Skypro's services for three years with the possibility of a bonus at the end, depending on the success of T-P's legal advertising during that time. The main points came next. There was to be complete confidentiality, of course, but the whole crux of the agreement, I believe, was the non-competition section. It was stipulated in no uncertain terms that during the agreement, and for at least two years after it ended, "Skypro was not to be involved, directly, or indirectly, as an officer, director or employee of, a consultant or lender to, or an investor in any entity, which shall carry on or engage in the business of publishing legal advertising, and from soliciting customers of the legal advertising publishing business in the parishes of Jefferson and Orleans."

In other words, from now on you are working for us and not those other guys! I'm sure David got the message. Actually, NOPG was taken care of and David had no intention of doing anything else in New Orleans at the time. He agreed to the contract offered and happily signed his illegible signature. For the next three years he dutifully reported to Ashton Phelps, but each time he was told there was nothing for him to do. This went on for three years. Maybe a few times he gave the publisher some ideas over the phone, but that was it. After the three years were over he got his bonus. The whole deal grossed Skypro about $100,000. Did David feel guilty about the lack of participation? I rather doubt it. He had done such a good job for *CityBusiness* it simply taught T-P a lesson. Don't mess with the "Green Hornet," as some of David's earlier associates used to call him.

Chapter 50

All the eighties seemed to be taken up with getting and keeping new clients for Adpro. In between, David discovered that his former writings could be the basis for more speech making, and he made a lot more speeches than ever before. Naturally, there was always somebody in the host group that wanted to hire him for his public relations knowledge. Sometimes he just spoke to organizations to which our friends belonged.

Holly Arvanites, one of my best friends and wife of Denny, who was president of Halle Bros. at the time, asked him to speak to the Planned Parenthood of Cleveland. Holly was president of the group and he couldn't say no. He knew little about the group at the time and had not given its work much thought until that moment. However, after boning up on its history and goals, he was able to give a great speech.

The big annual meeting took place in the president's quarters of the Federal Reserve Bank. It marked the 58th year of the group's service in Northeast Ohio, and many dignitaries were there, as well as new board members. David's keynote address was powerful, and reflected the problems of the times. Remember, this was 1986; he could have been addressing the audience in 2012 as well. He urged the Planned Parenthood board and staff to "...challenge the sophisticated attack on its image by the ultra-conservative movement by employing modern marketing techniques to the agency's own benefit."

He presented convincing evidence that the organization must move aggressively to shape its own public image with a major campaign for visibility. He pointed out that the good and valuable work of Planned Parenthood nationally had been damaged and subverted by the success of "Ultra Right" groups who have made fetal politics the emotionally charged issue of the 80s. David concluded his talk by reminding everyone that their mission of pregnancy prevention, if expanded would deter abortions better than all the anti-abortion picketers in the world.

This was a well-accepted speech. It is amazing that people like Mitt Romney can still be considered in the anti-abortion, Ultra Right category, wanting to get rid of Planned Parenthood 27 years later. Maybe some of David's input worked its way through the various divisions of the group. Someone heeded David's advice, because Mitt Romney couldn't make it with the good old middle class.

Other speeches reflected his old love of advertising and public relations. One of his favorite all-time articles was titled: "How Do You Rate as a Client?" He turned it into a roaring speech that incited audience participation. The first time he gave that speech it was as a substitution for another one, which was derived from an article in *Industrial Marketing* magazine. He told his audience he changed the subject because he was upset with an issue which had occurred that week with what became known as the "TWA Affair." That is what it was called by one of David's flying friends, who said, "If your parachute doesn't work, turn it in for a replacement when you hit the ground." David reminded the group that the theme of all their meetings that year was "the Stimulators," and he wanted to tickle their imagination while getting his feelings off his chest.

The story was that TWA invited eight agencies to solicit their $14 million account. Then they decided after all to retain their present agency, Foote, Cone and Belding. In an *Advertising*

Age article at the time, the issue was covered fully. "Representatives of the losers, all of them keenly disappointed since they made 'outstanding presentations,' according to Trans World Airlines, suggested in conversations with *Advertising Age* that TWA hadn't planned to make any change, but had been 'on an idea gathering expedition,' or perhaps TWA thought this would be a good way to goose Foote, Cone.

"Asked if TWA would reimburse the agencies for any of this work, a TWA public relations executive said, 'No. They were invited to make presentation, period.'" That was the end of the *Ad Age* quote.

David explained at the time that he did some checking and found out that the agencies involved spent almost a million dollars out of pocket for these presentations, not counting the thousands of creative hours. He wondered when the advertising agency business would come of age, and quit chasing after accounts like a dog in heat, or stop acting like a streetwalker peddling its wares for a price.

At the time, David said he didn't understand the thinking of these agencies. The gross income of the TWA account would be about $2,000,000, and the agency could make 10% or so. They were willing to gamble their profits for a year or two to get this account.

David explained in his own agency they felt they didn't have to go overboard in pursuing an account. He said that many times a prospect would pay for a total creative presentation, if this was what they wanted to hear. He said he had negotiated such arrangements and they had proved mutually advantageous. David asked his audience to stop and think what a TWA affair does to the image of the agency business, and what a precedent it sets. Apparently, he felt that all one had to do in the competitive world of ad agencies was dangle a million-dollar bait and we'd jump through hoops, strain our creative forces in speculative efforts, and give birth to instant ads.

He noted that he didn't like this image. He went on to say,

"I'm sick and tired of people in advertising agencies who keep apologizing for the fact that they are in advertising agencies. And being ashamed of it. I'm sick and tired of all the jokes and jibes and jeers. I'm sick of the pose—the gray flannel pose—and the idea that, because you're in advertising, you have to play along with the gags of the foolish image of yourself—over-sophisticated and over-sexed, and over-paid and over your depth—in a very shallow job. Someone who drinks double martinis and leads a double life, and talks double talk. (ed. note. Amazing—these are the very characteristics that made up the premise for the TV show *"MadMen"* fifty years later.)

David continued by saying he knew he couldn't change the system by shouting about it, but he thought it was time the agencies reversed positions. He suggested that before an agency accepted an account, they ask the prospect to take a test. He wondered if they had the "guts" to tell an account: "We won't work for you unless you shape up." He thought it was time to tell them we wanted more input, cooperation, and attention.

At this point in his speech, David announced that he has devised a test called "How Do You Rate as a Client." He explained that tests were all the rage then, and he was sure such tests like, "Are You a Good Husband?" "Will You Make a Good Lover?" or six questions to test you honesty, had been available in many publications.

He told the group, "If you're an agency man, rate one of your clients. If you are not an advertiser or an agency man, rate an advertiser you know. And he started asking the questions.

That was the beginning of all the quiz speeches. Since it was still a pertinent idea after so many years, David could tailor the questions for any clients. I think David invented the word "recycle." For any of you readers who may be interested, the twenty question quiz is included. It is still relevant in the 21st century.

HOW DO YOU RATE AS A CLIENT?

This is a 20 questions do-it-yourself test. Rate yourself as you really perform today -- not what you think you are.

If you get more than 80 points, you're one of the good guys and your agency is returning your attitude with good work.

1. Do you make your agency's work more effective by providing clear-cut, well-thought-out, written marketing plans?

> Give yourself 10 points for a "yes". If you want
> your advertising to go somewhere, you have to figure
> out where you want to go. A solid, sound marketing plan
> is as indispensable in getting there as a road map is to
> a driver traveling new territory.

2. Are your advertising objectives realistic, attainable and clearly stated?

> Give yourself ten points for a "yes". But think carefully
> before you pat yourself on the back. Vague objectives
> that fall into the classification of hack generalities
> -- such as "increased sales" -- do not qualify. Keep
> in mind that advertising cannot actually sell the product,
> unless you're in the mail order business. But advertising
> can move the share of mind in your favor.

3. Do you work with your agency in planning advertising programs a year or two ahead -- or do you keep them guessing with ad-at-a-time assignments?

> Five points if your plans project a year or two ahead
> or so. Give your agency the chance to marshall all of
> their resources -- and yours-- by letting them in on
> your longer range goals.

4. Do you encourage your agency team to meet with your sales and technical people and top management?

> Subtract ten points if you do not. This is an absolute
> essential. Whatever your skills as a lottery marketing
> manager, it is terribly difficult to translate your
> management's intentions to your agency. Nothing but
> nothing beats first hand exposure.

5. Do you have a long list of advertising "do's" and "don'ts"?

Subtract ten points if you do. Verbotens are like fences -- they may keep your agency from straying into a swamp, but they also prevent your agency from possibly stumbling into a gold mine. The great campaigns you admire so much often ignore all of the pat rules that can be raised. Safe, mediocre advertising is neither risky or uncomfortable, but it might be boring.

6. Can you name the art director who actually creates your advertising?

Give yourself five points for a "yes". There's a new breed of art director in the advertising business today -- and he's as much a businessman as he is a specialist in graphic design. But he can't be expected to exercise his business sense in a vacuum.

7. Can you name the copywriter who actually creates your advertising?

Give yourself five points for a "yes." By and large, the great ideas come from great copywriters. But a great copywriter gets that way only from continued exposure to the razor edge of reality. Make your man or woman have that advantage.

8. How often do you meet with either the art director and/or the copywriter for the purpose of discussing your advertising?

Give yourself one point for each meeting held within the past year, to a maximum of ten points. If you don't meet with the creative people personally, you must be depending on your account executives to translate your intentions to them -- and this is something even Berlitz doesn't teach.

9. Has your agency's creative team ever met with your total commission?

Ten points for a "yes" answer ... and here's why: You wouldn't expect a writer to write an article about Thailand if he'd never been out of Pittsburgh would you? Ditto for a writer who attempts to tell your state's story. More great campaigns have been born on the floor of a retailer than within the confines of a conference room. Experience is often the midwife that delivers the inspired idea.

10. Do you ever have arguments with your agency's creative people?

> Five points for a "yes". While it's important to get along with the agency people who work on your account, it can be deadly if you get along too well. It is damned near impossible to create heat without a little friction.

11. In such arguments, how often does the account executive assigned to your account take your side?

> Subtract ten points if the answer is most or all of the time. Chances are, you've encouraged your account man to become an echo, not an independent voice.

12. Has your agency ever told you you were wrong in a decision you made?

> Ten points if the answer is "yes". Good clients create a climate in which agency people are not afraid to run against the grain of your opinion.

13. Has your agency ever told you you were right in a decision you made?

> Ten points if the answer is "yes". If you have the right climate for your agency to function in, their performance will be distinguished by independence and objectivity. Logically, you cannot be so brilliant that all your decisions are correct. But, just as logically, you cannot be so stupid that all your decisions are wrong.

14. What is your reaction when your agency gives you an advertisement which you instinctively feel is right, but which you know will cause a great deal of trouble for you? (Multiple choice):

> ** If you reject the ad and tell the agency to come up with something a little safer... subtract ten points.

> ** If you ask the agency to make a few changes so the ad will be more acceptable to your management... subtract five points.

> ** If you tell the agency you'll do your damndest to get approval -- and you work hard to do it...give yourself ten points.

> > It does little good to encourage your agency to come up with great ideas if you don't really intend to do anything with them. Face it, it takes two to tango

-- a great agency and a great client. And greatness, in part, is the courage to o.k. -- or fight for -- controversial ideas. Do you really think you could have approved an ad which counseled readers to think small, or one which labeled your product as "lemon", or one which granted that your company was only number two?

15. Has the chief executive of your agency ever battled with the management of your restaurant over the matter of what your ads say, or how they say it?

Good clients get their agencies involved -- and this includes to totality of their agencies, right up to the top guy. After all, the chief executive of your agency should be their best man, after all is said and done. Five points for a "yes".

16. When you reject an ad, do you make it clear what your objection is?

"I just don't like it", isn't valid. Blind hogs cannot consistently root up acorns. Keep your agency in the dark and you're apt to wind up in a blind alley. Subtract ten points if you're vague.

17. Once you've approved an ad, does your agency ever suggest changing it for the better? If they do, are you pleased or irritated?

Five points if they change ads after they're approved: five more points if you're pleased. Bad clients foster the agency theory that any "sold" ad is a good ad. If you're to get the maximum from your agency, you must encourage boat rocking, world shaking, an attitude that the agency must supply you with their very best efforts.

18. When you feel an ad is not right, do you believe it is your job to rewrite the headline or change the visual or edit the copy?

Ten points for a negative answer. If you're that good at writing copy or at art directing an ad, you ought to be working in a creative capacity at an ad agency. Otherwise, you're trying to compete with professionals who have been retained for their professional skills.

The result is inevitably amateurish.

19.   Do you force your agency to use your suppliers?

> Subtract ten points for a "yes". The execution of an
> advertisement often depends on the suppliers - photo-
> graphers, typesetters, illustrators, TV production
> houses -- involved. Tamper with those who will be used,
> and you provide your agency with a built-in alibi if
> the piece fails to work. It's tantamount to going to
> a doctor for an appendectomy, and then insisting that
> he use your choice of a hospital, nurse, anesthetist,
> etc.

20.   If your very best friend was responsible for the
advertising of a corporation,   could you recommend your present
advertising agency without reservation?

> Fifteen points for a "yes". Good clients inevitably
> get good performance from their agencies. If you've
> got reservations about your agency, you've either got
> the wrong agency, and should have changed before now
> -- or the reservations really reflect problems in how
> you are working with your agency. In either case, you
> haven't done your job.

O.K. now add up your score. If you gave yourself over 80 points,
you're doing a good job and your agency is reciprocating.

If you rated less than 75 points -- shame on you!

Remember that old line -- it takes a great client to recognize
and approve great advertising.

Chapter 51

avid always got enthusiastic about deal proposals that friends brought to him. Some of them required a financial investment, but many were just queries for his expertise in promotion, and might or might not end in some remuneration. I liked those deals the best. I could see my husband's brain working overtime to come up with the right approaches.

Leonard Cohan, one of his friends, told him of a young electronic whiz kid who was putting together a prototype of an electronic backgammon set. He needed some backing, of course, and the two guys pitched right in to help. Even though neither one of the men were game aficionados, they were completely sold on the concept. They first scouted out the big electronic show in Chicago to see what the trends were. There was no electronic backgammon; that's when they really got busy.

One of them, or both, came up with the idea that Omar Sharif should be brought into the picture. It was easier than expected to accomplish that. Sharif liked their idea to call the new game "Omar," and he enthusiastically authorized them to build a prototype for him to see. A time was arranged to meet in New York two months later.

The meeting occurred at lunch in the Regency Hotel dining room. Sharif brought along his partner, Tannah Hirsch, who was, and still is, the renowned bridge expert. While the four men were eating their chopped steak or Caesar salads they went through all the details of the deal with occasional note taking on a napkin. Len Cohan said he doesn't even remember when a contract was drawn up.

As the negotiations were drawing to a close, a small party of men walked into the dining room and were directed to a table adjacent to theirs. Sharif looked up and saw one of the men, and with a loud exclamation he rose from his chair and gave the man a bear hug, calling out, "My friend, my friend," in two different languages. The friend turned out to be Ezer Weizman, the Israeli Minister of Science and Technology at the time, and the future president of Israel. It was like a U.N. briefing with Arabic, Hebrew, French and English being used for introductions and conversation. The men with Weizman were bodyguards, and probably Mossad. It was a good thing that the most important details were discussed before the interruption, because nothing could be accomplished afterward.

When David and Len left the luncheon they were in good spirits. They had previously contacted several retailers, and two of the biggest were right there in New York: Macy's and Bloomingdales. They were on their way to Bloomingdales for a late afternoon appointment when David had a thought.

"Len, why don't you take this appointment. You are such a great salesman. I have to run over to the *Times*. I just remembered I had to check a story for Turner."

"Okay, I'll meet you back at the hotel in a couple of hours. Tomorrow, we'd better both go to Macy's. We'll need a big marketing pitch from you." They each went their separate ways and met up again at 6:00 p.m.

"Bloomindales really flipped for Omar and gave us a nice order," Len said gleefully. "They wanted to start with a 'small' order of four gross."

David looked at him and burst out laughing. "That's small?" he said. "That's sensational!" And since it was time to eat again, they continued their excited talk all the way to The

Palm. The next day got even a bigger order from Macy's. Now the work was really to begin.

The next step was another trip to the consumer electronics show, this time in Las Vegas. Barbara Cohan and I tagged along. It's what wives did in those days. The "boys" were able to pick up reps from around the country and tips on merchandising this type of product. They did a little spying as well to see if there were any serious competitors. So far there weren't. Things were looking up.

One of the other new customers was 47th Street Photo in N.Y. They had major dealings with Service Merchandise Showrooms, so David and Len went to Minneapolis in January to talk to the catalogue showroom people. That was another successful, albeit freezing, jaunt. "Omar" was to be included in the spring catalogue. David and Len worked hard in the next couple of months to coordinate the marketing and the reps, and the new customers they were gathering.

Then came the phone call. The wunderkind inventors announced they couldn't get the chip for the backgammon anymore—they had to stop production. David and Len were furious that they weren't told sooner. They had only shipped a dozen or so games to their major customers. It was quite an embarrassment for them. The retailers were angry, but nothing could be done about it. They hadn't lost anything, but their schedule was changed. But it was another story with the catalogue people. The catalogue had been printed and sent out all over the country. It was also a tough call to make to Omar Sharif. After all, it was his face on the box, which held the little backgammon computer. A regular backgammon board was sent along with the handheld computer so the moves could be set up as they were played.

David and Len carried on to other deals, as it were. Skylar still had Adpro and consulted for REVCO and Turner Construction Co., and several other lesser known clients, but he always enjoyed hearing about a new idea or product that could be expanded into something successful.

A few years before the Omar fiasco, David and Len, and I believe our dear friend and attorney Byron Krantz, started another endeavor called Sportsco. This was a company set up to handle financial, legal, and personal agendas for athletes. As I recall, their first clients were basketball players on the Cleveland Cavaliers team. The only names I remember are Austin Carr, Jim Brewer, and Bingo Smith. I believe Sportsco got a few other athletes as clients, but I don't have any records on them.

Before the company ran out of steam, Brewer and Carr joined Len and David, and a low-level golfer named John Haas, in another deal. I think there were some of the same investors as before. This time the group wanted to get the BMW franchise for Cleveland. The car dealership they were buying was Precision Motors in a far north suburb of Cleveland. The catch in obtaining this franchise for Precision was that it had to be approved by the parent company.

It so happened that the BMW district manager who was coming to interview the investors was an avid basketball fan, and when he heard that there were players in the group he was ecstatic.

"I want to take you and your group out for lunch when I get in," he said. "What's the best restaurant in town? You pick it and I'll pay. I can't wait to meet Austin Carr and Jim Brewer!" And so the longest lunch Giovanni's ever served came to pass.

Here is the story. Both Carr and Brewer, who were 6' 5" and 6' 7" respectively, were hearty eaters. They each ordered a couple of entrees and side orders. David and Len were aghast. After all, this BMW big whig was buying, and it might look a little piggish to take advantage they thought. But the district manager didn't mind at all, even when a few desserts were placed in front of them!

The dealership was won. John Haas became manager. Things went well for a change. We all were driving BMWs. It was not too popular an auto back in the late 70s, and early 80s it was still in its infancy, so to speak. There weren't a record amount of cars sold, but it was coming along everyone thought, until somebody looked at the books. There were major discrepancies. Nobody could prove anything. The dealership went down the drain. John was no longer manager. All we got out of it were a few secondhand BMWs. One of those went to our daughter, Stephanie. She couldn't bear to leave her large Belgian Bouvier dog home alone when she got her first job at a TV station. She took him to work and left him in the car with the windows open. She figured she could take him out on her breaks and all would be fine. It turned out not fine at all. After a few days she saw that the sweet pet had started eating the leather upholstery. It didn't take long for the interior to be a total wreck. The cost for repair was prohibitive. I don't remember what happened to the other two cars. David started saying that from then on he would only get into deals where he ran the show. And he kept to his word.

There was one more act to the David and Len show. This was going to be a really big endeavor. They found out about a company that was experimenting with a titanium golf club shaft. They tracked down a man named Joe Abeles and his company KBI, which stood for Kawecki Berylco Industries. The headquarters was in the *Daily News* building on 42nd Street in N.Y. It was an extremely reputable company. Skylar and Cohan proposed that titanium could work for a tennis racket as well as a club shaft. Joe Abeles agreed and an experimental racket was designed out in California at one of his subsidiaries.

Everything fell into place. There was to be a factory built in Cleveland. KBI would supply the building and the metal; David and Len would do the marketing, sales and fundraising. There were all sorts of meetings, market studies, lots of travel back and forth, and all the issues on the Ohio front were coming together. Suddenly one day when they tried calling Abeles, they never got a call back. They tried several times and no one would take their call. The only thing left to do was fly to N.Y. to see what was going on. When they got there they barged into the office. They were told that they were in the midst of selling KBI and couldn't possibly spend time on a project that was no longer viable. The Cleveland contingent was more disgusted than devastated. It was a waste of at least eight months of their time. They each came out of the deal with an experimental tennis racket. I used David's for a long time, even after all the giant rackets were in style. It didn't have a name, only some numbers scratched in the metal at the bottom of the handle. I was keeping it for posterity. A couple of years ago, my son-in-law gave it to the Salvation Army when I didn't know about it. I was furious. Len still has his. He can put it on eBay for big bucks, I bet.

There were a few other businesses that David glanced at, including a travel agency he named Travaco, where he put me to work to watch how things were going. He thought we could get trips as owners, but that didn't pan out as it should. He got busy again and didn't have time to think about start-ups. That was fine as far as I was concerned. I think this chapter should be called "Pie in the Sky Syndrome," or something like that.

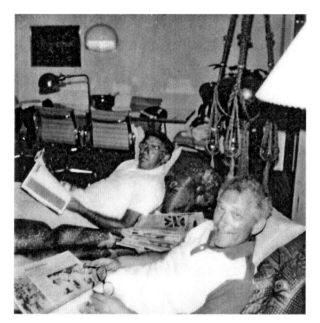

David and Leonard Cohan lounging between deals.

Chapter 52

*A*s the decade of the 80s was drawing to a close, we were
delighted that no more major illnesses were coming our
way. David was still actively involved at Adpro, and the full service footprint of the company was increasingly successful.
David's advertising, public relations and marketing experience
melded well with Michael Jacobson's packaging and sales ability. Special clients like Revco and Turner Construction were on
retainer, and were comfortable with the all-around service package.

David always had an opinion on my work as an interior
designer, so it didn't surprise me when he became interested in
one of my sources. It so happened that a family owned firm that
wholesaled "to the trade only," was steered to David to get
them out of a rut. The company was still one of the top suppliers, but was losing ground to the new design showrooms that
were popping up in the area. The name of the company was
"Western Furniture."

The first meeting took place at their freestanding showroom out in the boonies, so to speak. David shook hands with
the brothers and cousins, and sat down in one of the display
chairs. "I hope you won't take this the wrong way, but what the
hell kind of name is Western Furniture?" he asked. "If you want
to get into the new mainstream of design you have to change
that name, and I mean soon. Tell me," he continued, "what is

wrong with using your family name? Cellura just rolls off your tongue, and it sounds very upscale."

The owners looked at each other as if they had just been given the key to the city. "Why, you are so right, Dave. It just never occurred to us," said Ray Cellura. The others shook their heads in agreement. That was the beginning of a great business relationship. The Cellura family listened to all of David's suggestions from then on. They changed their way of doing business after at least a half-century. Toward the latter part of the new setup is where Michael got into the act. He had golf shirts made up with the Cellura logo that they gave to their customers. Whenever I got a new client in my little business, I took them out to Cellura to pick out fabrics and the like.

We were still considered snowbirds when we spent time in Florida. In 1979, we visited a place in Hollywood, Florida, called Emerald Hills. There was an excellent golf course and the villa we stayed in belonged to Harry and Lois Horvitz, whose family built all of Hollywood, it seems, since they owned a paving company that paved all the streets. We liked it so much that we put a deposit on the last phase of townhouses to be built. We chose a two-story model and we were able to designate whatever we wanted in the way of flooring, carpet and fixtures. We had been married 30 years at the time, and decided that it was a convenient place for a second home. Since David spent the next 28 years commuting, he always wanted to be near an airport. This first house was eight minutes from the Ft. Lauderdale airport. He loved the idea that he could be in Florida and on the first tee by about 12:30 p.m., and he left his overcoat in the car in Cleveland.

It wasn't unusual to invite clients and friends down to play golf, eat out, and just generally enjoy themselves. We spent the first ten years in Hollywood enjoying every minute of every trip. I mostly stayed down, because flying every week was not my thing. In 1989, I went home with David for a change. It had been a brutal week weather-wise in Shaker Heights. There was no problem starting the car when we arrived, since it had been in the parking garage. When we arrived home after a harrowing drive to the east side, we couldn't get in the driveway. It seems that the trusted snowplow guy didn't get around to us. We walked through knee-deep snow to the house and had to leave the car out front. That was one of the times (Oh, there were a few!) David was furious. He also made some decision I was not happy about. His pronouncement to me went something like this: "We have to sell this place. What do we need it for? It's too big and the upkeep is ridiculous, etc., etc."

I cannot for the life of me understand why I didn't make a big fuss about it. This was my dream house from day one. Just thinking about it now makes me sad. David was always a convincing guy, so I guess I went along with it. He was ready for a new challenge, I guess.

It came all too soon. Our beautiful house sold at the second highest price in Shaker Heights at the time. The first highest had an indoor pool. There were at least three indoor pools on the street, and about four or five outdoor ones. There was no comparable street in the area.

David got word of a two-story condo that a developer built for himself when he developed the elegant three-building complex called Three Village in Lyndhurst, another suburb of Cleveland. It was quite unusual and needed some architectural face lifting. David overnighted some photos to Claudia, who sketched some ideas on a piece of paper and sent it back post haste. We loved what she did, and David showed it to Al Sanchez who headed the Turner division in Ohio. He offered the services of his company and we were thrilled.

They billed us about two-thirds less than we thought possible. When a big outfit like that does a job there is no messing around—no days off the job; no excuses, period. It was fantastic the way they followed Claudia's plans. Originally, there were two staircases that led to an upper hall closed in with a wall; and a bedroom suite was on either side. Claudia's design knocked out the staircases, put up a half wall, put a stairway hidden behind the wall, and constructed an open loft with access to both bedrooms. There was even a sauna in one of the upper baths, which never got used. Looking back, every place in which we ever lived was great. David made himself a home office in each abode, and he was always king of his castle.

I'll never forget one thing in the remodeling of that condo. The painter wore stilts to paint the ceiling because it was 22 feet high. It was fun to watch him wield that paint roller, dipping it into paint cans sitting on a huge scaffold.

In the construction business there are sometimes serious problems that arise. Perhaps a worker is hurt or a structural problem arises. Turner had its share like any other company of its size. David stepped into the picture and resolved these issues with his "crises management" techniques. Sanchez and Skylar became fast friends. Turner's central division under Sanchez's direction soon learned how to make better market share projections. David came up with suggestions to make a new list of project categories, and how to evaluate the importance of new business that is sought after as to whether it is advantageous or profitable to the company.

David also helped Al in some of his speech writing and speaking. I remember some research he did on skyscrapers and hurricanes so that Al could make a successful talk in South America.

Turner's retainer continued for several years. The central division got better and better. It was always great to see how successful a client could become. It was then a pleasure to have them go out on their own with their new knowledge. As 1990 loomed, David was busier than ever. He was 65 years old and never gave a thought to retirement. Of course he would not think of taking a social security check yet; he had so much more to do!

David in our Three Village condo in Cleveland, OH.

Chapter 53

At the start of 1990, David got a surprise call from The Advertising Club of Cleveland. They were going to induct him into the Advertising Hall of Fame. He was working out of Florida at the time, so it meant an extra trip up north. Naturally, I wanted to attend the luncheon.

It was easy to make the trip, since we still had a condo to go to and didn't need a hotel room. With all of David's commuting we also had a lot of mileage on the books for free transportation. The induction was to take place on March 14 during the club's monthly meeting, so we had several weeks to think about the trip. Meanwhile, I had to alert everyone I knew to attend the luncheon, as guests were allowed. The club loved big crowds.

When we got home we found out that the year's inductions also included Andrew Meldrum, who had retired from agencies that he founded, and Louis B. Seltzer, long-time editor of the *Cleveland Press*, who had passed away many years before. David was cool about being chosen, but I could tell he was quite excited about it.

He dressed in a perfect dark suit for the occasion and one of his Liberty of London ties, and of course, one of his monogrammed shirts. When we arrived there was already a huge group of people milling around in the ballroom of the Statler Office Tower. After greeting many of his old friends, he was escorted to a seat at the dais, and I was seated at a table in the middle of the pack with some strange men and a few ladies. The usual food was served, and then the minutes of the meeting and new business was discussed

Finally, Bruce Akers, President of the Ad Club, rose to introduce the inductees: "This month we honor three new inductees into the Cleveland Advertising Club Hall of Fame. All three have left their mark on the communications industry of this community, and have rightly earned this acclaim to join those giants of the industry who have preceded them on this honor roll."

He spoke of the attributes of Meldrum and Seltzer, and then brought up David's history in the ad and newspaper business.

"In reviewing David's career, one aspect which kept coming out loud and clear was the fact that Dave was a super-achiever. Whatever he set out to do, he accomplished. He took public relations to a new level within an ad agency." Later, he remarked that he first heard of David's talents from his father, Kenneth Akers, who hired him at Griswold Eshleman when he was 24 years old.

Andy Meldrum made the first acceptance speech. A former associate of Louis Seltzer accepted the award in his honor. Then David's name was called and he got up, shook Pres. Bruce Aker's hand, and performed the usual ritual of taking off his jacket when he started most of his speeches.

"As you probably all realize by now, advertising is a shirt-sleeve business." That was one of his best openings for his speeches. He then tailored the pronouncement to the group he was addressing. In this case he mentioned his many years as an ad man, and the joys and trials of the business. Then the line that he often used that I dreaded: "I've been happily married for 25 years... *pause*... and that's not bad out of 40." I always had to smile and shake my head as a room full of chauvinistic males laughed and applauded. After a short discussion of his advertising beliefs, he humbly accepted his honor with thanks to all of the board that nominated him.

And so David slipped another feather in his cap.

The Hall of Fame induction was, and still is, an annual program to further the recognition of Cleveland as a major advertising center, and to honor the people who have contributed to its advertising greatness. David still considered himself the guru who could make corporate business judgments all they could be, with his help, naturally.

David receives Advertising Hall of Fame award from Bruce Akers, Ad Club president.

David giving a speech in shirt sleeves.

Chapter 54

*I*n 1990, Big Dave Skylar turned 65 years old. He had no intention of retiring again. He'd tried that at 51, and found it wasn't for him. He had to keep busy. There was just so much golf or tennis he could play.

It seemed like a milestone birthday at the time, so I planned a super brunch for him in the party room of our new condo. I invited all of our friends, as well as his business associates and clients. The guest list was huge, and I expected the usual refusals, but it seemed that didn't happen. There were only a couple of no-shows. I guess champagne brunches were rare at the time.

The grandkids that were old enough sang a parody dedicated to Gramp, and some friends took turns to "roast" him. Everyone got a piece of the birthday cake, and soon after took off for their various Sunday sports. It was great having the family come to town. I think we had the event just to see the children. We only seemed to be up north in the summer; it was hard for our grown children to leave their work in the winter to come to us in Florida.

David's Cleveland clients saw a lot more of him in the summer also. Fortunately, they didn't seem to mind. He could take care of their needs from wherever he was at the time, even on the high seas.

That is another story you might enjoy. Someone told David that the cruise ships were always looking for people who were experts in any field—sports, lecturing, bridge—you name it; they offered passage for $30 a day on any of their cruises. David obtained the name of the recruiter for Cunard and it wasn't long before we got the call. For two hours a day my husband became a golf pro and shuffleboard coordinator. I was allowed to join him on the trip. At $60 per diem for both of us, it was cheaper than staying home and going out to dinner. And David loves all the exotic food on cruises!

Our first time on the HMS Vistaford they gave us decent accommodations. The second and third times they were just okay. It was the fourth trip that we were given what was called an "inside cabin," and it really got to me. I take Dramamine and wear patches on my wrist, so not having windows was rather difficult for me. David could care less where he slept, and at the end of his working day (two hours!) and all that food, he had no problem sleeping. I was afraid to complain, but David asked if our cabin could be changed because of his wife's health.

After that I wasn't so sure I liked being the pro's wife. We had been back and forth in the Caribbean so many times that it was boring. It seemed that David was always attached to the same ship. It was home to him in a sense. When the opportunity came for a crossing to Europe, I agreed wholeheartedly. We sailed to Venice, got off the ship and trained to Milan for a couple of days, then met the ship again to cruise the Mediterranean. That wasn't the end of it. The ship went all the way back to Ft. Lauderdale by a circuitous route that took 16 days. By the time we were halfway back, we both decided we would stay on land for a long, long time. Enough was enough. We were away for a month.

We did a bit more traveling though. David decided he wanted to go to a Muslim country that wasn't too far away, or in the midst of riots and such. He came up with a ten-day trip to Morocco. It sounded exciting and exotic—Casablanca, you know? We flew to Malaga, Spain, where we were to meet our tour guide and other participants. We boarded a bus, which we had never done before, and we were off for an adventure. It was the worst trip we have ever taken. We rode in this old-fashioned vehicle with no bathroom for about eight hours every day just looking at dirty buildings and sand. At night we could not shower or rest, as we had to eat with the group mostly at the mediocre hotels where the tour booked. In a few places we stayed a couple of days so we could look around. I found nothing to eat anywhere.

One enjoyable day we went to the Kasbah in Fez where I purchased rugs for myself and for my children. I'm sure I didn't haggle enough, but they didn't cheat us too much. Amazingly, the rugs arrived three months later and David went to pick them up, and had to pay a duty for them even though they had an antique designation, which would make them duty free according to the Moroccan salesman!

After being on a bus for so many days we stayed at Costa Del Sol to rest up. We felt human again. I wonder if all Arab countries are so dirty. We will never know. Our traveling days are over.

After that trip David got a call from Andy Futey who worked for Governor Voinovich of Ohio. The call came at a perfect time. David was getting anxious for a new challenge. The governor wanted to know if David would be interested in being a commissioner of the Ohio Lottery. It looked like payback time after all the help he had given the governor. David told Andy that he would be delighted, and soon after, the announcement appeared in the *Plain Dealer*.

I should preface this appointment by telling you that Governor Voinovich often called upon David to talk up his administration. One such time occurred when the State of Ohio put out the word that it needed a new advertising agency to promote tourism. For some unknown reason, the media, including the principal newspaper, branded the process as "political" and showing "favoritism," and similar negative criticisms.

David took up the fight for the governor and the state by writing an op-ed piece which the newspaper could not reject, since the author had the background and knowledge to explain the process of choosing an agency so succinctly. He pointed out that "...it is most important that the state's tourism promotion funds be spent how and where they get the most bang for the buck. This means that the agencies that choose to participate in this selection process are actually bidding." This bidding, according to David, was not in a financial sense, but with talent and ideas, with layouts and copy, with photography and TV story boards, and with radio commercials and media schedules.

The article continued by saying that "...instead of being critical of the Voinovich administration and the way the state intends to spend tourism dollars, the media, especially the *Plain Dealer*, should compliment their efforts. When the *Plain Dealer* changed agencies it followed almost the same process."

The paper had to print the piece even with the above remark. At the end it said Skylar is a business consultant and a member of the Cleveland Advertising Hall of Fame.

The governor obviously liked David's style. Even though he was just a commissioner and not the director of the lottery, he assumed the position of spokesman for the department. The director was a little out of his element in the job and needed David's experience in dealing with the media, and also coming up with new ideas and proposals.

All the commissioners were political appointments. They represented all the main districts of Ohio. They were chosen for many reasons; many because they were big donors, but others like David because they had been helpful to the governor in the past.

The original three-year term of David's appointment was renewed several times. During the nineties he kept the job while others were passed over. In 1993, he pushed hard for the removal of the cap on winnings for an individual. He wrote articles for the local papers that detailed the bad effects of keeping such a cap. When it was advertised that a Super Lotto jackpot would be a large amount, but the payout could only be $26 million, it was not the way to gain more players. It took a few months of convincing before the commission got the state to remove the cap. Many more people began to play Super Lotto, as well as the other games that were introduced.

One chore of the commissioners was to give out big prizes if they were won in their districts. David got a big kick out of awarding the prize money to a middle-aged couple in Toledo, who really needed the money. Another time a young man was given a $10 million prize and really enjoyed the publicity. A couple of years later, David saw him at the airport with two attractive girls hanging onto him. David managed to take him aside for a minute to see how everything was going. He told Skylar that he was almost broke, but enjoyed every minute of his wealthy interlude. David could not imagine spending all that money.

Toward the end of the decade there was a commissioner who owned a large yacht. He invited all of his fellow members on a nighttime dinner cruise on the Cuyahoga River. That was the first time I'd ever heard of karaoke. The first officer on the boat was in charge of the entertainment. It was a bit awkward for the guests, since none of them had such splendid facilities with which to reciprocate. The lottery job was probably David's last service to the state and its politicos. Shortly after he became a resident of Florida, but still kept his clients up north. We moved again.

Ohio Lottery publicity shot to announce David's appointment to the Commission.

Stephanie says goodbye to David after her wedding in 1985.

Chapter 55

It would be negligent of me if I didn't tell you about another side of David Skylar. He had a great curiosity for all types of knowledge, with the exception of anything musical. Since he was tone deaf, that could have been the reason for his disinterest in music.

In our early days together he decided that we should take a course in photography. I thought it was a good idea also, but it never intrigued me the way it did him. One phase of the course at the art museum dealt with strobe light. Unfortunately, neither he nor I took many pictures after the classes were over. Every year he gave me a new camera, as if I were the one who was interested initially. Somehow cameras seemed to disappear in our household. There is one left in a desk drawer that probably still has film in it from 20 years ago.

When we had been married for 10 years, we moved to our second home. It was a large English Tudor that needed remodeling. That's when David's drafting skills became relevant. He drew up some plans for attaching a family room and other changes in the bedrooms. We hired a single carpenter, who was fantastic, to do the work on the difficult stuff. We found a paperhanger/painter to bring the walls up to date. The best part was the deal David made with an upscale kitchen cabinetmaker and an exclusive furniture store that entailed getting our purchases at cost if we opened our home to the public after the remodel. That was a real coup for us financially, but even at cost we found our good taste prevented us from adding the family room at that time.

David prepared the brochures to be given out at the open house, which was to last for about three weeks. It turned out that the weather was so bad at the time it only lasted for about nine days. All this time we were still in our old house, since we couldn't sell it. Whatever furniture we were living with was destined for the basement rec room. The designer from the furniture store put in some accessories for show, which I gave back to them after the open house.

One day I took the children over during the public showing, as they hadn't seen the final product of all the labor. Claudia was eight years old, and already was socially confident among strangers. She walked into the dining room where people were admiring the chandelier and blurted out, "My mommy isn't sure we will keep that because it costs $495 and she's not sure we can afford it!" I was walking right behind her and was slightly embarrassed. As it turned out, we have taken that chandelier to every home we could for the last 54 years.

By the time we built the family room, David was already eager to have a greenhouse. The plans we had fit it against the sliding glass doors of the new room. It proved to be a glorious addition. Most nights when David was in town he would work on the plants that we grew from seeds, or trim the dead leaves from full-grown hanging baskets. One of our friends who built an even larger greenhouse, sneaked in cuttings from the Caribbean once in his sweat socks and shared them with us. Those cuttings were the beginnings of our innumerous gifts to friends of the night-blooming cereus plants. To this day we get photos of the magnificent blossoms that have bloomed for friends late at night. The friends have had better luck with the plants than we had.

The next plant hobby started when we moved to the dream house. There was already a greenhouse attached to the side of the garage. It wasn't as convenient for us to maintain, as we had to walk through the garage to get there. It also was hard to start new seedlings, since we were in and out of town for about six months of the year. However, it was handy for storing big house plants that could be watered occasionally by a plant sitter.

It was during this period that David started making terrariums after extensive research. He bought those large bottles from a water company and lined them up in the garage on a work bench. He couldn't find the proper tools to reach into the small nozzles of the bottles, so he made them himself. On one long stick there were tiny scissors; on another were miniature tongs; and on still another there was a toothbrush connected. It was extremely difficult to put seedlings into the soil and secure them. I don't know where he got the patience. In other endeavors he was not a patient man. This, then, was a calming hobby for his type one personality. When each terrarium was finished, he presented it to a friend with explicit instructions for its care. He was often asked to make house calls on his gifts, as most people were not as knowledgeable on the subject.

It was a little incongruous that David, who was known to be a tough businessman, could be so enamored of flowers and all things botanical. He was happiest in those days just to put on old khakis and shirts; just to putter around the yard, which was almost an acre of trees and shrubs bordering on Canterbury Golf Club's thirteenth hole. There was even a pond for which he traveled to the other end of the city, to buy special water lilies and fish. He was the lord of his little fiefdom, and he loved every minute of his downtime, as he called it.

As I have said so many times in these passages, this last Ohio home of ours had everything, or almost everything. It didn't have a hot tub. That prompted David to call upon our daughter Claudia again to design a small room jutting out on the back brick terrace. She did a great job of making it just like the room out of which it extends. Two walls consisted of French windows like the rest of the house, and two walls were paneled and stained. The roof was some kind of special material that Claudia had researched when she was at MIT. It was a great addition, especially after David picked out a seven-foot round hot tub for the end of the space. Every night we got in the tub and watched the eleven o'clock news on a wall-mounted TV. We slept like babies in those days. It was one of David's best ideas.

It's sad that when we went to see the house after it had been sold three times, the owner didn't know why there was a water connection in the floor. They never knew there had been a hot tub in the room. There was also a worse travesty. Some owner along the way had painted all the wormy chestnut moldings, doors cabinets and bannisters! As the saying goes, you can't go home again.

Many years later David found another interest. He attended Bonsai classes in West Palm Beach. He bought interesting specimens at exhibits around Florida. Soon he realized it was more economical to start his own. Somehow he couldn't excel at this hobby, and so we were left with lots of unusual shaped stone containers.

There were a few other attempts at hobbies, but golf, tennis, and consulting seemed to fill his days. There were also a couple of southern moves that took up his time. He became a neighborhood politician in a country club setting. He was a president again for the third time!

In 1992, David found out about a development in Boca Raton which had gone into bankruptcy. A nephew who was a builder wanted to buy one of the neighborhoods that had only completed a half dozen of the 95 homes originally scheduled. We found a shell of a house that looked perfect for our needs. After a great deal of negotiation, our nephew was outbid, but we decided to finish the house anyway. The new builder made a deal that he would do the job according to the old builders specifications before he began building a different set of units than the original group.

We were able to pick out anything we wanted, and were delighted at the prospect of moving north to a newer area. When the house was finished and we moved in, the area was still like a wasteland with no streetlights and still some shells that had not sold. We were real pioneers at Woodfield Country Club. That's when David became president of our neighborhood association. As the other neighborhoods got built up with more elaborate and expensive homes, the atmosphere changed drastically.

David even started advising people on the main board of the development after the Canadian company developers left, and the members took over. He wrote speeches for the new president and got involved in all the politics. We lived there for seven and one half years. The rest of this story comes later. It isn't very pleasant.

Hot Tub Room

This 9'x18' room was added in 1986. It has a solar roof of Lexon plastic and glass doors which can be opened fully in the summer. The hot tub is a 7ft Jacuzzi brand with heater and special controls. It is covered by a custom foam insulated cover. This room has a heater and exhaust fan. It is lighted by two antique sconces.

Basement

This area is used for storage only. It contains the furnace, hot water heater, and water controls. The dimensions are 18'x29'. The workbench and lighting will remain with the house, as will the shelving. The bathroom, which is currently a photography darkroom, will be restored to it's original purpose. This bathroom contains a soaking sink. A locked closet is on the other side of the room.

Picture of hot tub room that Claudia designed for the Canterbury Lane house in Cleveland.

WELCOME TO SHAKER HEIGHTS'

"HOME FOR MODERN LIVING"

2863 MONTGOMERY ROAD

SHAKER HEIGHTS, OHIO

A practical demonstration
of what can be accomplished in a
gracious old home

SPONSORED BY:

THE BUILDERS EXCHANGE, INC.

THE ILLUMINATING COMPANY

OPEN TO THE PUBLIC — DEC. 5 THROUGH DEC. 13

WEEKDAY HOURS — 3 TO 8

SATURDAYS AND SUNDAYS — 1 TO 8

David set up an arrangement to get remodeling done at cost. We lived in that house longer than any other.

258

Chapter 56

Even after moving to Boca Raton and getting into country club politics, David still didn't feel he had enough to do. He was continuing his travel to Cleveland where he had some major clients; and he visited Ashton Phelps in New Orleans from time to time to try to fulfill some of the contractual mumbo jumbo that the editor had written. It became more obvious with the passage of time that the idea was to keep David away from the Picayune's competitors. Since we still had the condo in Ohio, it was not a chore to visit his clients there. They were always having problems of some sort.

It looked like the best occupation for him in Florida was to go back to teaching advertising and marketing, a side job he performed gratis for the Cleveland Advertising Club when he started working in an agency. At that time, his students were adults interested in the "glamorous" field of advertising, because years later people would come up to him and tell him how much they enjoyed his classes.

He approached the department head at a university which was located nearby. He met this head honcho and found him to be a real academic. The man had never worked in the field and was not a creative type at all. Since David did not have a Masters, he was not readily accepted to teach. This man kept insisting that David prove to him that he could handle the courses required.

Since David really wanted to teach, he went along with these requests for experience. He put together a portfolio of all the published articles he had, plus an abundance of speeches he had made; he felt like a kid who was trying to get into a special college. Actually, he knew he had published more in the field of real advertising than the department head. David also knew that academic knowledge didn't always work in the business world, but he kept those thoughts to himself. He knew he could be a good teacher. He had been around.

When he got the job, he set up the curriculum and chose the books he needed for backup. He took the job very seriously; after all, he felt he could give his young students some of the real-life experience he had obtained after forty years in the business.

Whatever he did, the students loved him. The classes were always filled to capacity. Students told others and he was a very popular instructor. The head man began to discuss ideas and problems with him. David was quite innovative in his approach to teaching. He put his heart into the job, which paid him $5,000 a semester! It was obvious that he was sincere.

It was worth all the effort, he felt, when the students sent in their evaluations for the course at the end of each semester, and they were all "excellent." He was quite proud of his record.

The courses that he set up were in tune with modern times. One of the first of its kind was a course called "Marketing in a Multi-cultural Society." Before he started to teach that one, he used some of his ideas in his teaching outlines. For example, what approach do you use for the gay and lesbian community; what about the various religious groups, and of course, the immigrant segment of society that was still searching for understanding of the American way.

David kept researching ideas, and so he learned about various groups before he passed on the knowledge to his students. One day he asked the class for a show of hands if they knew what a "rainbow" sign in store windows signifies. Only one person raised his hand. David had just recently found out himself that it meant a gay owner welcomed others like himself. In another session he sent the students out to find the shopping habits of Orthodox Jews. Most of the class had not even known any kind of Jewish person. Through this exercise they found that this segment of the religion did not drive or ride in a car on Saturday, let alone shop on that day. David expanded the minds of these kids. He made his assignments interesting as well as instructive.

As for the rules and regulations of academia, David had no respect. Some guidelines were so archaic that he felt frustrated. He didn't associate with many of his fellow teachers. One time, though, he had to attend an open house at the home of the chairman of the department. I'm not sure what the occasion was, but it was a compulsory event. The residence was about 10 minutes from our home, so David thought we could just pop in, have a drink, and take our leave without anyone noticing. It didn't exactly work out that way.

The house looked nice and new on the outside, but when you walked in the door it was like an Addams Family set. I have never seen anything like it. It was very dim inside, although it was still afternoon. Every stick of furniture was oversized and black, as I recall. There were dark curtains on the windows. I must have put the specifics out of my mind because they were so frightening. Somehow we smiled through it all and met some of the pompous guests, had our diet Cokes, and were ready to sneak out. Just then, someone (the chairman or his wife) suggested we might like a tour of the house. David and I both rolled our eyes at each other and knew we had to go along with it.

We went upstairs and saw the bedrooms, and looked into the office that was near the head of the stairs. The door had been open as we peered into the dark room. Then the owner proudly closed the door, which had a windowed top. Printed on the door was "John Jones, PhD." We couldn't believe anyone could do that in his own home! And he thought it was clever. As you see, the name is changed to protect the innocent; not him, but us, as he might buy this book!

Eventually, David was asked to transfer to the honors college about 25 miles away. The driving time began to wear on him, especially when he had night classes. Late at night I-95 is like the Indianapolis Speedway. That is when he decided we should move closer to the school. That decision turned out to cause us a lot of aggravation and money. The new house that we found was wonderful, but our exit from the Woodfield Country Club development was a nightmare. I'll get into that a little later.

Chapter 57

*A*ll my discussion of the articles David had written in the last chapter should possibly be clarified. As a public relations guru, he knew how to promote his ideas. After making one of his speeches, he would put it in article form and query the publications most likely to print it. At least four out of five journals or newspapers accepted his work. Here is a typical letter that he wrote to the editors:

> *Dear Jack,*
> *Here's a copy of a speech I made at the American Management Association in Chicago Friday at noon.*
> *If there's anything in it for Ad Age, please feel free to use what you can.*
> *Best Regards.*
> *Very Truly Yours,*

He would add his signature underneath whatever title he held at the time. In this case it was Executive Vice President, Director of Client Service, The Griswold Eshleman Co. As for his signature, it was just an unreadable scribble. Many times his secretary signed his name legibly, but only in correspondence that was unimportant.

While going through the notebook containing most of David's work, I came across the exact speech, which later appeared in several publications. It is interesting to note that he was always a little ahead of the field in his subject matter. Some of the articles he wrote could just as well be written today, some 40 years later. I would like to share the speech that the above query was about. It was entitled: "Agency Client Finances—A New Day is Dawning."

Agency finances, once a secret as closely guarded as a bride's virginity, is now rapidly becoming an open book.

And the title of that open book is called a <u>Prospectus for the Sale of Stock</u>.

Not only is the secrecy of agency finances falling by the wayside, but the sacredness of the traditional 15% commission is beginning to crumble also.

As more and more agencies rush to underwriters "to go public" -- more information and financial data on the advertising business is being made available. And riding right in on the tail of this atmosphere of disclosure is the accelerated rapid acceptance by both agency and client of some form of negotiating fee system of compensation which will soon replace the 15% commission.

Today there are some 15 agencies whose stock is available to the public. On Wall Street and other financial centers, Security Analysts are peering at these companies through the professional gaze of a "money engineer". There's no more hanky-panky or cute tricks with a sharp pencil. These publicly held companies must tell it like it is. Even the overwhelming combination of super star Mary Wells and her investment bankers got their wrists slapped by investors when they tried the now famous "long write-off gambit."

It used to be that agencies reported their financial results to themselves, I.R.S. and the 4A's -- and often three sets of books were used.

Agency Finances

I can now look smack into Maxwell Dane's financial statement through his annual report and know his operating profit to the penny.

And this trend is accelerating. In addition to the 15 agencies now "public" another 10 or so are in registration. And I'll bet that right now 100 or more agencies are seriously studying this approach.

Just think of this fact for a minute. The 30 and 40 year olds who came back from World War II to start agencies or join going operations are now in their late 50's and 60's. These guys want out of the rat race and one of the only ways they can maximize their investment is through the public offering route.

Most agencies value their stock at book value, or book plus a premium, say 10%, for good will. An executive can get three, four times book, when his company's stock goes public.

That's why I feel that the Gold Rush of 1969 is off and running and in terms of dollars made -- it will make previous gold rushes look like penny ante poker.

And the wonderful part of all of this is that it's advantageous for everybody. As the agencies learn to live under prompt and total disclosure, their clients will benefit by sharing with the agency a responsibility for profit.

One of the most complex of all business relationships is the client-agency "marriage."

Agency Finances

The word "marriage" at first glance seems out of place, but a client-agency relationship must be more than a commercial shack-up; it must be more than a casual summer romance.

It is a business marriage, and is subject to all the stresses and strains, and contains similar rewards and responsibilities, as the nuptial contract.

Some of these business marriages fail because like individuals, the going gets tough after the honeymoon is over. The trouble starts when they get down to the business of living together.

That's when the suspicions, the deficiencies, the irritations, the personality clashes, the grinding over money matters must be met and mastered.

According to marriage counsellors, the major cause of divorce in this country is money; the lack of it, the mis-use of it, the need for more of it, and the general confusion that surrounds it.

Although "money" is never the reason given for an agency-client separation, you can bet that somewhere in the shadows there have been misunderstandings about who pays for what and why, which have led to an ever deepening break in the relationship. Nothing irritates a business-man more than "... to be had without enjoying it ... and then I wind up paying for it ..."

Any relationship between a client and an agency is affected by day-to-day problems both parties encounter. The single most pressing problem affecting compensation arrangements today is the agency profit squeeze.

Agency Finances

The climate at the opening ceremonies of a new relationship is not always ideal for poking around for bad habits or for conducting indoctrination seminars about business -- any more than walking
down the aisle with your beloved is quite the time to inquire about
snoring, cracker crumbs in bed or past romances.

The most important single factor affecting the agency-client
relationship is pricing, based on a clear and concise advance understanding by both agency and client of what is expected of whom. Most
break-ups will have the common denominator of the absence of a clear and
concise advance understanding.

Here, for example, are some common errors and pitfalls which
grow out of hazy negotiations.

Layouts. What do we mean by a rough? What does the client
mean?

Revisions. What's the limit? Who pays?

Meetings. Who is expected to attend? The art director, the
copy writer, the researcher? That's fine -- it just costs more and does
the financial arrangement cover it?

17.65. Most advertisers understand this one, but there are
still plenty who don't.

In simple terms, 17.65% of net is the same as 15% of gross.
If the agency has a craftsman's bill for $243.00 and take 17.65% of net,
the service charge is $42.88. This is the same amount you get when you
take 15% of gross, which in this case is $285.88 ($243.00 plus $42.88).
15% of $285.88 = $42.88. And photostats, and overtime, and photography,
and talent mark-ups, and travel expenses, etcetera!

Agency Finances

There are eight general compensation arrangements between agencies and their clients. Well over 99% of all compensation arrangements between agencies and their clients fall into these eight classifications:

    1. Media Commissions

        plus charges on outside purchases.

        plus charges for inside services.

This arrangement provides the agency with the combination of media commissions, plus percentage or other charges on materials and services purchased for clients, plus fees or other charges for some specific services performed inside the agency.

    2. Media Commissions

        plus charges on outside services.

This is the same as number one, that is, the combination of media commissions plus percentage or other charges on materials and services purchased, but with no fees or other charges for any inside services.

    3. Media Commissions only

Under the third arrangement, the agency's compensation consists of media commissions only.

    4. 1, 2, or 3 plus overall additional fee.

    5. 1, 2, or 3 with minimum/maximum profit percentage.

This arrangement is the same as 1, 2, or 3 but with the addition of a guaranteed minimum profit percentage on the accounts, and a controlled maximum profit percentage. This arrangement was used by agencies for the first time in 1965.

Agency Finances

6. Minimum Fee

Here the agency bills the client the amount, if any, by which commissions fall short of the agreed-upon minimum. When media commissions and the percentage on purchases, if any, grow to the point where they exceed the minimum, the fee arrangement is dropped.

7. Fee Crediting Commissions

This is an overall fee on the entire account, the agency receiving no other compensation. This fee is agreed upon in advance and billed periodically. Media commissions are credited, or media and production are billed net.

8. Cost Crediting Commissions

This is the overall cost of handling the entire account, or cost plus. Media commissions are credited, or the client is billed net for media and production. This is the same as number seven except that the amount of the fee in this case is determined after the work is done.

Of these eight different compensation arrangements, No. 1, the combination of media commissions, plus charges on outside purchases, plus charges on some inside services, is used most frequently, an estimated 90% of the time.

The ordinary minimum fee is the second most popular arrangement followed closely by No. 4, the combination of media commissions, plus charges for outside and some inside services, plus an overall additional fee.

There is no "standard" method of agency compensation. The average agency will use two or three of these arrangements and perhaps more.

Agency Finances

- 8 -

In recent years, the fee arrangements have been gaining popularity at the expense of the media commission arrangements.

Whatever the financial arrangement between client and agency, it has to satisfy these four points:

1. Does it reflect the value of the service?

2. Is it based on a correct definition of the work to be done?

3. Is it competitive?

4. Is it MAKING A PROFIT which is reasonable to the agency and satisfactory to the clients?

The final test for a long, happy marriage between client and agency comes with these two questions:

1. Does the agency and client at the very outset understand reasonably well the scope and manner of the services to be rendered and who pays for what?

2. Does the client respect the agency's desire to make a fair profit?

When the answer to both of these questions is an unequivocal yes, you can tear up the tickets to Reno and count on living happily ever after ......

Agency Finances

His speech "Arise Ye Women," written in 1965, was later updated in 1984. He had an uncanny sense of what should be done by women to better society, as well as their own positions. Though the texts were different in those years, the content could be used in the twenty-first century. To give you an idea, some of the final paragraphs in the 1984 speech ended like this:

"You have the issues that seem to concern women most—issues like reducing the income gap between men and women, helping the poor, strengthening civil rights, gun control, environmental preservation, nuclear power, preventing increased foreign intervention, salvaging social security...."

His main advice for women was that both politicians and business executives get quite concerned when they get communications from women, as now that they see the power that they have.

He urged his female audiences to understand that power begins with 20/20, "...not your eyesight, but twenty minutes and 20 cents (ha!) for a stamp to get out your opinion in a letter."

A lot of women's organizations heard that speech. It still has timely content.

There were so many other articles that seemed to peer into the future. One of them was written after his stint in publishing. "Why Newspapers Die" came out well before the big internet push when newspapers were just beginning to fade away. That article was published in the *Quill Magazine* in 1984. It was widely read by journalists across the states, many of whom had found themselves jobless after years of distinctive writing.

I wish I could duplicate that piece for you, but it was extremely long. However, there were some observations that really dissected the problems that caused newspapers to fail. According to the main preface of the article, he stated simply that "...some newspapers have been murdered, some mugged, some raped, and some sabotaged. Some committed suicide, and some just faded away because of management malnutrition.

"Failing publishers have a number of excuses for why newspapers die. These are cliché reasons given to stunned employees by a stone-faced executive as he reads the newspaper's death notice.

"First, television is killing newspapers. This is an easy out for a behind-the-times publisher. Newspapers don't compete against TV at all; they compete for readers who read, as opposed to watchers who watch." David went on to say that other publications have grown in readership while many newspapers have fallen behind. He believes that they have forgotten that the quality of their writers has sometimes deteriorated. Good newspapers have gone for 'star quality' systems; others have become bland and dull.

"Secondly, afternoon papers are doomed." Since Detroit, Cleveland, and Pittsburgh all have the same demographics he claimed, could the demise of the very successful *Cleveland Press* have been the fault of the new management? Subsequent investigations showed that to be true.

Third, the excuse that newspapers are facing hard times. David felt this was another cliché for the public's attention. He said that newspaper publishing was an extremely profitable business, and it seemed ridiculous that they always talk 'poor.' He cited all the statistics for the time, and showed that newspaper publishing companies were well accepted on Wall Street. He admitted that costs have gone up, but they have gone up for everything. He felt that publishers have not been able to cope with marketing changes. David named the big companies that have sophisticated marketing technicians that can anticipate change and deal with it.

He believed it has become obvious that for several decades the industry's accountants and lawyers have become smarter and more powerful than the publishers and editors. There is much more in the article about individual newspaper closures, and he focused on the *Cleveland Press* dissolution, because it was in his home town. In the present day, it looks like the morning paper, the *Plain Dealer*, which refused a joint operating deal with *The Press*, may now go to three days a week. Maybe the Newhouse group blames the computer age. That's the excuse of the 21st century.

David ended his article by asking "...could the *Philadelphia Bulletin*, the *Buffalo Courier-Express*, and the *Cleveland Press* have been saved? A lot of people think so. I am one of them."

One of the most clairvoyant speeches I discovered in David's large collection I had never seen before. It was written in 1990, but it could have been written in 2008. It was titled "The Conservative Right Moves Again." It was written 23 years ago, but the subject matter mirrors the news of today. I would like to present this speech for your review.

THE CONSERVATIVE RIGHT MOVES AGAIN

by David Skylar

Although President Bush promised a more "gentle" approach to the country's many social and economic problems, his cohorts in the ultra-conservative movement seem to be doing otherwise.

Here it is 1990, two years before the next significant national elections, and the "New Right" is already gearing up to demonstrate their power.

If we can anticipate anything in the next several years, one thing is certain, we will see a strong challenge from the Reactionary Right," the "New Right," the conservative movement -- call it what you may. In all elections, moderate and liberal, candidates will be targeted.

In Washington, DC, and in state houses across the country, they will pressure law makers to bend in their direction. And most important of all, the Reactionary Right will win in the courts -- at every level including the Supreme Court.

For a candidate to be targeted is not a mark of distinction, but possible extinction. Over the last decade, in the U.S. Senate alone, the Reactionary Right has had some startling successes. The litany of losers includes Senators McIntyre, Clark, Haskell, Case, Hathaway, Anderson, Bayh, Church, Cluver, Durkin, Nelson and McGovern. In addition to the national politicians, hundreds of state and local races have felt the impact of the Reactionary Right.

Conservative Right speech

To understand this movement is to fear its power. The Reactionary Right is not a new phenomenon. It is simply a collection of old line, ultra-conservatives with catchy new names. The difference is that they are having an impact on this country that far exceeds their actual strength.

It is important to remember that the Reactionary Right is a collection of separate single issue groups and traditional ultra-conservative organizations.

Men and women close to the White House do the planning and coordinating of activities. With their ties to the Republican National Committee and the Republican (Congressional) Steering Committee, they bring a semblance of sophistication to the Reactionary Right.

CLONED COMMITTEES

The actual impetus for the Reactionary Right comes from a small influential circle of individuals. One of the most important is Richard Viguerie, the direct mail fundraiser whose computerized lists generate the cash to run the various organizations. The Committee for the Survival of a Free Congress, is the brains behind the Reactionary Right. The Conservative Caucus and the National Conservative Political Action Committee respectively, are the organizational geniuses of the movement. Most of the other committees have been "cloned" by these groups.

The explosion of cloned committees is by design. The Reactionary Right addresses each of the "hot button" issues with its own committee. Thus, the opponents of gun control, the Equal Rights Amendment, organized labor, affirmative action, gay rights and abortion have their own committee.

Conservative Right speech

The hot button issues and cloned committees are the key to the Reactionary Right's strategy, which is essentially a marriage of expediency between Americans disgruntled about an issue and the ultra-conservative cause.

The right-wingers know that their brand of politics is repugnant to the vast majority of Americans. They have learned that they can successfully exploit the hot button issues. And they recognize that those issues will attract votes from the constituencies they could not otherwise reach.

It is simply coalition politics. The difference is that the Reactionary Right is organizing, funding and directing the committees that comprise the coalition. While the partners in this marriage of expediency may not be enamored with each other, they know that the combination can produce results. <u>And results are what coalition politics is all about.</u>

The Reactionary Right is not monolithic. It consists of individuals with varying degrees of commitment to the conservative cause. Some <u>are</u> clones, but many are well-meaning, committed people who believe in their issue. To lump them all together would be a mistake.

Middle America is Target

While the Reactionary Right may make headlines targeting moderate and liberal politicians, they make more headway targeting the traditional constituencies of those politicians. Their target is Middle America ... ethnic, Catholic and working class Americans. This targeted group has been described as:

> "...basically decent and honest, neither paranoid nor bigoted, but who are anxiety ridden over what frequently appears to them to be an assault on their total personal value system."

> Conservative Right speech

The targeted group has also been described as "cultural fundamentalists." A cultural fundamentalist is someone who takes their values from the traditions of local society. Moral and religious values are vital ingredients in their political decisions and their approach to social and economic problems. Cultural fundamentalists are more oriented towards production, work and saving, than consumption and enjoyment.

They have traditionally been in the Democratic corner. They have supported liberals __because of__ their progressive stance on economic issues __and in spite of__ their attempts at social engineering. But these same people are wondering why America needs abortion and gun control to stop crime. It is those doubts and fears upon which the Reactionary Right preys.

The Reactionary Right has learned that traditional democratic constituencies are approachable on the basis of non-economic values -- religion, culture, morals and race relations. The hot button issues give them ready access to ethnics, Catholics and trade unionists that were heretofore unapproachable, to individuals that would have turned a deaf ear to the Reactionary Right's appeal a decade ago.

With the hot button issues, they are able to persuade these people to vote against moderate and liberal politicians. They were able to persuade union members, ethnics and Catholics to jump ship.

Their strategy then is to "pick off" enough traditional Democratic votes to elect a conservative Republican candidate.

The Religions Right

The "Religious Right" may well be more dangerous than their political counterparts. The most vocal components of the Reactionary Right are the organizations built around religious issues.

Conservative Right speech

For the past number of years, the religious rightwing has concentrated on the abortion issue. Fetal politics occupied center stage. The National Right to Life Committee and the Life Amendment Political Action Committees held the spotlight. The Right to Lifers, however, now share that spotlight with the Christian Evangelicals.

The Reactionary Right has cloned committees (the Moral Majority, Christian Voice, Religious Roundtable and National Christian Action) to aid the Evangelical preachers organize. Unlike the narrower issue of abortion, the Evangelicals have attacked "humanism" and the "permissiveness of our society."

Without any doubt, the "rank-and-file" Right to Lifers and Born again Christians believe in the righteousness of their causes. Their fervor arises from deep-seated, moral convictions. For the most part, they are not motivated by traditional political concerns; they are not striving for political power. And therein lies the crux of the problem.

The Right to Lifers depend on grass roots activities -- door to door campaigning, papering parking lots, and more sophisticated media events. How they are actively recruiting Right to Life candidates. The Right to Lifers have become sophisticated and effective campaigners.

On the other hand, the Evangelicals were not active in politics until 1988. While Evangelical preachers have a large TV and radio listenership, it was unclear how effective they would be in getting their "flocks" to register and then to vote for the preferred candidate. Large amounts of money can be raised by these preachers, but their effectiveness was untested.

Conservative Right speech

Although the Evangelicals failed their first presidential political test in 1990, they are still a force to b concerned about. The real threat from this ally of the Reactionary Right is that they attract individuals to the political process who have never before participated. Registration campaigns conducted from the pulpit have been successful. We know that these preachers can turn folks on. We know they can turn them out.

Tactics of the Reactionary Right

The Reactionary Right's tactics are as simple and direct as its strategy. They can be summarized as: start early, always stress the negative and repeat the message often.

An early start has become the hallmark of the Reactionary Right. Unlike most political action committees, the Reactionary Right selects its targets long before the filing deadlines. They target their opponents early. Almost simultaneously, Viguerie's computers began to spew direct mail attacks into the targeted candidates states. Somewhat later, radio and TV ads begin to run in those states.

How does the Reactionary Right operate? Very simply stated -- The Reactionary Right attacks. Whether in the form of direct mail or paid media, the attacks are usually sharp and strident. They are always negative. Their ads are designed to generate hatred and fear in the audience.

To boost its hatred/fear campaign, the Reactionary Right relies on the "big lie" school of propaganda. The bigger the lie, the more it sounds like the truth. The Reactionary Right believes that if the misstatements are repeated often enough, their credibility is enhanced.

While the Reactionary Right will occasionally alter the content of its ads, the tag lines -- the real negative themes never change. The ads keep pounding away at the same themes.

Conservative Right speech

And pound away they do. The Reactionary Right believes in repetition. They hope "the negatives will stick ... that there will be people voting against the targeted candidate without remembering why."

To implement their strategy and tactics, the Reactionary Right has developed a five point campaign program. They are not bashful nor secretive about it. Basically the program consists of:

1. A series of scientific voter surveys designed to detect the strengths and weaknesses of the targeted candidate.

2. Hiring a field coordinator who is supposed to marshall "all the forces who are opposing the incumbent," start distribution of materials detailing his record and coordinate the "free media program" against the incumbent.

3. A direct mail campaign that asks voters to contribute and/or get involved in a small way to help defeat the targeted candidate.

4. An extensive advertising campaign, aimed at "exploiting the weaknesses of the incumbent."

5. Recruitment of a candidate best able to represent the conservative viewpoint.

This five point program is complimented and supplemented by the other groups of the Reactionary Right. However, each committee will mail its own fundraising appeal. All groups share the results of the voter surveys and the research into the incumbent's record.

Conservative Right speech

The funds to finance the various activities of the New Right come from Viguerie's direct mail campaigns. The fundraising efforts are national in scope but a large portion of the letters find their way into the targeted states. The direct mail campaign serves the dual purpose of getting out a negative message and raising money.

In recent elections, the Reactionary Right's various committees spent over 10 million dollars -- not including fundraising costs. The Reactionary Right's war chest is extensive.

The bottom line is that the Reactionary Right is a formidable opponent. It is well financed and fanatical. What it lacks in size it makes up in tenacity and aggressiveness. But above all else, the Reactionary Right has the ability to undermine a candidate's natural electoral base. The Reactionary Right is not to be taken lightly.

On the Positive Side....
Every political movement has its share of Achilles heels. The Reactionary Right is no exception. In fact, this movement probably has more exploitable weaknesses than most.

The Reactionary Right's major weakness is its narrow base. While its leaders have been effective in creating an image of widespread support, the impression is mostly due to manipulating "blue smoke and mirrors." The Reactionary Right, in spite of press clippings to the contrary, is a distinct incestuous minority.

The Reactionary Right is the same old collection of ultra-conservatives. Its true believers are small in number.

Conservative Right speech

The Reactionary Right cannot comprise more than ten percent of the electorate. Up to now their brand of negative politics and reactionary stands have attracted few adherents. Standing alone, they would have troupe electing the county dog warden.

But the Reactionary Right has managed to create the impression of strength by multiplying its committees and convincing the press that it is engaging in coalition politics. Nothing could be further from the truth. The committees of the Reactionary Right are created by mitosis -- the process of dividing a cell to create two. They all stem from the same core group. They have interlocking directors, activists and membership lists. It is a distinct, incestuous minority.

The second major weakness is the Reactionary Right's <u>ideological purity</u>. The leadership brooks no deviation from the published line. On each issue, the Reactionary Right requires 110 percent. It is a purity that borders on fanaticism and creates internal problems for the movement.

It is not just the ideological purity that weakens the Reactionary Right, but its penchant for taking the most extreme position on an issue. On a vast array of issues -- from labor law reform to abortion -- the Reactionary Right adopts a radical, intransigent position. Their stance is so far right as to be repugnant to a majority of Americans. This is particularly true with respect to economic issues. If the Reactionary Right's position on most issues is given wide publication, then it loses more votes than it attracts.

The extreme positions may aid fundraising, but it hampers attempts to find new adherents to the faith. Its ideological purity forces the Reactionary Right to proselytize, not persuade. And it is easier to preach than convert.

Conservative Right speech

The third weakness involves the Reactionary Right's <u>tactics</u>. While Americans love a good fight, they detest a dirty fighter. The Reactionary Right's tactics often fall into the category of fighting dirty.

The Reactionary Right's tactics smack of fanaticism. They have been described as "radicals, working to overturn the present power structure in this country." Their tactics often exceed the bounds of fair play and acceptable campaign mores. Therefore, their tactics will draw criticism from the press and will be labeled "unfair," "despicable," etc.

The final weakness of the Reactionary Right is its leadership, who are men without pride or principle.

Meeting the Challenge of the Reactionary Right

The Reactionary Right, through its cloned off shoots, has had alarming success. They have been instrumental in defeating a number of important Senators and Congressmen. They have been pivotal in blocking all manner of legislation, and imposing their ideas on local community school boards, library boards and state legislatures. They have grown into a rich and powerful force. This force must be met by still another force. A strong watchdog group is needed.

Every state should have a bi-partisan committee to monitor and then publicly comment on the tactics of the Reactionary Right committees active in that state. This group would also attempt to control those committees by bringing law suits and filing complaints with Fair Campaign Practices Commission in each state. This watchdog committee should be formed in each state and immediately serve notice that they will not tolerate underhanded tactics used by the Reactionary Right and any other committee or group. This committee should have legal status as a Political Action Committee so that it can raise and spend monies.

Conservative Right speech

A fundraising effort should start immediately so that stationery, brochures, etc. can be produced. A lawyer well versed in state campaign law should be retained, as well as a spokesperson for the committee. The committee chairperson and Board of Director should be bi-partisan and represent a cross-section of management, labor, etc.

The committee would immediately organize statewide to monitor radio/TV talk shows, respond to letters to the editor, flag obnoxious advertising and, in general, be aware and respond to Reactionary Right tactics.

It's not what they say -- it's how they say it. And it would be the goal of this committee to respond to uncouth and poor taste advertising. It would also be the goal of this committee to provide the environment for fair and decent elections.

The Reactionary Right might appear invincible, but they are not. The battleground is the courts and the media.

You have to fight their fire with your own.

Conservative Right speech

As you can perceive, David had basically liberal views. His best friends were mostly Republicans, but not those of tea party caliber. He got along well with them at the club or social functions, because he didn't discuss politics except when he was counseling various politicians of either party.

There were many other articles and speeches that I found preserved by his loyal secretaries through the years, especially an older lady named Blanche Young, who protected him like a son. When he moved from the ad agency business to the newspaper business, she joined him immediately. It was truly a sad day when she died.

Chapter 58

When David decided to move closer to the honors college where he was teaching, I realized it made sense for him not to drive the highway for 25 miles each way at night. The realtors started showing us houses right around the campus, but nothing appealed to us.

One day after a disappointing tour of the environs, the newest agent happened to see another unfinished house listed in a development in what would be considered the "boonies" of West Palm Beach. It was a community that had lavish homes, but lots of vacant spaces. It was on one of the PGA golf courses far from the main PGA center. There was a small wooden pro shop and no decent sign out front to show it had borrowed the prestigious name of Bay Hill Estates.

When we saw the house it was set back on an acre of land with the back grounds butting up to the 12th green of the golf course. All the plastered walls were in, but there were no appliances in the kitchen. All the doors had to be put in and some of the wiring, and we were able to have it painted in our choice of colors. There was more landscaping to go in and several minor details to work out. There was no pool, and we knew we would have to build one. The builder wanted out of the development and he gave us a decent price.

It took six months to finish the place. We were getting anxious, but it didn't matter that much, since we hadn't sold the house in Woodfield yet. In late summer we got one of the gardeners with a truck to drive two single beds, two inside chairs, and two lawn chairs up to the new house. Once the refrigerator got in we spent weekends up there camping out. We brought basic food up for breakfasts and dined out the rest of the time.

We sold our house in early fall and got out by October 27th. The actual closing was to be November 1st. The buyer was a single lawyer who was engaged to a lady. Both he and the woman had children. Just thinking of this man makes me angry 13 years later. After the deal was made, he called us with his fiancé on the other line begging us to lower the price. He said he had a child going to college and so many expenses, etc.; then she started with the same sob story, and like fools that we can be, we dropped the price another five thousand. On the day before the movers were to arrive, our realtor came in with a telegram from this buyer saying he wanted out, and the realtor had told him he would lose his $20 thousand dollar deposit. Apparently, he had broken up with the lady, but he went along with the sale, as he couldn't bear to lose $20 thousand.

The day of the closing he was his usual self, but we were relieved that the house was sold. When I saw him drive away in a new Mercedes convertible, I was livid. At that time David told me to cool it. We had discounted the house for him and we made a mistake, so "just forget it." It was a little later that David was furious with the man's arrogance.

After we moved away, we started getting bills from Woodfield for lockers, cart path fees, food minimum fees, and the regular monthly dues. David kept making trips down to meet with the manager, who then told him he was working on straightening out the various problems. David also spoke to the president, whom he thought was a good friend. He asked David to play in the member/guest golf tournament that was coming up that month. Unfortunately, a board member named Kathy Griffith quashed the invitation by declaring that David was still a member and couldn't be a guest. Technically, that couldn't be possible, because one of the club laws said you had to live on the premises in order to be a member of the club. From what we gathered, his friend resigned as president and there was a big fight brewing. David obtained minutes of the meeting where they were discussing "Skylar's problem."

By that time David was sick of writing polite letters to the board. They sold off our golf membership for around $27 thousand plus, and sent us a check for about five thousand after deducting all the improbable fees. We hired a lawyer that our new neighbor recommended and we rejected that check. From then on we were put at the bottom of a list for the equity return due us, even though we were the first golf members to resign. There was no law in the development that said you had to sell your house with a social membership. That didn't happen for at least two more years.

The problem seemed to be that Woodfield had made deals with several builders offering them social memberships that they could give out to their customers who bought houses from them. As the development mushroomed, all of these social memberships got utilized. Nobody else needed them. In what our attorney believed at the time, it was slightly illegal to hold us hostage because they hadn't sold our social membership. At that point in time it was suggested to David that he approach that buyer of our house and offer him a couple thousand dollars to become a social member.

David drove down to Boca to meet this guy and did as he was advised to do. It was a genuine offer, and you would think the man would accept with pleasure, since it would give him the opportunity to dine and play tennis, and use all the facilities, with the exception of golf. Even that was allowed a few times a year, but the mean-spirited individual wanted upwards of eight thousand dollars, and David walked away swearing. If he had accepted the offer, we wouldn't have lost $49 thousand in the owed equity, plus seven years of litigation that went nowhere. At the end our attorney, who ignored David's letters and calls, quit because we stopped paying him. The judge let him quit without the slightest bit of concern for our welfare.

I wonder if Woodfield's lawyer, whose name was George W. Bush, pulled every dirty trick in the book, and our counselor was too overwhelmed to try harder. Whatever the reason, I ended up signing away the right to sue the club, because he intimidated me by saying if we lost our case I would have to pay Woodfield's legal fees as well. You see, I believe David had a stroke after trying to get this problem settled. I had to take over, and I had no clue how to fight back.

While all this was going on, a friend suggested that one of his friends could help me if I sent him all the paperwork that we had collected. He was teaching law courses at a local private college. I thought he was doing us a favor—the kind of favor where you buy the man dinner in appreciation. No way. After he read my material and offered a few ideas over the phone, we got a bill from his son's law office which noted we were getting a discount, so the total was just under one thousand dollars. I should have questioned it, but since it was a friend of a friend, I had to pay it. I don't think David would have let him get away with it.

I have probably bored you with all my vindictiveness (if there is such a word!), but it's a part of growing up or growing old. As far as Woodfield is concerned, I rue the day the members took over from Canada Square, the people who bailed out the Barber family who started the development. The arrogance of the people who became board members, believing that running a club was like having their own fiefdom. Can you believe that in the beginning of our struggle to resign, we were sent a 1099 for the full sale price of our golf membership, which we never received?

As for the buyer of our house, he proved to be a terrible neighbor. I was told that he had often run out of the house chasing his wife (he had finally married that woman) and grabbing her by the hair, yelling, etc. I was embarrassed to think people like that lived in what was once our delightful house.

There were a few good years in our new house before all hell broke loose. I'll tell you about them next.

Chapter 59

At the start of the 21st century, David was still working pretty much as always, but he was primarily doing it from Florida. Since some of his Ohio clients had absorbed all that he had taught them, and had become extremely successful, they mutually agreed to discontinue their relationships. So with a pared-down client list, David sought new business in Florida.

New business was delayed somewhat, as the first of several health issues took place. In a routine physical, a comprehensive x-ray was taken that showed David's spleen seemed to be abnormally enlarged. His primary doctor sent him to an oncologist, who concluded that it should be removed immediately. There is no way that it could be biopsied, as it is a blood-filled organ.

Since we had not yet gained any feelings of trust for Florida doctors, we made arrangements to return to Cleveland for the surgery at University Hospital where a young physician was becoming known for his innovative surgical techniques. He drew out the spleen laparoscopically, a procedure that was just becoming available. The young man who performed the surgery was Dr. Raymond P. Onders. For some reason, David called him his "cowboy doctor." They hit it off immediately, and David was able to get an appointment in a few days. When it was over, it turned out there was nothing at all wrong with the spleen, and all the anguish was for nothing. And it left David with a weaker immune system. Two years later, Dr. Onders operated on Christopher Reeve, implanting a diaphragm pacing device which allowed "Superman" to breathe off the ventilator. We were lucky to find him.

We rented an apartment in Cleveland for the remainder of the summer, and David took it easy until he felt a bit stronger. He didn't have classes in the summer, so it worked out well. As soon as he was back on his feet he made some calls to his remaining clients, and naturally they had work for him to do. Except for the tight accommodations, it wasn't a bad summer. We still had our club and our friends to keep us busy.

We began to get anxious to get back to our new home. When we left for Cleveland, the pool contractor had disappeared, and we didn't have time to hire some other company to finish it. When contractors disappear in Florida, there is no way to find them. Sub-contractors were not getting paid, and we started getting letters putting liens on our property, so we had to get legal advice. Everything seems like a scam in Florida. At any rate, David was anxious to get the pool finished and get back in his old routine of teaching and consulting, and golf.

We flew back home as originally planned, because we knew he wouldn't have been allowed to drive anyway; we had left both cars in Florida and had a rental in Cleveland. It was great sleeping in our own bed again. David immediately found a reputable pool contractor who was willing to finish the job that had begun almost a year before. In less than two months it was finally completed. We could begin to enjoy the outdoor setting of our home about eight miles away from West Palm Beach civilization.

It was just about that time that David consulted our next-door neighbor about finding a reputable lawyer to sue Woodfield. He gave us the name of a man he had done business with when he was a banker before his retirement. David and I met the man and he agreed that we had a case. Thus began the saga of the "disappearing equity," which I have discussed before.

David continued his teaching and wrote several business stories that the *Sun Sentinel* was happy to print, since he had good credentials, as well as good material. Sometimes stories were just written about him and his innovative teaching. One such story refers to his new course that I previously mentioned. It was titled "Marketing to the Melting Pot," with a subhead "New FAU Class to Focus on Sales to Subcultures."

The article starts out "...last spring David Skylar, an adjunct professor at Florida Atlantic University, assigned one of his students to study a Jewish kosher butcher shop. How, he asked, would the student advertise that store on a Saturday, which is generally a big shopping day?

"The student came back to Skylar and explained there was a problem. Many Orthodox Jews don't shop on Saturday, the Jewish Sabbath.

"Skylar, a marketing professional who is a member of the national Advertising Hall of Fame, already knew that, but his student learned a valuable lesson about subculture advertising." The article went on to say that Skylar explained that one must know intimate details of various subcultures in order to market to them successfully. He noted that with South Florida's rapidly changing multicultural population, old marketing schemes based on the one-ad-fits-all formula are being thrown out the window.

Consequently, the piece continued, FAU would offer for the first time, "Marketing in a Multi-cultural Society" beginning the next semester at the Jupiter campus "'All new courses are taught away from the main campus in Boca Raton, like Broadway shows tried out of town, to determine their value and student interest,' Skylar said."

David was quoted as saying that with more minorities than ever moving into the middle class, it is imperative to market to them. Not doing so could make or break an individual business.

There were several statistics in the story about various ethnic groups in Florida, citing Broward County as an example of almost a tripling of Caribbean communities in one decade.

"'Gays and Lesbians are a significant market that can't be ignored, because they, too, have millions of dollars to spend, and understand such things as fashion trends,'" Skylar said." There were other remarks that David made, but the fact that he convinced the school to offer his course was quite a coup. It was such a conservative department up until then.

Permit me to go back a few years to an event which culminated in a deep, trusting business relationship in 2003. It started in a small Ohio city where our daughter Stephanie and her then husband, Martin Gould, ran two radio stations. They had become well accepted in Lima, and participated in many city activities, both professionally and socially. At one point they were in the midst of a discussion as to how the Lima Technical College could become more prestigious, as well as popular.

They called in David to help them with the problem. He checked with his sources and found out former Governor James A. Rhodes, who had recently died in 2001, had never had an educational institution named after him. David felt that by using that name the school would get the prestige it deserved. It was also perfect for the city, because Lima was a big Republican community, for the most part, and would get built-in support by its citizens.

The idea was quickly embraced by the head of the college, and steps began to seek permission from the family. David and Martin found out that Rhodes had a daughter in Ft. Lauderdale and they contacted her. She was married to the Broward County Property Assessor, William Markham. They agreed to meet with The Lima contingent, including David, who was in West Palm Beach.

The meeting took place in Florida, and the Markhams thought the idea was great. They were quite willing to give the clearance to go ahead with the name change. They relied on

David and Marty to set up the dedication. The date was set and then the preparation began. There were innumerable details to work out. Think all the documents, stationary, signage that needed changing, besides the notifications to suppliers and other institution. It was a mammoth job, but it turned out to be well worth the effort.

On the actual day of the dedication, dignitaries from all over the state were invited. The Rhodes family was delighted, and Lima had its own college to nurture. Rhodes College had a nice ring to it

Soon after the Lima event, Markham got in touch with David and asked if he would be interested in helping his county department with some problems. It seems that he was impressed with his ability to get things done in a business-like and timely fashion. David agreed and it was the beginning of a great relationship.. After his classes were over, on several days a week David would drive from Jupiter to Ft. Lauderdale and back. I marveled at his great energy; he was in his mid-70s after all.

The problem in the Broward Assessor's department was they needed to find a way to derive income. For years all sorts of information had been disseminated to the public for free. They had to find a way to sell maps, deeds, appraisals, and the like. It was a drain on their finances to prepare these requested documents. Think also of the cost of aerial photographs!

David proposed that they set up a website, and when he got the okay to do so, he hired the appropriate experts to set it up. He worked with these people as well as Markham's staff to set up prices and online information on the products offered.

I was told that the first month the website was in operation, the department earned in the neighborhood of $100,000.

Just prior to this period David had received a phone call. It was from another adjunct professor at FAU. I would like to share Dick Wingerson's own recollection of how the two advertising guys met.

I had just signed up for another stint as an adjunct professor of advertising at Florida Atlantic University. The faculty secretary had given me some syllabi of other profs to give me an idea of how to write mine. And I was on the beach reading them. They were all academic blah, blah, blah, UNTIL I came across Dave Skylar's syllabus. Wow! This guy sounds like me, I thought. Obviously well experienced, original, and funny! I knew I had to meet him, so I called. He was delighted to get my call and suggested we meet for breakfast at the Original Pancake House at US-1 and Hillsborough, midway between his Boca Raton home and my Pompano Beach condo.

So we met. And this big, booming, jolly guy and I clicked right away. We compared careers; mine in Detroit, Australia, and Ft. Lauderdale, and his in Cleveland, Chicago, and New York. I mentioned a guy I had worked with, Carlos Vasquez. Dave had worked with him, too. I mentioned an ad guy who was in my sister's Cleveland wedding. Dave had worked with him, too. Plus, he had been Liberace's manager in the early days! (ed. note. Not exactly.)

Dave asked me to be a guest lecturer at his class. I said sure and asked him to guest at mine. No surprise, he was a big success. Other guest gigs followed. I even subbed for him once or twice. "Our teaching methods are totally opposite, but equally effective," he remarked once.

After he and his wife, Marilyn, moved to West Palm Beach, he invited my wife, Maria, and I to visit. A beautiful home, beautifully and artfully decorated. Smart, interesting, and funny friends. Maria remembers the Bailey's Irish Crème. I remember the White House Apple Butter. (a brunch?)

I sold Dave some of my old Lionel trains for his Chicago son-in-law's collection. Later, he suggested we form a team, AdPros. (Pros was short for professionals, NOT short for prostitutes.)

An Australian graphic designer I know came up with a logo: a capital A with ringer being thrown over it. "Uncommon

Common Sense" was our slogan. Our most memorable campaign was for Benefits Outsource run by a friend of mine in Hallandale. I designed the logo and tag "Your Outsource Resource." Dave did the marketing and wrote the copy. "A perfect example that image is everything," David remarked on the project's successful completion. Later, we were misled and stiffed by a young weasel who wanted a free lunch and some free ad advice.

We also had a great lunch at Sonny's with Elsy, a Venezuelan art director we worked with. I moved to Tallahassee in 2003, and asked Dave and another old ad buddy to be judges at the Ad Fed Awards. We had a good time reconnecting, dining, socializing, and we kept in touch by phone later.

Unfortunately, not long after, David had a stroke while fixing breakfast for Marilyn. I talked to him a couple of times after that. The stroke had stolen his conversational abilities, but not his humor. His last words to me were, "Either I'm going to get better, or I'm going to be one pissed off 80 year old."

So now it is obvious why I am telling these tales instead of David. I think it is important to describe how this debilitating illness began, and how it affected his life and the lives of his family. Maybe telling David's story might make people more aware of the illness, and that would be a good thing.

Chapter 60

It is impossible to determine what single event could trigger a major health issue like a stroke. Looking back it could have been a wayward pill that I found on the bathroom floor occasionally after David tossed his morning supply into his mouth too hastily. It could have been stress from flying back and forth between Ft. Lauderdale and Cleveland, or other cities.

However, I believe it was both of those triggers, plus one more. David called Bill Markham's office one morning to confirm his appointment and found out that the well-known, much younger Broward County appraiser had succumbed to a heart attack the night before. He was totally shocked by the news. How could this be? he thought. He was in his early 60s and seemed so healthy. Soon after, David made the long stressful nighttime trip to attend Bill's wake in Ft. Lauderdale.

Three days later he had a stroke. It was a gorgeous, sunny, Sunday morning when we slept until about 10:30. That was unusual for David. He normally got up to read his precious newspapers out by the pool until I awoke. It was also unusual because his sister and her husband were visiting, and already out at the pool, and David liked to be a gracious host and attend to their needs. But on that day I noticed when he awoke he put on khakis and a golf shirt. "How come you didn't put your bathing suit on?" I asked.

"I've got a lot of student papers to grade," he said. "I'm going to make you French toast first, so you have 15 more minutes to sleep," he called over his shoulder as he left the room. I dozed for a while more, then realized it was over fifteen minutes and I hadn't gotten a hurry-up call. I put on my bathing suit and sauntered into the kitchen to see if he needed help. When I came into the open family room bar area, which was adjacent to the kitchen, he was sitting on a barstool slumped over and tried to talk, but the words did not come out. I opened the door and yelled out to my sister-in-law, and called 911. As she sat with him, I grabbed a pair of sweatpants and an old, lightweight, terrycloth jacket. My in-laws threw on smarter clothes. They must have known how cold hospitals could be.

We lived quite far out of the closest town, Palm Beach Gardens, where the hospital was located. It only took the ambulance about 15 minutes to arrive, but it seemed like an hour. We kept trying to talk to David in order to console him, but he was not able to respond. When help arrived, they knew just what to do. I wanted to ride back with him, but the driver had me sit next to him, because the guys in the back were working on David and communicating with hospital personnel. Sitting up front was a bit frightening, as the driver was bad-mouthing the bad drivers he had to skirt around. I had to give all the medical information to admitting when we arrived while David was taken into emergency. I don't remember having my credentials with me. I guess I wasn't very cool.

I remember calling Stephanie back in Lima, who in turn got hold of Dean in Chicago, but somehow big sister Claudia couldn't be reached for a few hours. The hospital called our primary doctor. A nice young man named Andrew Moffitt came to the hospital immediately and got all the proper procedures going. He got the cardiologist and the neurologist on duty at the time. The team had to get all the tests done to determine the type of stroke so the proper treatment could be given.

Just about a half hour before the three-hour deadline for treatment of an ischemic stroke, David received the injection called TPA, which dissolves blood clots in the area of the brain. I was anxious for the tests to be finished, because if the injection went even a few minutes past the "golden three hour TPA limit" it could cause dangerous bleeding. I was warned and I made the right decision.

Even with the injection, David was a very sick guy. I was glad there was somebody from the family with us. I wondered if the kids could get there.

So much went on during the next few hours. There were all sorts of consultations. They found that David could not swallow, and it was decided that he had to have a feeding tube so he could be fed intravenously. I kept trying to hold his hand and talk to him, but I don't think it did any good.

After a whole day of intensive care, he was partly awake. His eyes looked so puzzled and sad. I felt so helpless. I was freezing in my bathing suit and open-necked cover-up. Around midnight Stephanie and Marty appeared. Then Dean and Claudia arrived from Chicago. We saw David perk up a bit when he saw his children. I felt a lot better too, knowing that I could share decision-making with my family. The first few days would have been a blur if it weren't for the daily notes that the kids took turns writing. We carried on with the dailies long after the initial trauma started. It seems that the doctors on the team had different ideas about certain medications. In the beginning it was not an option to give oral medications, because David couldn't swallow. All the medications had to be crushed and put into the IV. The tubes began to jam up at times, and they had to be flushed out.

At this point the medical team started talking about a peg to be inserted directly into the stomach. The speech therapists could not work with David with the tubes in the way. They could not do all the tests to check swallowing.

Each day we found that David could understand us a little better, as we did him. It was very difficult for him to talk, so when we heard some mumbling we listened very carefully. On the fifth day, David asked what happened to him, and wondered what he was attached to. Another time he asked the age of our grandson, Jackson.

On that day Dr. Knez, who was our original cardiologist, made his daily appearance and gave us a little more information. He said they couldn't give David any blood thinners now because bleeding chances were much higher than any benefit they might give. He said it was a "big" stroke and terrible looking on the scan. He said David would walk with a limp, and would eventually swallow and speak with a good attitude. He said he was progressively getting better, but the changes would be slight and slow.

At one point we were told that it might not have been atrial fibrillation that caused the stroke, but more likely it was related to vascular disease. It was just one point of confusion we endured the first 10 days of David's illness. Doctor's disagreed on just about all the forms of treatment.

After taking x-rays of the swallowing process, most agreed that he should have a stomach peg inserted in his abdomen. There was much back and forth decision making about this procedure, but it hadn't happened yet. Finally, Dr. Moffitt said it would be taken care of the next day, which would be day eleven for the patient.

The next morning Claudia was the unlucky family member attending David when the surgeon taking the place of Dr. Taub came into the room. Claudia said he was very annoyed that he was only called that morning, since Taub and another two surgeons were out of town. I came in about then and got into the conversation. He told us he planned to do the surgery for the peg at 1:30 p.m. the next day. When Claudia casually said that Dr. Moffitt had told her these surgeons did these procedures all the time and "they could do them with their eyes closed," he was even more noticeably miffed. He went into a long explanation about how difficult it was, etc. He also said they only did this to people that they thought wouldn't eat for months. That really surprised us, and the tone of the conversation was somewhat hostile and disturbed David as much as he understood it. He also hadn't known David was on Plavix up until three days before. He said he would talk to the neurosurgeon about how long David was off the Plavix. We heard the neurosurgeon paged, and that was one conversation we didn't want to hear.

A little later, Dr. Schallop (the neurosurgeon) came in and said David's cat scan hadn't changed. We took that to be a good sign. David got another air bed to prevent any skin damage. He grabbed and tried to drink some ice water when we stepped out of the room. The nurse was there, but couldn't stop him fast enough. He also tried to grab the Pepsi that they used to clear the feeding tubes, which clogged several times that day. He could only use his left hand. He was extremely thirsty, but the risk of the water going into his lungs was high.

He was put on intravenous liquids, as the doctor felt he needed more hydration. Then a catheter was inserted again, as he wasn't "going" by himself. He was hazy about what happened to him, and seemed to think he had more than one stroke. He did okay with the speech therapist, but to us he seemed the same as he did over a week ago. He slept most of the time and didn't do any exercises. It was not a good day.

The next morning the usual therapists arrived. First, the physical therapist came in and managed to transfer David to a chair. He moved the weak leg up and down, and did some of the occupational therapist's exercises with David's right arm. It was still swollen and in a sling at this point. David was resisting the therapy at first, and then went along with it. When the speech therapist came in, she wanted him to make certain sounds that strengthen facial muscles, and he started resisting those, too. When I attempted to help the therapist by trying to show him how to do the exercises, he told me to "get out of here." I didn't realize it then, but that was the beginning of his hostility toward me.

Before lunch, Dr. Moffitt came in and said all was well and the procedure would take place as planned. Claudia asked him about the remarks of the gastro surgeon and he said not to worry about it. He said the peg would come out when we were ready, but it had to be at a safe time. He said he had the pegs put into people that he deemed "salvageable," and "David is salvageable."

The procedure took about twenty minutes, and David was brought back to the room just before 3:00 p.m. He was still asleep from the anesthetic. The tube was out of his nose, but the "milkshake like liquid" would not be started until the next day.

Our nephew, Dr. Kenneth Grossman, called while David was still sleeping. We are so lucky to have this man in the family. Anytime anyone is sick we call Ken, and he speaks to our attending physicians and then reports the diagnosis in plain talk. He told us then that David had been put on Clonidine, and that was why he was so sleepy all the time. He then called the nurses on duty to remind them that some sort of injection had to be given that night, because he could not be given his crushed meds since the intravenous feeding wouldn't start until the next day.

When we arrived late the next morning, our patient seemed a little better; at least he told Dr. Schallop that he felt better. The doctor said that he would get an x-ray of the swallowing when the speech therapist came in the following Monday. Dr. Moffitt heard that someone had tried to give David applesauce in the middle of the night, but was stopped just in time. When we heard that, we shook our heads in disbelief. Sometimes hospital mistakes can really hurt you.

A couple of David's friends came to visit. You could see he enjoyed the visits, even though the communication wasn't too good. After they left he asked me to get a nurse to put him back in bed. It usually took a few minutes to get anybody to do it.

Meanwhile, he kept sucking on the sponge sticks like crazy. He was so thirsty. At one point we thought he said something about swallowing, but we couldn't be sure. We discussed some business issues with him and he seemed to understand.

On April 3rd, 16 days after he entered Palm Beach Gardens Hospital, he was to be transferred to St. Mary's Hospital for extensive therapy. When we came into his room, David was completely exhausted and we weren't sure of the reason. When he pointed to the belt left by the therapist, we found out he had walked for the first time down the hall. I guess they wanted to be sure he could go through the paces at St. Mary's.

Both Dr. Schallop and Dr. Knez said we could call them at any time, even though they were not affiliated with the other hospital. Dr. Knez put the bug in David's ear about getting a pacemaker. He said it wasn't needed right then, but we should definitely keep it in mind. He said it would prevent any other sudden heart problems, and would stop another stroke.

We got some legal papers signed: power of attorney and health care surrogate. We got a notary and witnesses, and we were ready to move on. Transportation came to pick up our patient about 3:00 p.m., and Claudia arranged to put the fee on her credit card because they said Medicare didn't pay for it. She also rode along with him while I followed. The second phase of what was to prove a long recovery was about to begin.

David was given a private room again without our requesting one. I kept quiet about that. I went through all the entry forms again, and patiently awaited the nurse to tend to her new patient. When she came in, she looked at the peg, poured water in it, and took his blood pressure. No one had started the feeding with or without crushed-up meds. We waited until 8:15 when the feeding things were hooked up at last.

We got to the hospital early the next morning in order for Claudia to say goodbye. David was already dressed in some khaki shorts and a golf shirt. The occupational therapist had shown David how to put on the shirt himself. It was slow going putting on the shorts, though. His right arm was still non-functioning, as it would be going forward. He seemed to cooperate, and that was important at the time. We met a young assistant to the new doctor, whom we were to meet in the evening, and he seemed like a caring practitioner.

When I returned from taking Claudia to the airport, they were taking David in for physical therapy. I stayed out of the way so he could concentrate on the hard therapy without my staring at him. After 45 minutes he was exhausted and wanted to get in bed. They were working on him while I stood out in the hall. I wasn't sure if they were flushing the peg or giving him more fluid. It was difficult to get answers when you wanted them, especially since I didn't know the doctor in charge. I also needed to find out if anything had been put on the cut we saw on his face early in the morning. The big question was: it looked like he had been shaved with a real blade when we were told to use only an electric shaver. It is not easy to be safe in a hospital. Patient notes don't seem to be read by the aides.

Shortly after his nap, David was taken for the swallowing test x-ray. They promised to let us know the results right away. Nobody let us know, but the next day David ate half of a turkey dinner. They insisted on putting thickener into his liquids, which David wasn't too happy about. He gradually ate more food, but the peg was used to give him his meds and more fluid.

For the next several days the different doctors all debated about whether he should go on Coumadin again. The new neurologist that was called in said he had to have it or he would get another stroke. When the old neurologist got into the act, he said that Plavix and aspirin were enough. Finally, after consulting with Kenny and Dr. Moffitt, the neurologist agreed to give Lovenox injections for a while. Then while David was still in the hospital he would get the Coumadin where he could be watched, and was unlikely to fall.

So much was going on in the early days of April. Our patient had been given Milk of Magnesia, which caused him to be miserable. When he had to "go," nobody was ever around despite ringing for nurses. I thought that I should get outside help if that kept up. Eventually, that problem got solved. Ken, our nephew, flew in to see David for himself, after having been on so many long-distance calls. He spent several hours with him, doing some of his own tests, and going over words and their meanings. He conferred with the attending physicians, explaining his interest in David. He said that the mind seemed alright, but the words could not come out the way David meant them. This was known as aphasia. There would be some improvement as time passed, but the problem would never be completely cured.

By April 15, David was doing about three hours of physical therapy daily. After each session he would be so tired that he asked to be put in bed. He was now walking in and out of the exercise room with the therapist hold the belt attached to his waist. There was still the problem of his motivation. The psychologist was a little too upbeat for David's taste. He was always making jokes and singing, and David would not have liked him even before he had a stroke. We asked that the psychiatrist be called in again, as she hadn't seen him since he arrived there. She told us that her first encounter with David had shown him to be uncooperative, and he balked at taking any medication for depression. He denies being depressed to this day.

Meanwhile, a new cat scan showed improvement in the brain. I guess that meant that the clot had more or less dissolved, and the therapy should start working better. It was not easy to deal with David. He was, and is, extremely set in his ways. The stroke only increased his belligerence, so it was interesting to us when we were upset about the lack of care, he told us to be patient. That was a first for sure!

It was increasingly hard to get help when we needed it. There was so much confusion when new caregivers came in and would start reading instructions written several days before. It was also difficult for David to see himself getting better, when one day they put a catheter on him and the next he was told he would be taken to the bathroom. Stephanie, who is seriously organized, was beginning to lose her cool with the attendants. She felt that the hospital was at fault for not doing their job to maintain continuity of care.

One day the psychologist was walking by and saw how frustrated we were trying to get someone to take David to the bathroom. He apologized and said they were short of help, and were trying to get some personnel from another floor. Forty minutes later someone came in and David said he didn't feel like going anymore. The attendant made an unforgettable remark that "he was whining for no reason." Stephanie and I could have punched her right then! We certainly didn't need that kind of attitude in a hospital.

When the urologist told us he had started David on antibiotics, we wondered why. He said David got a bladder infection from the catheter use, but it wasn't anything to worry about. All sorts of little traumas came up while there. Now the doctors started talking to us about whether we could care for David at home or whether he should go to a sub-acute facility when his three weeks were over in the present hospital.

After much discussion it was decided that they would keep David for an extra week or so. Since I admitted that I could not care for him while he was still in this stage of recuperation, the hospital said they would try to intensify his treatment. We also had to wait to get him admitted to the sub-acute facility that we chose closer to home. It was difficult to drive the distance from St. Mary's to our house at night, and I didn't always have a family member in town to help me. We also needed to get all the paperwork together for the transfer, as again there would be a different set of doctors in case of an emergency. My daughter-in-law, Chris Ledbetter, was due in next, and she would help me get things together for the next phase.

When Chris arrived, David was delighted. He didn't know she was coming. I must say David did light up when he saw Claudia, Dean, or Stephanie. He seemed to relate to their conversations, and he still tried to give advice as he always had in the past. Chris was the last family member to visit at St. Mary's. She, too, was disgusted with the non-therapy help. These hospital dealings were all unfamiliar to her. At that time she was feature editor of the *Chicago Sun-Times* with several dozen writers under her authority. She went back to Chicago with a full heart, and wrote a beautiful piece about David. It said it like it was. Read it for yourself and see how she captured the whole spirit of her father-in-law.

CHICAGO SUN-TIMES • WEDNESDAY, JUNE 16, 2004

SHOWCASE 67

Some snapshots of a father's life

SHE SAID

BY CHRISTINE LEDBETTER

Taped family pictures adorn the wall opposite his hospital bed. Neatly printed beneath each photo are the names of those pictured and — in parentheses — their relationship to the patient. There's Dean (son) and Rachel (Dean's daughter) wearing their gloves after a softball game. Syd (Dean's son) dances to a piece he choreographed in New York. Outfitted in kimonos are Oriana and Alix (Claudia's daughters) vacationing in Japan; Jack (Stephanie's son) in shades and a leather jacket strums his guitar; Skylar (Stephanie's daughter) kicks a leg straight up in a brown-belt maneuver. There's even one of me (Dean's wife) smiling with my father-in-law, the patient.

David Skylar, the patriarch of this family, lies in a bed in a Florida rehabilitation clinic, trying to remember the people on the wall and so much more. The stroke he suffered weeks earlier killed a massive number of brain cells, weakened his right side and caused short-term memory loss.

Nurses and aides bustle in and out; they handle him efficiently and quickly. They call him dear and honey as if they know him. Doctors and social workers visit occasionally; they speak loudly and slowly. They talk about him but look at his wife, Marilyn, or me during this April visit.

He is a big man, diminished physically and spiritually by an illness that will affect nearly 700,000 Americans this year. Experts say his ability to regain all his functions depends partially on his willingness to believe he can get better. He must work hard, they say, to relearn how to walk and use his arm, which hangs limply in a sling. He seems daunted by the huge task before him. "I'm not the man I was," he says. But we don't believe him.

He has faced enormous challenges before. At 78, he can be proud of a life that took him from playing stickball with his mother's mop on the streets of the Bronx to shaking the hands of presidents. He was born in New York to Jewish immigrants from Russia. His father worked seven days a week in a grocery store. The family lived in a bottom-floor

David Skylar and his daughter-in-law, Christine Ledbetter.

apartment where he and his sister shared a bedroom with their cat and dog. After serving in the Air Force during World War II, he studied journalism at the University of Missouri-Columbia on the GI Bill.

His statewide investigative stories earned him the distinction of being the only journalism student on campus with an expense account. There, he met Marilyn, also a journalism student, and when they married, they moved to her hometown of Cleveland.

He launched a group of suburban newspapers that made national news in 1972 for supporting George McGovern for president, one of the senator's few endorsements against Richard Nixon. When David sold the papers, he worked as Sen. Howard Metzenbaum's campaign director before retiring to Florida.

The resume is only part of his story. A rugged version of Paul Newman-handsome, he possesses a voice as deep as Moses. He golfs with a 12 handicap, which leaves him perennially tan. He wears a blue blazer as if he was born in

it, and way before it was cool, he wore Gucci loafers without socks. At any gathering, he is its center.

I met David when he returned to Columbia to lecture at the Journalism School. His son and I were both journalism students there and dating. We went to dinner together and I was so thoroughly intimidated by the man with the booming voice and the passionate opinions, I spoke fewer than 10 words the entire evening. That would change as I learned he could listen as well as he could speak.

As a father and grandfather, he has always kept a respectful distance unless called on for help. One golden August, Dean and I were vacationing in the Hamptons and ran out of money. David wired enough for us to stay a few more days, just long enough for us to decide to marry. There were many obstacles — we were still in school, both unemployed, and I wasn't Jewish — but David was never a hurdle. He was always ready to catch his children if they fell. As sometimes they did.

They're with him now — Dean, Claudia and Stephanie — taking turns flying to Florida to help as he makes the transition from rehab center to home. Growing older can't be easy for a man who is larger than life. While being confined to a wheelchair has limited his world, he can still wheel himself into his home office.

On the wall above his desk are framed pictures. In one he's introducing Gerald Ford, and in another, he's shaking hands with Lyndon Johnson. Ike's there, too, and George McGovern, of course. There are photos from golf outings, civic events and fund-raisers. And there are the family portraits, in which he's surrounded by his wife of 55 years, his three children, their spouses and the six grandchildren. He's in the middle, the family's core. The wall isn't filled yet. There's room for so much more.

Christine Ledbetter wrote this article after visiting
David in the hospital in West Palm Beach, 2004.

Chapter 61

On April 27, 2004, after 43 days in hospitals, David arrived at Chatsworth, a sub-acute facility better known as a nursing home. It was a straight shot of eight miles down the road from our home, and in a nicer neighborhood than St. Mary's. I was able to visit earlier and stay later. There was not much for me to do for him, as the schedule of therapies and naps filled his day. Gradually, I started doing some of my chores while he was so occupied. I wish I hadn't given up our club membership at Ibis so fast. I could have played a few rounds. What prompted my decision, I guess, was that I was unsure about income and all the expenses we were incurring. I needn't have worried so much.

The people at Chatsworth were excellent therapists. The other problem of the lack of aides was the same as in the hospitals. Nobody should be without family or other support when confined to a health institution. I could see a lot of improvement in David's walking and arm control. One of the therapists had taken care of me when I had a knee replacement. I was pleased that she was assigned to David. He listened to her, and for once made better progress.

It was easier for friends to visit when he was at Chatsworth, because most of them that wintered in Palm Beach County had not gone home yet. He always seemed a little more relaxed when his friends came. There was just one problem that

I felt needed addressing. An in-house medical doctor only came to the facility once a week, unless there was a dire emergency. Our doctor no longer went to nursing homes, so if a problem arose we had to rely on a nurse calling the doctor in charge of the facility. Needless to say, it was hard to get help when you needed it.

After two weeks, the staff evaluated David's progress. He needed more work on his standing alone and balancing. He did much better in the dressing category. He was taught how to put on a shirt again, and how to slip on a pair of slacks. The staff seemed to think he could go home in two or three weeks. He kept asking when he could go home, and I told him it depended on his cooperation. He didn't like that. As far as he was concerned, that wasn't an acceptable answer.

Finally, the day came when we did take him home. He was using a three-footed base cane that they called a hemi-walker. We didn't need a ramp, as he was able to make it up the two small steps to the front door. We marched him right into the bedroom so he could rest. Once he was tucked in, he called me over to him and took my hand. That was probably the only time I saw any "sweet" emotion in his eyes. David is not the emotional type.

We fell into a routine similar to those in the various health facilities, but somehow it was more stimulating, because the therapists were more cheerful and they had a nice, bright, open area in which to work with their patient. We also had a visiting nurse who took David's vitals and took blood samples twice a week when he came home. I found a young Jamaican college boy who came in every day for a few hours and took care of showers and shaving, and just helping me a lot. It wasn't too long before David could do some things for himself. He got a little too comfortable with his wheelchair, and it was tough to get him walking around.

It had been over three months since he'd had the stroke. Being home was so much better for his walk in the water back then. Now the doctors recommend it and he won't go in the condo pool; he just sits in his wheelchair and observes! In August, Stephanie and Marty and the kids became Florida residents. They chose Ft. Lauderdale, which was over an hour drive from us. They visited usually on weekends, but it was a hassle, as Stephanie flew back and forth every week to her job in Ohio, as she didn't want to give it up until she found something in Florida.

Then came Hurricane Frances. Our first! We did have plenty of warning, though. By chance, one of our kids' friends from Lima, Ohio, had an empty house in Naples. The kids told me to pack up clothes for at least a week, and they drove us and their children in two cars across the state. We had an unplanned adventure when everyone on the east coast was caught in a terrible storm. When the reports said "all clear," we drove back to the Lauderdale house first and saw the damage to the trees and landscape. We stayed there overnight and then got driven home. Stephanie drove us and Marty followed with Jack and Skye. When we got home we found that the fifty-two foot screen enclosure was collapsed in the pool. We took pictures and called the insurance company. We happened to be one of the first to see damage, and we got the new screen up in a few weeks. Some people had to wait months for service.

We were not affected by "Charlie," which came before Frances, but soon after came "Ivan" and "Jeanne," which were too close for comfort. We stayed down in Cooper City with Stephanie for those. I remember how the whole family stayed in one room away from the window for hours at a time. Some arrangement with a neighbor two doors away got us connected to his generator, so we had a light on in the room. Every once in a while one of us would sneak into the next room where we could see outside. It was really frightening to see bushes and yard debris flying through the air. The rain was heavy and blinding. So, we made it through three hurricanes, and David remained as stoic as ever.

By the next month we felt David could travel to Chicago for Thanksgiving. It was customary for our family to gather on that holiday, because Dean and Chris and their children spent Christmas with her parents. With Stephanie's family in Florida, it was so much easier for us to travel. We both got wheelchairs at O'Hare, because although I wasn't ill, I couldn't make the long walk.

I can't call Claudia's home a "house" because it has 18,000 square feet, including the basement. Before David's stroke we used to stay in the grandparents' suite that was actually designed for us. It has a separate staircase and exit, and is now used for guests. The home is a gutted factory, done over beautifully by Claudia and her husband, James Mastro, who have been acclaimed across the U.S. for their innovative architecture.

On this holiday we stayed in a huge room on the first floor that James had used for his train collection. Claudia also arranged for David to get a week's therapy at the Chicago Rehabilitation Institute. It was excellent therapy, and they got him off the hemi-walker and on a real cane. We had a great time that trip. My son-in-law took all the men and boys for special haircuts while the women prepared for Thanksgiving dinner. There really wasn't that much to do, since Claudia had worked hard in advance to get all the gourmet touches started for which she was known.

It was a very special time, and then we got a phone call from our realtor in Palm Beach saying that we had an offer on our house. That really made the day. I was happy and sad at the same time, because I knew we had to sell, but I really didn't want to leave that lovely place. We countered the offer a bit and said we would be coming home to finalize the deal. I thought about so many of our former house sales when David was in charge, and he always said, "We'll flip a coin for the difference."

As soon as we got home, we took care of the preliminary paperwork on the sale. It was so sad to see my husband struggle to print his name with his left hand. He couldn't even hold the pen with his right one. Shortly after, we started looking for a rental in Weston closer to our children. We found an almost brand new, hardly used house owned by a couple from Puerto Rico. Our agent took care of the details; we needed some window blinds and a few other small things done before we could move in. There was no pool, but a little patio faced a lake and David could access it easily. There was no pressure on us, but we started packing immediately.

We also managed to have a house sale for neighbors only, and we were able to unload some art we didn't need, and many other household items. I never realized we had so much left to sell, as we had been sending furniture to our children for years. When the movers came, we sat David down on a chair and let him direct traffic. It took hours to get everything on the truck; then it was another hour and a half for them to drive to Weston. Since we cleaned each room as it was cleared, we were able to leave shortly after the truck. It was my daughter's job to drive us down. I don't know what I would have done without Stephanie and Marty in Florida. As we drove to our new place, I thought about the last-minute decision I had to make selling our sitting mower for only $200. It's a good thing David was not aware of the transaction. Before the stroke he would have had a fit. I guess before the stroke, however, we wouldn't have been selling the mower in the first place.

Needless to say, the movers didn't finish until 11:00 p.m. All the yet unknown neighbors and their children kept gawking at my furniture. Our wonderful helper at the time, Julia Mayne, helped us settle in that night and slept over before making the trip back home. The little house was perfect for our needs. It was five minutes from the Cleveland Clinic Florida where we set up all new doctors and tests. I was also five minutes from the Weston Recreation Center where there were bridge games every Monday afternoon. At that time I was able to leave David alone, as he was able to get around with his cane and take care of his basic needs for a few hours. We were also about fifteen minutes away from family, and that was one of the reasons for the move away from Palm Beach County. David had a short stay in the hospital with pneumonia, but he recuperated just fine before the year's lease was up and the absentee landlords decided to sell the house. I was not too upset, as I wanted to be even closer to my daughter.

We moved again. This time to a bigger house a half-mile from the kids. It was an older house, and I thought it would be good for David as it had a pool. It was not to be. The South American landlady and her mostly unseen husband did not honor the contract to do specific improvements, such as putting up a railing at the pool steps. Without one, David could not use the pool at all. The landlady was impossible. We had a bad leak in one of the bedrooms, and after six months she finally got the next-door neighbor to fix it. It still leaked afterwards.

We finally mutually agreed to move after a year and a half. She reneged on part of the security deposit, and I had to take her to court. We won the judgment, but never got paid. Three collection agencies were unsuccessful in getting through to her. She was a mean one for sure. This was another case when my husband told me to forget about it. I can't let things go so easily. After six years another collection guy called me and said he would like to try to get something from her. I told him it was impossible, but "be my guest!"

Other than the bad house situation, it was a great year for travel. We got to Chicago again; this time for our granddaughter Rachel's high school graduation. After that we went to Palo Alto for granddaughter Oriana's graduation from Stanford. David also got to visit his oldest friend Lee Pitt, who lived on top of a mountain nearby. It was a happy trip with no illness and no mishaps.

In August we made the trip to Durham, England, for Alexandra's wedding. I'm not sure how we managed by ourselves, but I carried enough five-dollar bills to cover our wheelchair "pushers," and David was still able to visit the airport restroom when he was wheeled up to it. We had to fly to Edinburgh, where the nearly weds picked us up for the 45-minute drive to Durham. The hotel was typically English, and it was delightful to meet and greet the 100 or so guests that arrived from Chicago, plus all the British friends and family of the groom. It was Alexandra and Alexander, and they became Alix and AJ after wearing out the "Boy Alex" moniker.

The wedding took place in the chapel of the university, and the reception was in a real castle adjoining the school. It was quite beautiful, and the medieval feeling of the surroundings was mindboggling. We couldn't make it to the picture taking at the front of the castle, as David felt a little overtired, so we were driven back to the hotel after the late festivities. We did get photos with our family, which were memorable.

After the wedding, Claudia and James took us to Edinburgh for a few days of sightseeing. We stayed in a rental apartment that Claudia had arranged and got around by cabs. It was a nice finish to an exciting week. We had an overnight flight home, so we managed to get some rest. We arrived just in time to finish the last three months of hurricane season. This time we were around the corner from family and it felt less stressful.

There were a few problems that fall. We still maintained our relationship with the Cleveland Clinic doctors, and they decided that David needed a pacemaker; it was actually a pacemaker/defibrillator combination. The medication was doing some of the heart regulation, but not enough. He had to go into the hospital for at least 24 hours. Even short stays take a lot out of him. We got more therapy every time he was discharged from a hospital, so it worked out to his advantage in a way. He just gets weak after any medical episode.

I started to get some aides from time to time if I wanted to do errands or even play golf a few times. I had a wonderful lady come in to stay with David for a few mornings when I joined some ladies at the early hour of 7:30 a.m. It was an ungodly time, and after being used to a private club, I went along with this group at the semi-private course about three minutes away from our house. I had this aide come at 7:15 a.m. a couple of times, and she was right on time. The third time I left David sleeping and the door open for her arrival. When I got home around noon, I found David sitting on the floor leaning against the kitchen door jam. The aide had never shown up and never called. I could not find out from him how long he had been sitting there. He was unable to tell me. Somehow I managed to get him up with some chair help, but I was concerned that he had really hurt himself. All I found was a deep bruise on his strong arm. He did not complain. I have never left him again unless someone was with him. He fell one more time when I was home and cut his arm. I had to call EMS, as I couldn't lift him. I put a pillow under his head and tried to clean up his wound. We learned the reason for his falling was the dosage of the anti-depressant the doctor had prescribed. When he fell again, we left that doctor and his medication. When asked, David said he was not depressed. He is just obstinate and angry sometimes, and won't help himself. To this day he hardly ever smiles.

After the decision to leave that miserable rental situation, I felt we had to buy our own place again. I remembered the small section of Hollywood that we once enjoyed as snowbirds. We had built a townhouse in Emerald Hills, because it had many Cleveland residents that we knew. It also overlooked two lakes of the golf course, which was one of the best in the area at the time. I recalled that a huge condo complex was built across the street from the townhouse section. I decided to look there for our new abode. It seems strange that most of my sentences are starting with "I." Most of our decisions in our life were made by "us." For the preceding four years all the decisions were made by a "reluctant me."

We found a condo that seemed to be a good deal at the time, but it was a real mess. The owner had passed away five years previously, and his large family had used it to store odds and ends of furniture and household items. For some reason they never had the time to sell the place. Once we decided to buy it, we called Claudia to get down there to do the sketches for blueprints for the remodel. She came down within a few days and got to work on the plans. We used the same contractor that Stephanie had used at her house. He started out okay, but gradually became less watchful, and we found out he had taken a job with the city also. Workers were not showing up regularly, and mistakes were being made. We thought we could be moved in by July 1, but it was not to be. We moved the furniture in, but we had to live at Stephanie and Marty's house for three weeks until we got someone to finish the kitchen. The problem was that the original carpenter was a little off the wall and mismatched the veneer on all the cabinets. He then installed them wrong.

When the cabinets were redone we were able to get the appliances put in their proper places so we could begin living there. We still had to have the beautiful glass tile done in the kitchen and a mirror put in the dressing room. Claudia said she had never had so many problems in any of her huge architectural jobs before this small one. She thought it must be the caliber of Florida workers. I had to agree with her!

When I chose Emerald Hills, I believed we would find some of our old friends. By the time we were settled enough to make a few calls, we found out that most people had moved away, and two others passed away within weeks of our residency Just about everyone we knew wintered in the area we came from in Palm Beach County. A psychologist who saw David a couple of times, concluded that he needed to be able to interact with his peers. What a joke! There was only one man from downstairs that became a friend, and he didn't have much in common with David. We depended on having dinner with the kids once a week or a pop-in from the grandchildren once in a while. It was always a joy to see Jack and Skye grow up before our eyes. We didn't have that privilege with the other grandchildren.

By summer of 2008, we existed by occasional visits from friends and our children taking turns in watching over us. The last trip that we made was to our grandson Sydney's wedding in New York. We hadn't been back there in years. It was a lovely ceremony where the couple read vows to each other and exchanged rings. There was no need for an official, as they had already been married in city hall a few days before. The guest list was heavily weighted with all Syd's dance friends and Leti's friends from NYU and Columbia. The two families did not know each other, except for dinner the night before given by the groom's parents.

The night of the wedding David did not feel well. Being in a strange city we took him to the emergency room at N.Y. Presbyterian Hospital, where he was seen right away. It was determined that he should be admitted for a day or two. X-rays showed he had a light case of pneumonia. Dean was the only one that was able to stay with us. After finding out the diagnosis, Claudia and Stephanie left the rest of the details to their brother, because they had business obligations they could not change unless it was a serious emergency. The doctor assigned to David told us that the antibiotics he put David on should clear up his condition in a few days. By the third day he reluctantly discharged us with orders to see our doctor when we got home. We spoke to Ken, our family's' medical guru, and he said he thought it was okay for David to return home.

The day was cloudy when we got to La Guardia. We were supposed to leave before Dean, who was going to Chicago. He got us wheelchairs and thought it would be a good idea if we went to the gate to be first in line for boarding. Unfortunately, he could not come through with us. The worse scenario was that we sat for eight hours alone while terrible storms were causing horrific delays on the East Coast. Dean kept calling us on his cell phone and vice versa to check on departure times. I think he got off before us. This incident soured us on traveling any more. Of course, other issues prevented us from going anywhere.

Since David's initial physical therapy in 2004, he had been walking with a cane. I could take care of him by myself with minimal problems. In 2010, everything changed. I had a botched-up surgery by Dr. Hoa Nuguyon, which was followed almost immediately by a remedial surgery. I was out of commission for a few months. I had to begin having constant aides to take care of us. Then, as I was back on my feet, David tripped on his quilt as he was returning from a nocturnal visit to the loo.

I couldn't get him off the carpet, and for the first time ever he groaned in pain. I didn't want to call EMS until I knew what was happening. I managed to convince the condo security guard to come help me put him in bed. He fell asleep, so I believed the worse was over. It wasn't. At 6:00 a.m. I called for help, and they knew right away that he had broken something because he was in such pain. When we got to the hospital I called my son-in-law, Marty, and he met us at the hospital. I also called Stephanie in Ohio, and Claudia and Dean in Chicago. David had fractured his right hip and needed immediate surgery.

Flash forward to the first surgery; he became infected and while he was in a nursing home recuperating, he was taken back to the hospital to fix the problem. After that surgery he was admitted to a more convenient nursing home next to the hospital. Other problems kept popping up and I had our long-time aide stay with him every day, even as I sat with him. I could not care for him like she could. Everything gets a little hazy as I think back to those autumn months. I remember Claudia arranged a private Thanksgiving at the nursing home with food that she prepared with Stephanie. I vaguely remember a couple of brief trips back to the hospital in December, but I don't recall the reason. And so we resumed more physical and occupational therapy. David became even more stubborn about walking and exercising. He has also become more mean spirited. I've been told not to take it personally. That is hard to do. With all this discussion of illnesses it makes for a boring retrospective. But as David used to say, "Old age sucks." I still say it "beats the alternative!"

David got cheered by Dean and Syd when he got out of rehab.

David gets a special Chicago haircut on his first trip after stroke.

All the guys at the barbershop in Chicago. James is taking the photo.

David and I went to Durham, England for our grandaughter
Alexandra's wedding to Alexander Corner.

Cruise ship family picture on Marilyn's 80th birthday.

Chapter 62

*H*ere we are in 2013. The days pass quickly, and we aren't having any fun. David is hanging in, as the expression goes. He still loves to eat, and he has learned to eat food without salt. That is the prime issue right now. He must not get bouts of congestive heart failure. He always wants to go out to dinner, but I have to nix that, as he eats as if he will never get the opportunity again. I also cannot tell every chef to eliminate the sodium. On special occasions we do go out. That is usually when our children visit.

Yes, there are new health issues that I won't get into now. And yes, it is getting harder and harder to get David to respond to therapists who try to help him. He will not walk down the hall with his walker, even though he is quite able to do so. He is showered and shaved every other day, and is wheeled down for his hour of observing the neighbors in the pool. It could be 99 degrees and he will not walk in the water with help. Sometimes I lose my temper when I try to convince him that he must not sit in his automatic recliner all day. He tells me to get away and I start to cry. I just can't help myself. I look at him now, with some ribs showing, and his skinny arms, and wonder how he could change so much. What happened to the big, tough guy I married 64 years ago? It is unbelievable to me that David watches *The Price is Right* and cooking shows every day when he never watched daytime TV in his life, with the exception of

Sunday Morning. I am never sure just what he understands or doesn't understand anymore. He does not have Alzheimer's, but it is hard to fathom what he is thinking.

Getting back to the coverage of his life, I am sure I missed a lot of interesting episodes. Maybe they will come to me before this goes into publication. However, David's day-to-day business career was not in my scope at the time. Thanks to the few people still around who could fill me in on his doings, I was able to move along.

I read somewhere that the creator of "*MadMen*" expects to take the lead actor into old age. I'm sure he cannot portray his character as still being a "hunk" in his old age. If the story has honest content, it will become as boring as real life. But boring is okay if you are still breathing. I think about all the friends who came to see David after his stroke, and realize that three-fourths of them have passed away. David is still with us. He is my very special survivor. One of these days I am going to say, "Get off your duff, goddammit, and let's dance and shuffle off to Buffalo or something." Maybe he might smile for a change.

Claudia takes David for an outing to Hollywood Beach for lunch on the boardwalk.

Four generations of beautiful blue eyed "boys" with Dean, Sydney and Lukas.

David in felt hat and suit, typical of the era, talking to a security guard.

David had some cool outfits.

Pres. Lyndon johnson autographed this photo for David's unknown good deed!

First official family photo. 1960.

Our family in Chicago before David's stroke.

Dean and Syd take David to Hooters but he shows his "So what!" look.

CPSIA information can be obtained at www.ICGtesting.com
Printed in the USA
BVOW03s2136130314

347633BV00001B/55/P

3/15